LISTEN TO THE DINOSAUR

David M. Fellman

As with everything else, this is for Lisa and Alix

ISBN 978-0-9823490-1-4

Contents

Listen To The
Dinosaur

An attendee at a recent seminar called me a dinosaur.

"I came here looking to find some new ideas," he said. "You didn't teach me anything about selling comprehensive solutions at the C-Level in the digital age and arena, just the same old 'prospect-and-follow-up-and-ask-good-questions' crap I've been hearing from my boss. Dinosaurs are extinct, man, and you're not helping me any by telling me to sell like one."

I think it's worth mentioning that this particular salesperson was sent to my seminar because he's an underachiever, plodding along at about 60% of his employer's expectations after a year and a half on the job. Personally, I think he's a whole lot closer to being extinct than I am.

But that's not what I want to talk to you about. I think a lot of salespeople are looking for a new way to sell, because their perception is that the old way isn't working anymore. This isn't a new phenomenon; it's probably been happening as long as there have been salespeople. Times change, products and services change, technology changes — so the fundamentals of selling must change too, right?

I think *wrong*. I also think that the more people look for a new way to sell, the farther they get from the fundamentals. And that's why their method of selling isn't working.

I believe in fundamentals. I also believe in creativity. And *that's* what I want to talk to you about. But the fundamentals come first, and if that makes me a dinosaur, well then, *maybe you should listen to the dinosaur!*

Inside, Outside, Etc.

I draw a distinction between inside selling and outside selling, and also between retail selling and commercial selling. This book is mostly meant for commercial salespeople, but I think there are lessons to be learned from the retail world. I think retail salespeople can also take lessons from the commercial world. The challenges are different, but I think the fundamentals are still largely the same. Inside, outside, retail or commercial, selling is about meeting or exceeding the buyer's needs and/or wants.

Needs and *wants* can be completely different animals, though. For example, a printing buyer needs a quantity of brochures. He wants them delivered by Friday. Why is that? One possibility is that he wants this particular project off his desk before the start of the weekend, just so he doesn't have to worry about it anymore. Another possibility is that he's leaving for a trade show on Saturday, and a new product launch might fall flat on its face if those brochures aren't there.

If you're a printing salesperson, you probably need to understand the *need/want equation*, right? If you're late with the delivery — or if you can't meet the buyer's stated delivery requirement in the first place — you might be OK if it's only a *want*. You're in trouble either way, though, if it's really a *need*. If you commit and don't deliver, you may very well lose the customer. And if you commit when you *know* you can't deliver, you *should* lose the customer! It doesn't matter whether you're an outside, commercial salesperson for a national printing company, or an inside, retail salesperson for a local quick printing/copyshop. The fundamentals are still the same!

Here's some Dinosaur Wisdom: *You must understand the need in order to meet or exceed it.* Here's some more Dinosaur Wisdom: *You'll be most successful when you can meet most of the* wants *in addition to all of the* needs.

Thank about that. You're probably not the only supplier for whatever it is that you sell. If the buyer has a choice, why should he/she choose you? Obviously a number of factors that go into that decision, and we'll talk much more about them later on. At a fundamental level, though, don't you like to buy from people who make it easy on you rather than hard? And don't you like to buy from people who go the extra mile?

On the other hand, would you continue to buy from someone who makes it easy *and* goes the extra mile during the sales process, but then lets you down on the delivery/execution of the product or service? In the great cosmic scheme of things, *need* is the absolute, and *want* falls into the added value category. You need to strive for both, but when push comes to shove — as it often does, right? — it's important to know the difference between the *wants* and the *needs*.

Buyers & Sellers

I used the term *buyer* a moment ago, and I'll be using it again throughout this book. I want to specify, though, that *buyer* is not a title, it's just a noun — unless, of course, it is a formal title with a capital "B". In the old days, that was pretty common, but in modern times, a Buyer-with-a-Capital-"B" will more commonly be titled *Purchasing* Agent or Manager or Director, or perhaps one of those rank indicators with *Acquisition* or *Procurement* or *Materiel* on the front end.

You may work mostly with *Purchasing/Acquisition/Procurement/Materiel* titles, but many salespeople do not. I think — and again, this is something we'll talk more about later — that it's very important to know the exact title of the people you're selling to. Why? Well, for starters, if your product or service has application in many industries, and you know that the Supply Chain Manager is the right person to be talking to in at least one of those industries, it simplifies your prospecting challenge when you're trying to develop new customers within that industry. I'm sure you'll agree that a lot of selling time gets wasted talking to the wrong person. Which conversation would you rather have with a gatekeeper-type: "Who would be responsible for ordering new inventory management technology for your company?" or "Can you give me the name of your Supply Chain Manager?"

Customers and Not-Customers

Here's some more important terminology. In the world of retail sales, it's probably OK to refer to anyone who walks into the store as a customer, but in the other categories — inside and outside commercial sales — I think you should reserve that term for people who are actually buying from you. In fact, I think there are *four categories* of people on the buying side of the commercial sales equation: *suspects, prospects, customers* and *maximized customers*.

Here's how the progression works. They are *suspects* when you think they might be *prospects*, but you can only call them prospects when you *know for sure* that they qualify. You should only call them *customers* when they're actually buying from you, and you can call them *maximized customers* when you're getting the maximum share of their business.

Why is that important? Because you have different challenges with unsold *prospects* than you do with established *customers*, and you don't even want to address some of those challenges until you know that a prospect is really qualified. And, you still have some selling to do to take a *customer* to the *maximized customer* level, whereas all you have to worry about with a truly maximized customer is customer service and satisfaction.

Fully Qualified

There's the seed of a critical definition of *selling* in there somewhere, but before I get to that, I want to define a qualified prospect. In order to be *fully* qualified, whoever we're talking about has to pass three tests. First, you have to know — not just think or hope! — that they buy, want or need exactly what you sell. Second, you have to know — again, not just think or hope! — that they have enough volume potential to make pursuing them worthwhile. (I think you'll also agree that a lot of selling time gets wasted on "minnows" when the salespeople should be casting for bigger fish!)

Third — and this is ultimately the most important consideration — they have to show some real interest in buying from you. Anything less than that, and they're not *fully qualified* prospects.

Now, that doesn't mean you walk away from anyone who isn't obviously fully qualified. It just means that there's more work to be done. You might need more research to determine if they qualify in terms of the first and second criteria. You might need to be more convincing — or more persistent, or more assertive, or more creative — in order to qualify them in terms of the third criteria. Most salespeople, I think, don't really question the quality of their suspect/prospect pipeline. Most salespeople, I think, don't even know the difference between a suspect and a prospect. This is more than just semantics! We're going to talk about *time management* later on, and one of the most important time management considerations for salespeople is to *invest* their time wisely.

What Is *Selling?*

OK, back to that critical definition of *selling*. There are many components to a selling job: prospecting, communicating, convincing and closing, handling pre-sale objections, handling post-sale issues or problems and maintaining customer relationships, just to name a few. The most critical definition of selling, though, is tied to the critical *objective* of selling, and that's to generate revenue. No matter what you sell or where you sell it, inside or outside, retail or commercial, your *prime directive* is to generate revenue.

In many cases, the prime directive goes beyond that — to generate *profitable* revenue! — but not every salesperson has control of the factors that affect profit. So for now, let's focus on generating *top line* revenue as a salesperson's reason for being. That means making the sale, and the bigger the sale the better. It also means developing customers, and the bigger the customer the better. Everybody stands to benefit when a salesperson generates revenue. The flip side of that, of course, is that nobody benefits when you don't (except maybe your competitors!)

Now let's talk about *how* you generate revenue. Sometimes it's simply *suggestive*, but at the highest levels of selling, it's usually *consultative*. What's the difference? The suggestive approach is *do you want one of these?* The consultative approach is *do you need one of these?* Admittedly, some products and/or services can be sold quite effectively using a suggestive approach. Here's some more Dinosaur Wisdom, though: *The more complex the product or service, the more likely it requires a consultative sale!*

Do You Want Fries With That?

The most famous example of suggestive selling in our time is probably: "Do you want fries with that?" I think you'll probably agree that most people don't *need* the fries, but those six words have sold a lot of potatoes! So here's a question. Does suggestive selling represent *added value*, or simply business greed?

Here's an answer, in the form of a story. I was driving from my home in Cary, NC to Kill Devil Hills, which is out on North Carolina's Outer Banks. I left just before 6:00 PM after a full day in the office, and I was scheduled to meet with a client at 8:00 the next morning. The weather was marginal to miserable for about the first two-thirds of my 200 mile drive, and construction and an accident turned what's normally a 3+ hour drive into a 5+ hour ordeal. I was grumpy and tired when I pulled into Plymouth, NC just after 10:00 PM, with at least another hour to go. I needed coffee, and the only thing open in town was McDonald's.

I parked, walked in, and ordered a large coffee. The server, a woman about my age, poured it and put the top on and then smiled sort of sweetly at me. "You know what would be really good with this?" she said. "A little box of our McCookies. Would you like one of those?

Now when I think McDonald's, I don't think about cookies. I guess I knew that they sold them, with that knowledge stored somewhere in the back of my mind, but I certainly didn't walk in there that night expecting to buy any. When I did think about cookies, though, my whole outlook changed. "Yes," I thought, "I *would* like some of those," so I ordered them, paid for them, walked back out to my car and opened the little box. The next 10-15 minutes was the best part of my drive, and I owed that to a salesperson who probably never thought of herself as a salesperson, but who did a very professional selling job nonetheless.

She generated revenue — *additional revenue!* — for her employer, and I received *added value.* That's the essence of win-win selling, right? And yes, it's probably true that a lot of suggestive selling is mostly motivated by business greed, but there are also times when the suggestion is appreciated. I think it's probably worth *asking* just about everybody if they might *want* something else that you sell, just to be sure that you don't miss anybody who would value the suggestion!

A Consultative Story

Here's another story, which also reflects a retail situation and a lesson for the commercial world. I bought a new desk some years back, and I wanted to set it up facing outward into the room. That meant dealing with all of the various cords and wires connected to my keyboard, mouse, monitor, telephone, etc., and unlike many modern desks, this one didn't have pre-cut holes. *No big deal*, I though, *I'll just drill myself a hole.*

I measured all of the cords and wires and determined that I'd need a 1½ inch hole, and since I didn't have a drill bit that big, I headed off to Ace Hardware. There I found a confusing array of drill bits and hole saws, ranging in price from $1.98 to $19.95. I narrowed my choice down to three, but that's as far as I could get on my own, so I was pretty happy when a salesperson came around the corner, into my aisle.

"How can I help you today?" he asked.

I told him: "I need a large drill bit, but I'm not sure which of these is the right one."

"OK," he said, "I can help you with that, but let's start here…you don't really need a drill bit."

I said: "Oh really?"

"No sir," he said. "What you actually need is a hole."

He was right of course. And then he said: "OK, first question…how big a hole do you need?"

"It needs to be an inch and a half wide," I told him.

"OK," he said. "So far, so good. Any of these three bits will drill you a one-and-a-half inch hole. Now, what do you need this hole drilled in?"

"My desk," I told him.

"OK," he said. "What's your desk made of…wood or metal?"

"Wood," I said. Then he asked: "Is it solid wood, or could it be a laminate material over pressboard?"

"That's what it is," I said. "A laminate over pressboard."

"OK," he said, "next question: How thick is the part of the desk you need the hole through?"

"Maybe an inch or an inch-and-a-quarter," I said.

"All right," he said. "Only one more question. How many of these holes do you expect to need?"

"Just one," I said. "I just want to be able to keep all the wires from my computer and my phone out of sight as much as possible."

"Yeah," he said, "that can be pretty messy with all of those wires hanging out all over your desk. OK, this drill bit right here is the one you want for the hole you need." He handed me one of three drill bits I'd been looking at — interestingly, it was by far the least expensive of the three.

I think he sensed that I'd appreciate a little bit more explanation. "If you'd needed your hole in something made of metal," he said, "you'd have had to buy this one here," — the most expensive of the three — "and if you'd needed to drill a lot of holes in wood or pressboard, I'd have recommended this one," — which cost almost as much — "but the one you've got there will drill you one hole through inch or inch-and-a-quarter pressboard without any problem, and if you need another hole or two like it sometime in the future, you ought to be able to count on that bit to handle those, too."

Positive Experience/Additional Revenue

I thanked him for his help, and then I asked: "Have you ever had any sales training?"

"Gosh, no," he said. "I'm not any kind of salesman, I'm just a clerk in a store."

So here we have another salesperson who doesn't think of himself as a salesperson, but who did a very professional job of selling nonetheless. He may never have heard terms like *needs assessment, consultative selling,* and *applications product knowledge,* but he managed to create a very positive buying experience for his customer.

Did he generate revenue? Yes, although it was only $1.98. Did he generate *additional* revenue? Not in the sense that I spent more than I had to or intended to that day, but the positive buying experience he created has brought me back to that Ace Hardware store many times, even after Lowe's and Home Depot moved into our town.

Thinking back on that day, though, I wonder if he couldn't have generated some *additional* revenue. He did ask me if there was anything else I needed, but he didn't offer anything *suggestive*. With the power of hindsight, I'm going to suggest the following scenario:

"What kind of shape is your drill in?" he might have asked me. "Is is corded or cordless? Would you like to look at some of the new cordless drills that are 2-3 times more powerful than the first generation of battery powered drills?" I'm not sure I would have bought a new drill that day, but I'm not sure I wouldn't have! Again, I think it's probably worth *asking* just about everybody if they might *want* something else that you sell, just to be sure that you don't miss anybody who would value the suggestion, or take advantage of the opportunity.

Applications Product Knowledge

I used a term a moment ago that I think requires some explanation. *Product knowledge* should be a familiar concept to any salesperson, but it turns out that there are two kinds of product knowledge: *specifications* product knowledge and *applications* product knowledge.

Specifications product knowledge is all about the product itself — what sizes and/ or versions and/or models and/or colors it's available in. Obviously, *specifications* product knowledge is important to every salesperson. You have to know what you sell in order to sell it successfully and effectively.

Applications product knowledge is all about how the product is used — in other words, which size or version or model or even which brand will work best for the buyer or user. Is one kind of product knowledge more important than the other? I think so. To me, the essence of consultative selling is to recommend the right tool for the job. And in my experience, the world is full of people who aren't really sure what they need. They're trying to decide which drill bit they want, without really understanding that the answer lies simply and completely in the nature of the hole they need!

If they're lucky, they'll find a salesperson with the requisite product knowledge — both *specifications* product knowledge and *applications* product knowledge — someone who will ask the right questions and listen to the answers and then process that information and come up with a recommendation for the best tool — the best product or service! — for the job.

How Can I Help You?

Before we leave my Ace Hardware story, I want to mention one more thing that this salesperson did brilliantly. When he approached me, he didn't ask: "Can I help you?" Instead, he asked: "How can I help you today?"

The semantic difference is a small one, but I want you to think about the attitudinal difference. All too often, "Can I help you?" is perceived by the customer as a challenge. (All too often, it's perceived that way because the salesperson is already having a bad day, and every customer introduces the possibility of making it even worse! Please note that if you're always having bad days, you probably don't belong in any kind of sales!)

The two additional words on either end of *"How* can I help you *today*?" make it a much warmer question. *I know that I can probably help you because you called or came in here, and I'm going to try to be right in the moment with you.* It has been said that you only get one chance to make a good first impression. Which question do you think creates a better impression?

To Be Great

That, by the way, was the first example of what you'll find to be a recurring theme in this book. My goal is to teach you some of what I know about selling, but beyond that, I hope to teach you something about what it means to be a salesperson — a *great* salesperson. I think you'll agree that there are lots of not-so-great salespeople in the world; some who lack talent, some who lack integrity, and some who lack both. The true professionals in sales have had to rise above the stigma created by the denizens of the bottom of the barrel in our profession, but I think it's fair to say that those true professionals are valued by the marketplace — both by their customers and by their employers!

So what does it mean to be a great salesperson? Here's an observation, it's not *one big thing* that makes most of them great, it's that they master the *little things that can make big differences*. That's what I think we have in the difference between "Can I help you?" and "How can I help you today?"

Another Theme

Another recurring theme is that it takes courage to be a great salesperson. In fact, I believe it takes three different kinds of courage: *courage of knowledge, courage for contact,* and *courage to question.*

Courage of knowledge is pretty straightforward — the more you know about what you're selling, the more likely it is that you'll be able to sell it with confidence. And as noted, that applies to both *specifications* product knowledge and *applications* product knowledge. This is probably the most plentiful kind of courage for many of the "reluctant" salespeople I've known — for example, small business owners who have to take on the sales role — and it's probably the least plentiful kind of courage for sales rookies.

That makes sense, right? It's a lot less frightening to make a sales call when you know what you're selling! I think *courage of knowledge* explains about half of why it's easy for a typical small business owner to go out and meet with a customer or prospect when it's that person who initiated the contact. The main topic of conversation is likely to be the product or service or project that prompted the call in the first place, and talking about something that familiar is well within most small business owners' comfort zones.

For rookies, talking about the product or service or project can be the scary part. That's why it's so important to work on your product knowledge — both *specifications* product knowledge and *applications* product knowledge — from Day One to the day you retire!

Courage for Contact

Courage for contact is probably the most plentiful kind of courage for sales employees — at least, for those who are well suited to a sales position in the first place — and probably the least plentiful for typical small business owners. The opposite of *courage for contact* is often called *call reluctance*, and it's a killer in the sales world. If you don't make the calls, you won't be very successful, and it's always very sad to me when a lack of *courage for contact* is all that keeps sales success from happening. It's a lot easier when they call you, of course, and that's the other half of why typical small business owners have so little trouble "selling" to customers or prospects who initiate the contact. It's not the "selling" that's scary to most reluctant salespeople, it's the act of making the first move toward a possible (likely?) rejection.

The cure for this affliction is pretty straightforward. You just have to understand that the rejection is not personal. In fact, it's really just a reflection of three elements of human nature — (1) resistance to change, (2) further resistance to adding anything to what's probably already a heavy workload, and (3) a general distrust of salespeople.

In the real world of sales, the odds are stacked against you when you pick up the telephone to try to make that first move. The chances of rejection are much greater than the chances of acceptance on any individual prospecting call, but it's usually no more personal than having a traffic light turn red as your car approaches an intersection.

So here's some more Dinosaur Wisdom: *If traffic lights don't keep you from driving, then the fear of rejection shouldn't keep you from selling!* Granted, you need *courage for contact*, but that courage really shouldn't be too hard to find. In fact, most successful salespeople will tell you that the fear goes away pretty quickly once you learn that it's not personal, and you learn that simply by experiencing it.

By the way, I'm going to teach you a process in which picking up the telephone is *not* your first move. I'm opposed to cold calls, both making them and receiving them. There's a better way to start your sale!

Courage to Question

The third kind of courage is *courage to question* — and by this, I mean the courage to ask provocative questions, and to demand answers! It's this kind of courage that really separates the top salespeople from everyone else. In other words, *courage of knowledge* and *courage for contact* provide a good start, but *courage to question* will take you to a whole different level.

The idea of *asking for the order* is familiar to most salespeople (although many salespeople never actually do it! We'll talk more about that later on.) The point I want to make here is that *asking for the order* is not really a provocative question! I was out on a sales call not too long ago with a network systems salesperson, and after walking the prospect through her proposal, she asked a far more assertive question than: "Can I have the order?" Instead, she said: "I feel like I've done a good job putting together the system you need, and a pretty good job in presenting it to you. Here's what I need to know now — do you feel like I really know what I'm talking about, and that you can trust my recommendations?"

The look on the prospect's face made it clear that he wasn't expecting that question, and he actually told the salesperson that he was impressed with her courage. "I'm in sales too," he said, "and I'm not sure I could stick my neck out as far as you just did. If I ask for the order and they say *no*, I don't have to take it personally. But if I ask if they trust me and they say *no*, that's a whole different story!"

"Well, my coach here," she said, pointing her thumb in my direction, "has been telling me that it takes courage to be a great salesperson, and that's what I want to be. And I think whether I make this sale or not really boils down to whether you trust me or not, so why not just ask you that question? What's the worst thing that could happen? I might learn that I still have some convincing to do, but at least I might get to do that before you make the decision to buy from someone else!"

Needless to say, I was pleased with my client's performance. She had the courage to embrace the best possible strategy — recognizing the most likely core obstacle and going right after it — and she also had the courage to explain her strategy to her prospect. I'm a very strong believer in *transparent* selling strategy, and I'll write more about that later on.

For now, I hope you'll see the importance of *courage to question*. Do you see how you can benefit from assertive and provocative questions, even if the answer to your question is *no*? Sure, it would be great to hear that your prospect is "sold" on you already, but if that's not the case, you're a lot better off learning that sooner rather than later — while you still have an opportunity to do something about that situation, or *before* you put more time and energy into a sales effort that might be doomed to fail! Here's some more Dinosaur Wisdom: *If you learn what the problem is, you have an opportunity to fix it. If you haven't got a clue, you also haven't got a prayer!*

Demanding Answers

As noted, *courage to question* must include the courage to demand answers. Maybe I'd better explain what I mean by that. If you're of a certain age, you'll remember Nikita Khrushchev. (If you're not of that age, he was the Premier of the Soviet Union back in the "bad old days" of the Cold War.) If you do remember Khrushchev, you'll almost certainly remember the image of him pounding his shoe on a table, and that's *not* what I mean by demanding answers!

What I do mean is having the patience and courage to wait for an answer, even (especially?) when an uncomfortable silence follows your provocative question. Most salespeople react to any silence by filling it, and that's usually the wrong strategy. Be patient. *Force* them to answer with your silence. Don't let them off the hook, especially when the answer to your question might be the key to identifying the pain or the problem or the hot button that will lead to the result you're looking for!

One more thought on this subject. Sometimes the silence is not their unwillingness to answer; sometimes it's because they're *thinking* about *how* to answer. If you come into my office and ask me a thoughtful and provocative question, and then start talking again while I'm considering a thoughtful and enlightening answer, I'm probably not going to like you very much!

A Recommendation

I'm sure you know how to ask questions, but you may have to develop the courage to ask more provocative questions. So here's what I recommend: At the end of your next prospecting sales call, ask your suspect or prospect *"How'd I do today? Did I make any progress toward turning you into a customer?"* If you get a positive answer, ask *"What specifically did I do right?"* and then ask *"What do you think I should do next?"* If you get a negative answer, ask *"What specifically did I do wrong?"* and then ask *"What do you think I should do next?"*

I think you'll find that many people will give you thoughtful and enlightening answers to questions like these, and those answers will either help you to reach your goal, or else they'll make it clear that you're unlikely to succeed with that particular prospect. Either way, you'll learn that the *courage to question* generally gets you the answers you need. Once you realize that — and realize that you're unlikely to suffer any physical harm from asking assertive and provocative questions — you can start questioning and challenging whatever objections you encounter.

I'm pretty sure you'll find that courage alone will make you a better salesperson! And courage plus improvement in strategy and technique should make for a really good combination.

2
Skillsets and Knowledge Bases

So far, I have touched on *product knowledge* and alluded to *questioning skills*. It probably won't surprise you that I have more to say about skillsets and knowledge bases. OK, so what do you have to *know* to be successful in sales? I believe that your *knowledge base* has four components: *product knowledge, market knowledge, operational knowledge* and *selling knowledge*.

Product Knowledge

As we've discussed, there are two kinds of *product knowledge*: *specifications* product knowledge and *applications* product knowledge. And as noted, I believe that *applications* product knowledge is the more important of the two. Think back on my drill bit story. Even a civilian like me was able to pick out three bits that seemed to have the right *specifications*, but I needed professional help to determine which one was the right tool for my specific *application*.

Please note the word *civilian*. That's my term for anyone who doesn't have *professional knowledge* of the application at hand. For example, a chef would probably not be considered a *civilian* when talking with a restaurant equipment salesperson, but an architect working at designing his/her first kitchen certainly would be. It's a reasonable assumption that the chef probably knows what he/she wants or needs — but then again, it's not a certainty!

I have first-hand knowledge of that situation, by the way, having worked my way through college in the kitchens of hotels and restaurants and then spending the next five years in restaurant management before taking a sales job with a restaurant equipment company. I learned two things on that job that I think qualify as Dinosaur Wisdom: *(1) that the chefs usually knew what they wanted, but not always what they needed,* and *(2) that it was usually about price if it wasn't about* better.

I remember a call from one of my regular customers: "Dave, I need another dozen sets of long tongs (a necessity for reaching into hot places, of which a commercial kitchen has many!) Do you still have those 16" lightweights on sale?"

"Yes, we do," I answered, "but didn't you buy a dozen of those 5-6 weeks ago?"

"Was it only 5-6 weeks?" he answered. "Well, the guys are either losing them or breaking them or stealing them, so I need more as soon as I can get them. They're only like a buck apiece, right?"

"No," I said, "they're like 6 bucks apiece. Chef, are they losing them or stealing them or breaking them? It makes a difference!"

"Yeah, you're probably right," he said. "I know I've broken a couple pair, so that's probably what's happening with the other guys. You're going to try to sell me better ones now, aren't you?"

"I'm going to suggest that option, yeah," I said. "They cost almost twice as much, but they're made of heavy-gauge steel, so they'll probably last 10 times as long. I think that's the solution to your problem!"

"OK," he said. "Send 'em over."

The real moral of this story is that the chef viewed the tongs as a *commodity* item, and the guiding principle for buying any commodity is *cheap and convenient.* There's not a lot of added value potential in the commodity sales equation (other than possibly the *convenient* part.) Beyond that, the chef knew what he wanted, but not what he needed — and he *needed* a professional salesperson to point that out to him!

Do you see how my *specifications* product knowledge and my *applications* product knowledge came together to provide real value to a fellow professional? Now think about how important it would be to a *civilian!*

(By the way, I would like you to note that the commonly accepted opposite of *professional* is *amateur,* but that's not the term I've chosen to use. I think *civilian* shows a greater respect for the suspect, prospect or customer — another one of those *little things* that I think makes a big difference!)

Solutions and Problems (and Jargon)

I want to talk next about *market* knowledge, but before we get there, I want to ask you to consider my use of the word *solution* in that last story. The point I want to make here is that too many salespeople use way too much jargon in their sales conversations. When I used that word, I was talking about the solution to a real problem, not a *solution* as the term is used by so many marketing and sales people these days.

Jargon is OK, I suppose, if both parties know exactly what the selling party is talking about, but that seems to be the exception rather than the rule. I think many salespeople use jargon and other "big words" in the hope that they'll sound knowledgeable, and the end result may be that they sound knowledgeable but they don't actually communicate.

I've started to cringe every time I hear a salesperson talking about *solutions*. I was out on a call with a printing salesperson recently, and he told his prospect: "I don't want you to think of me as a printing salesman. I want you to think of me as a solutions provider."

I jumped in and asked the prospect what that term meant to him. "In all honesty," he said, "I don't know. We even advertise that we sell 'sleep solutions' — a term we got from one of our suppliers — but I'm not 100% sure what it means." (I think it's worth mentioning that this prospect was the owner of a very successful chain of mattress stores, and my impression was that he was a very bright guy.)

"How about you?" I asked the salesperson. "What exactly were you trying to communicate when you used that term?"

"Mostly that we're different," he said. "I've been reading that you need to differentiate yourself from all the other suppliers by focusing on solutions rather than transactions."

"So basically," I said, "you were hoping to look different and sound smart by saying something vague that even you didn't really understand. Is that a fair statement?"

The salesperson didn't say a word — although it's probably fair to say that if looks could kill, I'd have been lying very dead on the floor. "Lighten up," I said. "You're learning an important lesson here, and I bet this guy actually likes you better right now than he did a minute and a half ago." The prospect smiled and said: "I probably do. I think we're all learning something here."

"OK then," I said, "let me change the subject. How's business?"

"We're down pretty significantly," he answered. "People aren't buying as many mattresses as they were a year ago."

"Here's what scares me," I said. "What if people *are* buying mattresses, but they're not buying them from you because you're talking about 'sleep solutions' and they don't know what that means — or maybe they perceive a 'sleep solution' to be a lot more expensive than just a new mattress?"

Then the salesperson jumped back in: "This is exactly what I'm talking about," he said. "I'll help you to identify issues like that and market more effectively!"

"Then why didn't you say that," I asked him, "instead of sounding like a million other jargonauts in your attempt to sound different? Now you're starting to communicate. We've identified a real problem and now you're positioned to suggest a real solution!"

Personal Crusade

I should admit that this whole *solutions* thing has become a personal crusade. I'm all for *solutions selling*, which is just another way to say *consultative selling* — identify a problem and propose a solution; identify pain and propose pain relief; identify a better way of doing something and propose that as a reason for using your products or services or capabilities!

This whole *solutions* thing has gotten out of hand, though, and I'm not the only one who feels that way. I offer the following as proof:

> so·lu·tion (noun) the act, method, or process of solving a problem; the answer to a problem. (yourdictionary.com, Webster's New World College Dictionary, © 2005, Wiley Publishing, Inc., Cleveland, OH)
> so·lu·tion (jargon) a marketroid term for something he (or she) wants to sell you without bothering you with the often dizzying distinctions between hardware, software, services, applications, file formats, companies, brand names, and operating systems. (The Free On-line Dictionary of Computing, © 1993-2007, Denis Howe)

If you think being a *solutions provider* is a differentiating factor, I think you might be wrong. Once something becomes jargon, you're probably better off getting away from it and going back to the fundamental concept. Remember, by the way, that guys like me are always looking for differentiating ideas, and the whole concept of *solutions selling* has been propagated by the same "sales gurus" — or perhaps the next generation of the species — who brought you *consultative selling, Spin*

Selling, Selling to VITO, etc. I'm not telling you that any of that stuff is bad. I'm just telling you that it needs to be based on the established fundamentals or else it's not going to work for you, however sexy it might seem and sound.

Another Concern

Here's another *solutions*-based concern. I have a postcard on my desk — a direct mailer from a local company — and the front face of the card features a picture of a man standing in front of an office building, the rather generic name of the company (Paul Johnson and Associates) and the tagline: "Your Business Solutions Provider!" Can you tell me what that company sells? For all the postcard tells you, it could be anything from accounting services to whatever kind of business need might start with the letter "Z"!

Fortunately, the other side of the postcard did a little better job of explaining Paul Johnson's area of expertise, but please consider this — with the massive information overload that most people have to deal with, is it wise to ask them to work any harder than absolutely necessary to figure out what they could be/should be buying from you? If you use clear and mainstream language to express your intent and your proposition, you'll probably have a lot greater success. Here's some more Dinosaur Wisdom: *It is not the buyer's responsibility to communicate with the seller, it's the other way around.* Lose the jargon and you'll win more sales!

Market Knowledge

OK, I fell better now, having gotten that out of my system, so let's get back to *your* knowledge base. *Market knowledge* is the second element, and just as with *product knowledge,* there are two kinds of market-related knowledge that are important to most salespeople. The first one is knowledge of the trends in your product/service/usage category. The second is knowledge of what's going on in your sales territory.

The trends I'm referring to are often related to *applications product knowledge.* For example, the food-service industry has come under pressure to remove some of the health risk factors associated with out-of-home eating. One of the things they've been working on is the removal of trans fats from frying oils. (Like I said earlier, most people don't *need* the fries, but we *want* them anyway, right?)

If you sell frying oils to restaurants, you should definitely know what's going on with that research. But what if you sell "fryolators" to restaurants, or backing up one step in the distribution chain, what if you sell "fryolators" to restaurant equipment companies who in turn sell them to restaurants. The knowledge of frying oils may not be critical to those jobs, but do you see how it would represent added value? Maybe the best way to express this is that *product knowledge* is mostly about the present, while *market knowledge* includes a vision of the future. I think most of us have experienced a piece of hardware that turned out to be incompatible with a later piece of software — or vice versa! — and it would have been nice if a salesperson's *market knowledge* had protected us from that situation.

Where do you get that sort of market knowledge? I think you start by *reading* any trade publications that support your industries. Please note the italics for emphasis. I think most salespeople maybe glance at their trade publications, but they don't really *read* them so they don't really *learn* anything. That's pretty sad, and it relates to another piece of Dinosaur Wisdom: *If your company — or your industry — doesn't provide formal* training *to teach you everything you need to know, you must take responsibility for* learning. Great salespeople do that. Sadly, most of the not-so-great salespeople do not.

Your Territory

The second element of *market knowledge* is about what's going on in your sales territory. What's that you say, you don't have a specifically defined territory? Well, then, here's some more Dinosaur Wisdom: *If your company doesn't* assign *you to a specific sales territory, you should* define *one for yourself!*

Before you get too alarmed over that statement, let me explain that my philosophy on defining a sales territory is not about *limitation*, it's about *focus*, and geography is only one of the factors that should define your sales territory. This is an issue that's related to *niche marketing*, and I have found there to be four kinds of *niches* in just about every market.

First, there are *geographic* niches; for example, you sell something big and heavy where shipping cost is a major issue. If your closest competitor is 100 miles away, the radius in which shipping cost tilts in your favor is approximately 50 miles. Obviously, you can call on people outside of that radius, but the question is, can you sell to them? At some point, the cost of shipping tilts in the competitor's favor and puts you at a disadvantage.

Next are *industry* niches, and this gets a little more complex. On one hand, you might sell something that is very specific to one industry; for example, a computer/

communications product explicitly designed for law enforcement. On the other hand, you might sell something much more general, like my father did. He was an office products salesperson for most of his working life, and his geographic territory extended from Boston to as far north as he wanted to go. There were thousands and thousands of businesses in that geographic area, and pretty much all of them had some need for office equipment and supplies, but my father developed a couple of pretty specific niches.

His best customer was the home office of a hotel chain, and he learned a lot about the office products requirements of hotel companies from his dealings with them. That led him to focus on other hotels and hotel companies. He was also an avid tennis player, and another niche he selected was swim and tennis clubs, much like the one we belonged to. His third niche was banks, and back in the day, every city and town in American had at least one locally-owned bank, so he had plenty of prospects in that niche segment alone. "I'm a specialist in banks," he would tell them — or hotels, or tennis clubs — and for the most part, the people who purchased the office supplies for those companies responded positively. They seemed to like the idea of dealing with a specialist in their industry.

Product Niches

The third category is *product* niches, and again, this is a situation where you might only sell a single product, or you might carve a product niche out of a larger line. One of my father's colleagues developed a product niche with typewriters. I never completely understood his unwillingness to sell more than just typewriters to his prospects and customers, but the fact of the matter is that he made a good living selling a very small part of the office equipment and supplies product line. He would target situations where a company or organization would be buying 20 or 30 or more machines, and he made a lot of big sales, especially during the transition from manual typewriters to electric machines.

I actually helped to deliver and install what I think was his all-time record order: 155 IBM Selectrics. I was maybe 14 at the time, and I think I earned $15 for carrying half of those machines to the offices they'd be used in, taking them out of their cartons, setting them on their desks, and hauling all the cartons away. (That was pretty good money in those days, by the way. The whole thing took about 6 hours if I remember right, and the minimum wage at that time was $1.25 per hour. There were not a lot of opportunities for a teen-age kid to earn twice the minimum wage!)

Personality Niches

The fourth niche category is *personality* niches, and this one gets a little eclectic. The basic idea is that you'll generally be most successful in selling when you have something in common with the people you're selling to. Most salespeople — and many buyers — will tell you that *people buy from people they like*, and there's certainly some truth to that. The *like factor* is not the most important factor, though, and we'll talk more about that later on.

It is, however, a contributing factor, so that raises the question of why people like other people, and I think that takes us back to the fundamental idea of having something in common. If you're interested in sports, you will probably enjoy common ground with other sports fans. If you're interested in ballet, you should experience the same dynamic with other ballet enthusiasts. Within broad interest categories, though, there's a greater possibility that your specific interest will not match theirs — for example, you favorite sport might be football and the buyer's favorite sport might be soccer. There's a general match there, but it might not be a specific-enough match to support a relationship.

In the ballet example, you might be a fan of George Balanchine, but the buyer might prefer Jerome Robbins. There's a considerable difference between their styles, but in terms of common ground, the Balanchine-Robbins gap is considerably smaller than the football-soccer gap. I think you'll also agree that there are probably more sports fans in the world than ballet fans.

That leads us to another element of Dinosaur Wisdom: *You should always be looking for common ground and common interests, but the strongest bonds will be formed around the most eclectic interests.* Here's what that means: You might never be more than just *one of* the salespeople a buyer talks football with, but you might well be the only one he/she talks about ballet with. Part of the artistry in selling is to identify those areas of common ground where you'll really stand out.

Specific Applications

Here are two specific applications of how *personality* niches can be factored into defining a territory. As I mentioned earlier, I live in Cary, NC, which is a suburb of Raleigh, which in turn is one of the cities which represents the points of the Research Triangle region — Raleigh, Durham and Chapel Hill. Each of those cities is the home to a great university — The University of North Carolina in Chapel Hill, Duke University in Durham, and North Carolina State University in Raleigh — and all three schools are members of the Atlantic Coast Conference, which means that they are *fierce* rivals. It's pretty well understood in this area that you're either a Carolina fan, a Duke fan, or a State fan — or else you're some bozo who just doesn't understand what's important in life!

One of my local clients has four salespeople. One went to Carolina, one went to Duke, one went to NC State, and the other went to Cornell, and their territories are not defined by geography, but rather by the fan affiliation of the buyer! Their "pre-approach research" includes that information, and suspects are assigned solely based on which salesperson will have that particular common ground. I have convinced them to reassign some suspects if it turns out that a fan affiliation is not enough common ground, but as an initial strategy, this has been working pretty well for that company.

Another local client has two salespeople. One is pretty buttoned-down and businesslike, and the other is a rock'n'roller for whom the sales job is only his "day gig." Their territories are defined by the business community and the artistic community. The buttoned-down salesperson focuses on the large corporations in the Research Triangle Park, and the rock'n'roller focuses on museums and theatres and other arts-related organizations and venues. Again, they sometimes swap suspects when they learn that there's another element of potential common ground, but both salespeople are starting out in what seems likely to be a complimentary personality niche.

One More Story

Here's one more *personality* niche story. A small business owner once dragged his son over to me after a seminar — literally pulling him by his ponytail! "I want you to tell him that he has to cut this thing off," the father said, "and get rid of this thing (a ring through his lower lip). He's going to be our salesman. He needs to look dignified!"

"I'm not going to tell him that," I said, "but here's what I will tell him. *The farther you are from the mainstream in terms of appearance, the harder you may have to work to find people who will take you seriously and eventually buy from you.*" I think that qualifies as another element of Dinosaur Wisdom.

Territory Knowledge

OK, I'll have more to say about defining a territory a little farther along. For now, let's get back to the issue of *market knowledge*. In addition to the knowledge of trends in your product/service/usage category, it's also important to be on top of the business conditions in your territory. For example, if you cover a broad geographic territory with a limited product line, is the economy stronger in some parts of that geography than in others? If you cover a small geographical territory with a large product line, are there industries in your territory that are doing better than others? In either of those scenarios, are there individual companies in your territory that are doing better than others — and perhaps the flip side of that is more important: are there individual companies who are in danger of failing, and leaving your company stuck with unpaid invoices?

The great salespeople operate with their eyes and ears wide open, and they're always conscious of the market knowledge issues — both *what's going on in the market* and *where the market's going!*

Operational Knowledge

There are many, many companies in which salespeople don't get along very well with administrative and operational people. Why is that? When I ask the salespeople, the answer usually has something to do with the level of support they think they get — or don't get. When I ask the administrative and operational people, they usually tell me that the salespeople are lazy, they never handle the details, and they still make more money than anyone else. I'm sure some of that is nothing more than envy related to the compensation gap, but I also know that some of it is because many salespeople are lazy, they never handle the details, and they still make more money than anyone else!

Here's something else I know. There's a middle ground between the great salespeople and the worthless, lazy dogs. Those are the salespeople whose transgressions are more a matter of ignorance than intent. Yes, they do things the wrong way, but it's because no one has shown them the right way!

That's what *operational knowledge* is all about — clearly understanding your responsibilities and authorities and knowing how to fit in with the rest of the organization. The great salespeople know what they need from their organizations, and they also know what their organizations need from them. It's truly a partnership, and because the great salespeople carry their full share of the load, there's a lot less of that sales-versus-everyone-else friction.

I teach quite a few sales management seminars every year, and one of the principles I teach in those seminars probably qualifies as Dinosaur Wisdom: *Any knowledge which is necessary for success, but not currently present, must be trained in.* The point I try to make to the sales managers is that they're probably not spending enough time on operational training, and the problems between sales, admin and operations are often a direct result.

Now, let's put that together with a previous piece of Dinosaur Wisdom, the one that states: *If your company — or your industry — doesn't provide formal* training *to teach you everything you need to know, you must take responsibility for* learning. I think there's a real leadership opportunity here for many salespeople, to take the initiative and work with the rest of the organization to define everyone's *needs* and *wants*. If you think about that, it's nothing more than a selling challenge, to identify the problem and sell the "buyer(s)" on a solution! And who's better equipped to do that than a professional, consultative salesperson?

Selling Knowledge

The final component of your knowledge base is *selling knowledge,* but to tell you the truth, I'm not 100% sure that *knowledge* is the right word. When we get to this part of the knowledge base, I think the word *skills* might be more appropriate. And just as there were two categories of *product knowledge* and *market knowledge,* I think the ideal skillset for a salesperson contains two distinct categories: *convincing* skills and *organizational* skills.

What are the *convincing* skills? Again, lets break this down into smaller components: *prospecting* skills (which includes research skills), *communication* skills (which includes both writing and speaking skills, and of course listening skills), *questioning* skills (which is certainly part of communication, but important enough to justify a separate listing), *presentation* skills (which includes both the development and the presentation of a proposal), *negotiation* skills (which again is part of communication, but important enough to justify a separate listing) and finally, *recovery* skills (which is important because even the greatest salespeople don't always win!)

We will cover all of these skills and associated strategies in detail as we move forward. But first, let's talk about getting you better organized.

3

Organization and Time Management

Time is money. Three simple words, but there may not be a more essential truth in all of life. Time is money in so many ways, starting with the way production or development time is part of the cost of any product, and ending with the importance of *time management* to the person trying to make a living by selling that product. So why is it that *organization* and *time management* are the subjects of so much talk and so little action?

If you're like most salespeople, you probably have *sort of* an understanding of the techniques, and you probably have the best of intentions — but time and details just seem to get away from you every day. Does that sound familiar?

If so, it takes us to a fundamental question: Do you really want to make more money? If you do, reaching your earnings goal probably has something to do with getting yourself better organized and making yourself a better manager of time.

Everything In Its Place

The secret to organization is simply to *put everything in its place*. The secret to time management is simply to *plan your work and work your plan*. Over the years, there have been all kinds of organizational and time management tools, but for a salesperson in the modern age, the most appropriate fundamental tool is a *contact management* program.

There are computerized contact management programs like ACT, Outlook (with Business Contact Manager), Goldmine, Maximizer and Salesforce.com. There are also handwritten contact management tools like Day-Timer or DayRunner. The handwritten systems provide you with two of the three essential time and contact management capabilities: calendar and tickler file. The computerized programs provide you with both of those and the third: a place to put everything in its place. They also provide you with a significant added capability: mail-merge that can work with both e-mail and traditional mail. I have been using ACT for many years — going all the way back to the DOS version, which I think will maintain my Dinosaur credibility! — and I often describe it as a bunch of boxes, one for each contact, where you can stuff in everything that relates to that contact *and* you can train the box to open up and tell you when it's time to call or write or do something regarding that contact.

This ties into two more elements of Dinosaur Wisdom: (1) *You won't gain new customers from prospecting; you will gain new customers from follow-up*, and (2) *Every current customer provides you with three distinct levels of value: the value of what they're buying from you now, the value of what they could be buying from you, and the value of influence.* We'll get back to those particular Dinosaur Wisdoms later on.

Best Strategy

I think the best overall organizational strategy for a salesperson is to make *contact* management lead to *time* management. Here's what that means. As I mentioned, one of the three essential capabilities of a contact management system is the tickler file. Using ACT, for example, I can schedule my next phone call, meeting or "to-do" activity with just a few mouse clicks. Let's say that I get a lead on a Friday, and I enter all of the contact information into my database. Let's also say that I have other important things to do on Friday, so I schedule a "to-do" for Monday to do some further research.

On Monday, ACT reminds me that I want to do that — along with all of the other things I've told ACT I want to do on that particular day. Now let's say that my "task list" for this Monday consists of 37 tasks: 4 meetings, 5 "to-do's" and 28 phone calls. In ACT's daily calendar view — the second essential capability! — I see the meetings blocked out with the amount of time I think they'll take, and from there, I start "blocking in" the rest of my tasks. My basic thought process is this: "How can I jam all of these tasks into the hours of this day?"

On this particular Monday, I might see right away that it's not going to happen. Too many tasks, too little time! So now my thought process is this: "Which of these tasks are the most important ones?" In other words, the ones most likely to put money in my pocket! (OK, you may not be motivated totally by money, but I hope you'll recognize that making money is the end result of doing everything right in a sales job. That means everything from prospecting effectively to making great presentations to managing your time effectively to closing the sale. Consider this, too; if you're an employee, making money is the end result of doing what your boss wants you to do, and what your co-workers depend on you to do. Even if *you* don't want or need the money, don't forget your obligation to others!)

Here's some more Dinosaur Wisdom: *A hard-working salesperson will always have more tasks than time.* That's perfectly OK, as long as *prioritization* takes place and the most important tasks are completed. Most salespeople end their days with low priorities completed and high priorities left undone. Those salespeople make less money than the ones who end their days the other way around.

First Things First

ACT is the first thing I look at when I start out in the morning, and I don't move on to anything else until I have established my plan for the day. I usually sit down at my desk at about 7:10 AM if I'm not on the road, and I usually have my planning completed by 7:30. The next thing I do — in a planned block from 7:30 to 8:00 AM! — is check my e-mail and a couple of other business-related websites I read every morning.

Please note that I establish my priorities and plan my day first, and that checking my e-mail is *part of that plan!* I give myself enough time to read and respond to any urgent and important messages that have come in overnight, and unless one of those e-mails justifies changing my plan for the day, I'm into that plan by 8:00. I might still be working in e-mail at that point, but I'm writing e-mails that I've scheduled as "to-do" tasks in ACT. In other words, if I have important *proactive* work, I do that before less important *reactive* work.

Steven Covey describes a time management matrix in *The Seven Habits of Highly Effective People* by which any task — or interruption! — falls into one of four categories: urgent and important, urgent but not important, important but not urgent, and neither urgent nor important. *(Covey, Stephen R, 1990. The 7 Habits of Highly Effective People, Free Press, ISBN 0-67-170863-5)*

Urgent and important is the only valid reason for deviating from your plan, and when that happens, it's perfectly OK to set aside *important but not urgent* work and get to it later. Just get to it before you launch into anything that's *urgent but not important* or *neither urgent nor important!*

Be honest for a minute and ask yourself how much time you spent on *urgent but not important* yesterday. Now be really honest and ask yourself how much time you spent on the real junk — *neither urgent nor important* — and make a commitment not to do as much of that in the future! Instead, establish your priorities early in the day, and bounce every interruption against the rest of your plan for the day. If the interruption is *urgent and important,* you should drop what you're doing and attend to it. If it is any of the other three categories, you should do what you originally planned to do and get to the interruption later, or not at all.

Not At All?

Let's look at "not at all" for just a moment. What will happen if a customer or prospect asks you to do something and you don't do it? You certainly risk losing their business, or in the case of a suspect or prospect, the opportunity to ever do business with them. Look back, though, to that last piece of Dinosaur Wisdom: *A hard-working salesperson will always have more tasks than time.* Another way to say that is *a hard-working salesperson will always have more* opportunity *than time.* If you're that hard-working salesperson, you must recognize that some opportunity will fall by the wayside because you just can't get to it. If you're doing this right, though, the only factors that will keep you from getting to any opportunity are higher priorities, which means they're already putting — or more likely to put! — money in your pocket.

What if your boss — or a co-worker or a subordinate — asks you to do something which conflicts with your priorities? It's been my experience that most time management decisions are made with incomplete information. In other words, the other person is usually asking based on his or her own priorities, without any knowledge of yours. With more information, a better decision can often be reached. "OK, boss, I understand that you want me to do X. Let me just tell you that it conflicts with Y. Knowing that, do you still want me to do X, or should I do Y, or should we consider Z?"

Sometimes the "big picture" will outweigh your personal priorities, but as noted, every salesperson has to know that some opportunity will fall by the wayside just because you can't get to it. It's been said that selling is a numbers game, and this is just another reflection of that fundamental truth. Here's the critical question, though. Who will make the most money, the salesperson who has 10 fully-qualified irons in the fire but loses out on 3 of them because he/she just couldn't make the time to capitalize on them, or the salesperson who only had 5 fully-qualified irons in the fire? (Remember the definition of *fully qualified prospects*: (1) they buy exactly what you sell, (2) they buy enough of it to make pursuing them worthwhile, and (3), they show some real interest in buying from you. Anyone who doesn't meet all three of those criteria is not *fully qualified*!)

Here's another critical question. Who will make the most money, the salesperson who builds a base of small customers who eat up all of his/her time, or the salesperson who "trades up" to larger and/or less demanding customers by taking some risks in terms of customer service/customer contact in order to create the time to grow? Again, it all comes down to whether you really want to make more money or not. Like lots of things in business and in life, accomplishing that will require some *risk vs. reward* decisions, which is just another way to say *prioritization*.

Some of my clients have found it helpful to carry a prop which helps them to make time management decisions. It's a small square of paper, printed and then laminated, and what's printed on the paper is Steven Covey's time management matrix: four quadrants labeled *urgent and important, urgent but not important, important but not urgent,* and *neither urgent nor important.* When an interruption comes up, they pull out the matrix and ask themselves "OK, where exactly does this fit in?" and then they decide how to handle it.

Back To ACT

As I mentioned earlier, I've been using ACT since the DOS version, and I've seen it evolve into a fairly complex program. Lots of features have been added, but in my opinion, many of them have added mass but not value. I have described the most recent version of ACT as a product that can do 100 things, but I only need 8 of them. Here are the really important features of ACT and how you should use them:

1. The Database Fields: The "upper pane" of the ACT window is where you keep all your contact information. The pre-designed layouts include fields for the basics (company name, contact name, address, phone/fax/email, etc.) and some not-so-basics (country, website address, spouse's name, birthday, etc.). Here are the fields that I think are essential for every contact:

- Company Name
- Contact Name
- Title
- Physical Address

- E-mail Address
- Telephone Number
- Fax Number
- ID/Status

By *essential*, I mean that you should make it your business to capture this information. If any of it isn't present yet on any of your current records, call and ask for it!

Beyond the essential information, ACT's database fields allow you to capture and store all kinds of other information, ranging from the not-so-basics I mentioned earlier to much more specific-to-your-business information. For example, you could use ACT's customizable "user fields" to identify prospects or customers who use specific elements of your product line, or who belong to various civic organizations, or even where they went to high school or college! (One of my clients has a lot of fun with college and high school affiliations during the football season. He sends out congratulatory — or commiserating — e-mails every weekend to a group of prospects and customers whom he knows to be interested in their Alma Mater's football fortunes. The Internet makes it easy for him to get all the scores.)

2. The Activities Icons: At the very top of the ACT window are the *menu bar* and an *icon bar*. The menus and sub-menus let you access all of ACT's features, and the icon bar gives you quick access to the most important features, such as scheduling a phone call (a telephone icon), scheduling a meeting (an icon showing two hands shaking) and scheduling a "to-do" activity (an icon showing a finger with a string tied around it). When you click on one of these icons, it brings up a dialog box which lets you enter the specifics of the task, including date, time, duration and the specific nature or objective of the task.

3. The Task List and Calendar: Once you've scheduled a task, you can access it in three ways. First of all, each task is listed under the Activities Tab for each contact. (More on tabs to follow.) Second, it will be listed on your overall Task List, which can be accessed through an icon on the left side of the ACT window. Third, it will also be listed in daily, weekly and monthly calendar views, which can also be accessed through an icon on the left side of the window. As noted earlier, the first thing I do every day is look at my task list and daily calendar view, to prioritize and "block in" all the activities for that day. From either view, I can go to the individual contact record each task is connected to with just one mouse click.

4. The Notes Tab: The "lower pane" of the ACT window is governed by a set of tabs titled (in Version 12) Notes, History, Activities, Opportunities, Groups/Companies, Secondary Contacts, Documents, Contact Info, User Fields, Home Address, Web Info and Marketing Results. As noted, every activity scheduled for an individual contact can be seen on that record's Activities tab, and as you might expect, the Notes tab is where you take notes on your dealings with each contact. When I initiate a phone call, for example, I go from the task list or daily calendar view to the individual contact record, and as I dial the phone, I click on an icon with an image of a notebook on the icon bar, which opens up a word processing box where I write notes during and after conversation. If the contact calls me, I use the Lookup menu to take me to the contact's record and then click the "insert note" icon to start taking notes. When I come back from a meeting, I enter my notes into the record the same way.

5. The Documents Tab: As noted earlier, I sometimes describe ACT as a bunch of boxes, one for each contact, where you can stuff in everything that relates to that contact. As you've seen, some of that "stuff" goes into the database fields and some goes into the Notes tab. You can also attach "stuff" in the Documents tab — literally any file that can be saved in a computer can be attached to an individual contact record. That can mean anything from letters you've sent them to quotes or graphics files, and then all you have to do to open the file is double-click it. As I wrote earlier, the secret to organization is simply to put everything in its place!

6. Clear Activity & Schedule Follow-Up: When used properly, ACT — or any of the other contact managers — will remind you of the activities you've scheduled. After you complete each activity (including notes!), ACT provides a process to clear it and schedule whatever comes next. One mouse click brings up a "Clear Activity" dialog box which allows you to send information on that activity to the History tab. A second mouse click — on the "Follow-Up" button located in the lower-left corner of the "Clear Activity" dialog box — brings up a "Schedule Activity" dialog box, just like the one you used to schedule the activity that you're now clearing. I wrote earlier that *you won't gain new customers from prospecting; you will gain new* *customers from follow-up* — an element of Dinosaur Wisdom that I'll write more about later on. When used properly, ACT is a follow-up machine! Schedule an activity. Complete the activity. Schedule the next activity. That's how you gain new customers, and also how you manage your relationships with current customers.

By the way, one of my ironclad rules for ACT is that every contact record must have at least one future activity scheduled, even if it's only to think about doing something with that contact at some point in the future. That scheduled activity will at least bring the contact to your attention, otherwise he or she would be pretty much invisible inside of your database. The only way you'd ever come across that contact would be to scroll all the way through your database. Remember, the best approach for a salesperson is to let *contact management* lead to *time management*.

Another of my rules for ACT is to set it to roll any uncleared activity over to the next day. You do that (in Version 12) from the Tools menu, by selecting Preferences/Calendars & Scheduling/Scheduling Preferences and clicking on "automatically roll over to today" for all activity types. That insures than no activity will ever fall through the cracks. If you don't complete and/or clear it on the day it's originally scheduled for, it will continue to roll over until you do. (In earlier versions of ACT, you may find "Preferences" under the Edit menu.)

7. The Write Menu: As noted earlier, computer-based contact managers provide you with a significant added capability over paper-based systems — mail-merge that can work with both e-mail and traditional mail. Using the *Write* menu in ACT, you can compose letters, e-mails and faxes, and merge them either with individual contacts or groups of contacts. You can save standard letters and e-mail messages as templates, making it very easy, for example, to send out a group of introductory letters.

ACT also has the ability to integrate with Microsoft Word and Microsoft Outlook. Integrating with Word gives you many more features than ACT's own internal word processor. Integrating with Outlook lets you share contact and calendar information, but more importantly, it lets you send and receive e-mails from inside of ACT and then saves each e-mail message under the History tab of the individual contact record. There are also a number of third-party add-ons available for ACT which allow you to automate an entire marketing campaign; for example, setting up a series of e-mail messages to be sent out at specific intervals.

8: The Opportunities Tab: Most salespeople face two core selling challenges. The first is to sell themselves. The second is to "close the sale" on a product or service. The Opportunities tab is where you can keep track of the individual orders you're competing for. A single mouse click opens up a "New Opportunity" dialog box where you can enter the specifics of the project and even generate a quote form (which will immediately be saved in the History tab!) This dialog box also contains a "Follow-Up" button in the lower-left corner, which lets you schedule a follow-up phone call or "to-do" activity, and after completing and clearing that activity, you'll go back to the Opportunities tab and update your progress on that specific opportunity. The Opportunities tab also feeds ACT's *Reports* function, which lets you call up a variety of reports including a list of all your open quotes. That ties in to another one of my ironclad rules for ACT: *Every opened opportunity must have closure.* In other words, you must record whether you won the order or not, and if not, why not.

Mobile Options: I think the best way for most salespeople to use ACT is on a notebook computer that can be connected to a network. In that way, the active database is completely portable — meaning it can be accessed from the office, from home, from on vacation, etc. — but it can be "synched" to the network every time it connects to the network. That way the company (which is the real owner of the database, right?) maintains a copy of the database that should never be too far out of date, and the salesperson benefits from having a "backup" copy on the network server. (It's worth mentioning that several contact management programs allow you to store your database on the Internet and access it from any computer connected to the Internet. Salesforce.com was the first product based on this capability.)

I have several clients who have copies of ACT on both their office computer and a home computer, and they "shuttle" their active database file between the two machines using a USB thumb drive. I even have a client who e-mails her active database back and forth between two machines.

ACT can also be "synched" to just about any PDA device, including most smart phones. This is a good way to carry your contact list and task list with you, without having to actually carry a computer. Another benefit is that PDAs and smart phones "boot" faster than notebook computers, but the corresponding downside is that you may have to deal with text-entry limitations — a tiny keyboard and/or a stylus-based entry system. I have used a PDA in the past, but I got tired of those limitations, and now I just print my task list and/or calendar and take it with me when I go out into the field. I take notes right on those paper documents, and clear activities, schedule follow-up activities and enter my notes into ACT when I get back to my office. (I guess I really am a dinosaur!)

Other Cool Features: As I wrote earlier, I often describe ACT as a product which can do 100 things but I only need 8 of them. Beyond "need," there are still some pretty cool features attached to ACT and other computer-based contact management products. For example, there's an icon which opens up a link to MapQuest and shows me the location of the address in that record. The Web Info tab in the most recent version of ACT (ACT 12.0) lets me open a contact's website right inside the lower pane of the ACT window, and I can even run a Google search from there, or view a contact's LinkedIn record or Facebook page.

I can also use the Lookup function to pull up individual records or groups of records. For example, as mentioned earlier, I can use one of ACT's "user fields" to identify contacts who are fans of a particular football team, and pull up all of their records as a group with just a couple of mouse clicks. I can also do that using ACT's "Groups" function. (ACT lets you do a lot of things in more than one way.)

Another feature I get a lot of use out of is "My Record," which ACT prompts you to establish any time you create a new database. This is simply a record containing all of your own personal contact information, but like any other ACT record, you can schedule future activities and attach documents to it. On the day that I wrote this, I had 99 future activities scheduled under My Record, most of them simply reminders of things I don't want to forget or forget to do. These activities include relatives' birthdays and anniversaries, doctors appointments, etc. — all sorts of things I want to be reminded of that don't justify setting up a complete database record for the people or organizations I want to do them with. The "nearest" is a reminder for today that I'm expecting a technician from DirecTV this afternoon. The "farthest" is a reminder for February 1, 2014 that my passport expires in April 2014.

Please note my use of the phrase "any time you create a new database." This is something you should really only do once. I have run into people who have separate databases for customers, prospects and even different mailing lists. That's bad organizational strategy! The right way to do this is to have all of your contact records in a single database, and use the ID/Status field — one of the fields I listed as essential earlier — to differentiate between customers and prospects and list sources and other categorizations. That way, you won't have to switch between databases to access tasks or records. If you need more ways to differentiate — for example, prospects from different list sources — you can categorize them as "prospects" in the ID/Status field and use one of the user fields to identify the list source.

As noted, I'm a long-time ACT user. I often tell people that I couldn't run my life without ACT, let alone my business. Having said that, though, I really don't care whether you use ACT or any other contact management product. It's not the brand name that's important here, it's the organizational capability which provides the foundation for you to make *contact management* lead to *time management.*

Business Owners and Sales Hats

Are you the owner of your business, or perhaps an employee who has other responsibilities in addition to sales responsibilities? The time management challenge is magnified when any individual has to wear multiple "hats", but the guiding concepts are still the same — to make contact management lead to time management and to plan your work and work your plan.

If you're one of those individuals, it's critically important to block out your selling time and protect that selling time from interruption, and the "hat" analogy can be a very valuable tool here. For the sake of discussion, let's say that you've blocked out 9:30 AM to 11:30 AM for sales activities. That means at 9:30 AM, you put your sales hat on, and at 11:30 AM you take it off, *and while you're wearing that sales hat, you don't do anything other than sales activity!*

You can wear that hat figuratively or literally, by the way. I have a few clients who've needed a physical reminder of which hat they're supposed to be wearing, and a few more who have found an actual hat to be an effective signal to their staff. I remember one of them telling his employees that when they saw him wearing the red baseball cap, he was *Phil the Salesman,* not *Phil the Owner.* "Don't come to me with anything that *Phil the Owner* needs to deal with," he said, "because *Phil the Salesman* can't help you with those things. If it's something really important, come and tell me that you need *Phil the Owner,* but if it isn't, wait until he comes back."

Phil posts his daily schedule on his office door every day, so his staff can always see when he'll be taking his sales hat off, and plan accordingly. On most days, there are several people or things waiting for his attention at the moment his sales hat comes off, but with very few exceptions, they are things that are neither urgent nor critically important.

Occasionally, there are things that Phil would have considered urgent and important. Part of the success of this strategy is that Phil treats these exceptions as training opportunities. "This is the sort of thing I would like you to interrupt me with," he'll say. In fact, Phil has learned to treat almost all of the questions as training opportunities, and after dealing with the issue, he will frequently say, "Next time something like this comes up, just handle it the same way." Over time, Phil's staff has developed a pretty clear understanding of his preferences and priorities, and that does more than simply minimize interruptions to his selling time. I think Phil will tell you that his business is a lot easier to manage these days because his people are so well trained.

Another client recently said this to me: "My people aren't as well trained as Phil's people, and I'm not sure I'm comfortable being 'out of touch' for two hours at a time." I countered with: "What happens if you're out for a couple of hours making deliveries, or at a doctor's appointment? Does the whole place fall apart?" His answer was: "Sometimes is does!" I said: "OK, then we'll schedule shorter selling blocks," and what we came up with was putting the sales hat on from 9:30 AM to 10:30 AM, then taking it off for half an hour to deal with whatever issues may have come up during that hour, then putting it back on from 11:00 AM to 12:00 Noon. He still puts in two hours of sales activity every day, and that strategy — coupled with a commitment to training! — seems to be working pretty well.

Organization Summary

The secret to organization is simply to *put everything in its place*. The secret to time management is simply to *plan your work and work your plan*. The best overall strategy for a salesperson is to make *contact* management lead to *time* management. All of that adds up to ACT or another contact management product/system. Used properly, your contact management system will tell you what you should be doing each day, and your prioritization process will tell you what to do first and what to do later and what to maybe not do at all.

Your initial prioritization of each day should be part of the start of each day, but those priorities can change during the day, and there may very well be issues that will require you to drop what you're doing and apply all of your resources to dealing with them. Just remember that important *proactive* work always comes before less important *reactive* work, and remember Steven Covey's four categories: urgent and important (*drop what you're doing and deal with it!*), urgent but not important (*don't get caught up in this time-wasting trap!*), important but not urgent (*deal with it in a timely manner*), and neither urgent nor important (*the real junk, and another time-wasting trap*). Time is money, so use yours wisely!

Organization — Closing Thoughts

I tell a story in my seminars about the initial training on my second selling job (with Moore Business Forms), how I flew down to New Jersey for a week-long training program, and how every day started with breakfast meetings at 6:00 AM and ended with beer-fueled — but still job-related! — conversations late into the evening at the hotel bar. I learned a great deal that week, but there was one thing nobody covered, and it surfaced as the last question I asked my boss when he dropped me off at the airport on Friday afternoon. "How many sales calls am I supposed to make every day?" I asked him. His answer: "My top guys average 8 solid calls every day."

I later found out that he was exaggerating, but I've never thought less of him for that. Because I still remember exactly what I was thinking, sitting there in his car that day. "OK," I thought, "I didn't join this company to be an average performer. I want to be one of those top guys. I want to get noticed, and I want to get ahead, and I want to make a ton of money! If everyone else is making 8 calls a day, I'm going to find a way to make 11 calls a day!"

The result of that commitment was a level of accomplishment that no one in my division had ever seen. I put up very strong first year numbers, and in my second full year on the job, I was the president of the Divisional Sales Achievement Club — Moore's recognition of the top producer against quota in the division. And I can tell you that I didn't achieve that level of success because I was a great salesman. More than anything else, it came simply from very hard work.

OK, there was also some luck involved, but maybe not the sort of luck you might think. I wasn't lucky in inheriting a great territory, or having a huge new customer fall into my lap. No, I was lucky that I was young, and naive, and if you want to know the truth, I was lucky that I was kind of stupid back then.

Here's an example of how stupid I was. I didn't know that no one wants to see or hear from a salesperson before 9:30 or 10:00 in the morning. There are plenty of "veteran" salespeople even today who seem to know that, but I didn't. So like an idiot, I'd be on the telephone at 8:00 in the morning, calling people and maybe asking them to meet with me at 8:00 or 8:30 AM later that week. What was interesting was that I found more than a few people who were early starters themselves, and if I was calling at 8:00 or 8:30, I wasn't interrupting their breakfast or their beauty sleep.

I was also too stupid to know that no one wants to see a salesperson after 2:30 or 3:00 PM, so again, I'd be calling people late in the day and often asking them to meet with me late in the day a few days later. Again, I found more than a few people who regularly worked into the evening, so I wasn't going to be holding any of them back from getting home. Bottom line? I found that if you're willing to work long hours yourself, you can find people who'll *work with you* at pretty much any hour of a long business day.

Here's something else I found. Those people who worked long hours themselves were inclined to take me seriously because we shared a similar work ethic. I think you know that salespeople in general don't have a great reputation for being hard-working, and I'm sad to say that the reputation for short days and short-cuts is generally well deserved. You have an opportunity to stand out in the crowd the same way that I did, simply by "stretching the envelope" that defines most salespeople's working day.

Now here's some Dinosaur *Attitude*: If the reason you're not at the volume level you should be — or the earnings level you want to be! — is that you're not putting in a full day every day, I have no sympathy for you. *Time is money* means that time can be turned into money. Time that's not spent efficiently or effectively will generate less money than time that is. And time that's not spent at all generates no money at all.

Sales, Science and Engineering

Here's a little insight into how my mind works. When I think about time management, I often find myself thinking about Albert Einstein, and when I think about Einstein, I often find myself thinking about Sir Isaac Newton too. They were both brilliant scientists, but now you may be thinking, what do either of them have to do with sales? It turns out that you can apply much of what Einstein and Newton theorized to the science and engineering of selling.

Before I go any farther with that notion, let's make sure that you understand the difference between science and engineering. Perhaps the most basic explanation is that scientists create knowledge; they study the world as it is and seek to understand and explain things. Engineers, on the other hand, apply that knowledge, often in an effort to change the world. Maybe another way to explain this is that scientists are mostly about *specifications* while engineers are all about *application*.

Newton's Laws of Motion

Sir Isaac Newton is probably best known for the discovery of gravity — according to legend, it all happened when an apple fell off of a tree and hit him on the head. His *Universal Law of Gravitation* was the accepted explanation for gravitational behavior for more than 200 years, until it was superseded by Einstein's *Theory of General Relativity*. Newton is also well known for defining three *Laws of Motion*, and that's where his main contribution to the science of selling can be found.

Newton's First Law — sometimes referred to as the "law of inertia"— is usually stated in this way: *An object at rest tends to stay at rest and an object in motion tends to stay in motion with the same speed and in the same direction unless acted upon by an unbalanced force.*

What does that mean to a salesperson? The best way to answer that question may be to ask you *what* you compete with when you're out looking for new business. Please note that I'm not asking you *who* you compete with, because while it's (hopefully!) true that you compete with other salespeople and other companies on a regular basis, at the most fundamental level, it's not those salespeople and their companies that you compete with. You're really in competition with what they represent: the *status quo*. Here's some more Dinosaur Wisdom: *You're always in competition with the current and existing state of affairs as it pertains to your products and/or services.* That may mean another supplier, but it also may mean that they've never purchased a product or service like yours before.

Either way, a big part of your challenge is to break the inertia. If your suspect is at rest, you need to get them into motion. If your suspect is already in motion, you need to turn that motion in your direction. You have to be the *unbalanced force* that acts on the status quo. You may be familiar with the term *change agent*. That's just another way of describing a great salesperson.

Newton's Second Law

Newton's Second Law Of Motion is usually stated this way: *The acceleration of an object as produced by a net force is directly proportional to the magnitude of the net force, in the same direction as the net force, and inversely proportional to the mass of the object.*

OK, I apologize, but that's exactly what it says in the basic physics textbook I used to do my research on this point. Newton's Second Law can also be expressed by the equation $F = M \times A$, or Force equals Mass times Acceleration.

What does that mean to a salesperson? Newton's Second Law tells us that the more satisfied a suspect is with the *status quo*, the harder a salesperson will have to work to create the motion that might turn that buyer into a customer. That takes us back to time management, because you always have to be asking yourself if any individual suspect is worth all that effort.

Pushing vs. Pulling

The application of *force* also represents a very direct connection to Newton's Third Law of Motion, which tells us: *For every action, there is an equal and opposite reaction.* In practice, the force you apply to a suspect/prospect can be processed in one of two ways. It can be reflected back at you in a classic "equal and opposite" reaction—in other words, the buyer is pushing you away—or it can be channeled toward working with you.

This points to the difference between *pushing* and *pulling*, and it's a significant difference in terms of selling strategy. The *pushers* talk mostly about their products and services. The *pullers* talk mostly about their suspects, prospects and customers. The *pushers* lead with statements — *my product has been proven to reduce carbon emissions so it's better for the environment!* The *pullers* lead with questions — *do you have issues or concerns with carbon emissions and their effect on the environment?*

I think the *pullers* are much better *engineers*, but let me come back to that in a moment.

Einstein's Theory of Relativity

Albert Einstein was born 152 years after Newton's death, and he had access to much improved observation and measurement technology — some of which was a direct result of the *application* of Newton's science. Einstein himself published more than 300 scientific works, but he is probably best known for the equation $E = mc^2$ — *Energy equals mass multiplied by the speed of light squared.*

$E = mc^2$ doesn't have any direct application to sales, but Einstein also theorized that space and time are *relative* — in other words, they depend on the motion of the observer who measures them — and that's where his main contribution to the science of selling can be found. One of the key elements of Einstein's Special Theory of Relativity is that the relative passage of time slows as the relative speed of the observer increases. The most common application of this theory suggests that a person who travels to the stars and back at near-lightspeed would be younger on his/her return than a person who stayed on earth during that journey.

What does that mean to a salesperson? I think Einstein's Special Theory of Relativity provides us with a really good explanation of what happens when a salesperson tries to move too quickly in building a relationship or making a sale. If the salesperson is selling at Warp 9 and the buyer is buying at 1/2 Impulse, the relative speed creates a spatial gap that's far more likely to grow than to shrink. The best selling happens when the seller and the buyer are *on the same page* — or at least somewhere close to the same place in the spacetime continuum!

Current Customers

Beyond these applications to suspects and prospects, both Einstein's Theory of Relativity and Newton's Laws of Motion have some bearing on the other half of your sales equation: keeping the customers you already have. The "law of inertia" tells us that that they'll stay with you if you keep them happy, and Newton's Second Law explains why some customers require — and are worth — a greater level of effort in order to keep them happy. Newton's Third Law demonstrates the equilibrium of a solid and profitable customer relationship; one where you get value from the relationship that's equal to the effort you put in.

Einstein's Theory of Relativity reminds us that it's critical to *stay* on that same page with your customers. If their needs change — or their *wants* for that matter! — they're going to *gravitate* to someone who can satisfy the new need/want equation. The best way to prevent that from happening is simply to stay in touch.

No, wait, *simply* is the wrong word. This is not just a staying *in touch* with the buyer issue — *Hey, how's it going? Are you enjoying the summer? Do you need any of my stuff today?* — it's an issue of staying *in front of* any changes in the buyer's situation. *Hey, how's it going? Are you enjoying the summer? Do you see anything changing in your usage of my products and/or services? Is there anything you need — or want, or may need or want — that you're not getting from me, or that you're not sure you can get from me? Please let me know if there's anything that can help me to stay out in front of your wants and needs!*

Physics & Psychology

OK, I hope I've made the point that there are valid scientific explanations for many of the phenomena of selling. I'm not suggesting that either Newton or Einstein was in any way driven by the possibility that his knowledge would be helpful to salespeople someday, but I am saying that it's important to understand the underlying physics and psychology of your craft. The better you understand the science, the more likely it is that you can *apply it* to improve your performance.

So far, we've only talked about the physics, but a great deal of scientific research has also been done to understand the psychology of selling — although it might be more correct to express that as the psychology of *buying*. Here's some more Dinosaur Wisdom: *The better your understanding of what makes a buyer tick, the greater your chances of turning that buyer into a customer.*

There has also been a great deal of general psychological research that can be applied to buying and selling. I remember a training course from my Moore Business Forms days, called *Connecting With People*, which was based on the Myers-Briggs and Keirsey personality assessment processes.

Katharine Cook Briggs and her daughter, Isabel Briggs Myers were American psychologists who devised a psychometric questionnaire to measure the psychological preferences in how people perceive the world and make decisions. Expanding on theories developed by Swiss psychiatrist Carl Jung, the Myers-Briggs assessment is based on 4 *preferences* which lead to 16 distinct *personality types*.

The *preferences* are Extraversion or Introversion, Sensing or Intuition, Thinking or Feeling and Judging or Perceiving. In the Myers-Briggs terminology, each of the *preferences* is represented by a single letter, and the 16 resulting *personality types* are represented by 4-letter combinations. If INTJ or ESFP ring any bells for you, you've probably been exposed to the Myers-Briggs assessment at some point.

David Kiersey is another American psychologist who has continued to develop Jung's original theories. He developed the Kiersey Temperament Sorter, and fleshed out the descriptions of the 16 personality types — even to the point of giving them names which are far more evocative than the Myers-Briggs acronyms. For example, Keirsey calls an INTJ (Introversion, Intuition, Thinking, Judging) a *Scientist*, and an ESFP (Extroversion, Sensing, Feeling, Perceiving) an *Entertainer*.

Connecting With People tried to teach us how to evaluate each buyer's personality type, and then how to sell to that specific personality type. As you can probably imagine, it was suggested that you go at a Scientist with *facts*, but you try to appeal more to an Entertainer's *feelings*.

Now the big question: Did this training program help any of us to be more effective and successful? In my own case, the best answer is that it probably didn't hurt. I remember one element of the training, though, that I definitely disagree with now. The instructor told us: "You have to make your evaluation of the buyer within the first 30 seconds, otherwise none of this will do you any good." That may be true in a retail environment, but in anything that involves a "commercial" sales cycle, I think it's far better to avoid a snap judgment. Here's some more Dinosaur Wisdom: *When you have time to get to know someone, take the time and* use *the time to develop the strongest possible relationship.* Remember what happens when a salesperson tries to move too quickly!

By the way, if you're interested in taking either the Myers-Briggs Type Indicator or the Keirsey Temperament Sorter to get to know *yourself* a little better, you can do either of those things online. My best recommendation might be to buy a copy of one of David Keirsey's books — *Please Understand Me* or *Please Understand Me II* — both of which contain versions of the Keirsey Temperament Sorter which you can take and score yourself.

Let me make it clear that these are not *sales books* — in fact, the emphasis is more on understanding and improving spouse and family relationships — but I think you'll find them interesting and informative, and like *Connecting With People*, they probably won't hurt your sales performance either!

Behavioral Psychology

While we're talking about psychology and psychologists, there's one more we should consider — B.F. Skinner. As a grad student at Harvard in 1928, Skinner built a device capable of measuring and recording the number of times a rat pressed a bar to receive a food pellet. This provided a means to collect much more objective data about behavior than scientists had ever been able to gather before, and Skinner's observations of rats convinced him that *any behavior which is rewarded will likely be repeated.*

Skinner's body of work defines four contexts of *operant conditioning*: *positive reinforcement* (when a behavior is followed by a favorable stimulus); *negative reinforcement* (when a behavior is followed by the removal of an aversive stimulus); *positive punishment* (when a behavior is followed by an aversive stimulus); and *negative punishment* (when a behavior is followed by the removal of a favorable stimulus).

I remember the *punishment* contexts from my own childhood. Once when I was about 3, I stuck my fingers into an electric socket, producing a *very* adverse stimulus. That's all it took to teach me never to do that again! My parents tended toward *negative punishment* when I misbehaved, and one result was that I watched a lot less television than most of my friends did.

The *reinforcement* contexts are much more relevant to the psychology of selling/ buying. Your *customers* continue to buy from you when that behavior is followed by a favorable stimulus, and some of your *prospects* will become customers if you convince them that you can remove any adverse stimulus from their lives — spell that: P-A-I-N. On the other side of that coin, your *customers* might start thinking about buying from someone else if you cause them pain!

There's another important application of behavioral psychology in the later stages of the selling process, but we'll get to that a little farther along. Right now, let's start a transition from *science* to *engineering*.

Process and Engineering

Here's some more Dinosaur Wisdom: *Making a sale is a process, not an event!* The process may be simple or complex, and it may happen quickly or require a long sales cycle. Either way, the secret to long-lasting success in selling is to *engineer* a process that will work for you. How do you do that? The answer starts with another part of the difference between science and engineering: *scientists start at the beginning, while engineers usually start at the end.*

I think the exploration of the moon provides us with a good example of what I'm talking about here. The first astronomers observed the moon, night after night, month after month. As they gained knowledge, they were able to establish some theories — like where the moon went during the day, and why you didn't see much of it some nights. Continued observation and better tools and techniques either proved or disproved those theories, and eventually brought mankind to the point where we knew everything we could know about the moon without actually going there.

Science wanted to do that, so *engineering* had to figure out *how* to do it. The goal was clear — fly some guys to the moon, land them there and then fly them back home along with some souvenirs. The *process* started with that goal and the engineers worked backward from there, building the tools they'd need to reach their goal and trying to anticipate every problem that might arise. Engineering a sales process should work exactly the same way.

Process and Strategy

I should probably clarify that *process* and *strategy* are not the same thing. When I talk about *process,* I'm talking about a defined series of actions — first I do A, then I do B, and then depending on the response to B, I do C^1, C^2 or C^3. When I talk about *strategy*, I'm talking more about a philosophical approach to selling.

For example, my own selling strategy is *consultative* rather than *declaratory* — in other words, I'm a *puller* not a *pusher*. I'm not trying to sell myself *to you*, but rather, to help you to sell yourself *on me*. My selling strategy is also highly *transparent*, and I'll expand on that later on.

It might also be helpful to explain that my overall *business strategy* is to grow my business by increasing my speaking revenues, and that this represents a fairly recent change. For the last 20 years, my business has been built on three components: speaking, consulting and publishing. The speaking part of my business has provided both a direct and an indirect revenue stream. In other words, I've been paid to give speeches and present seminars, and then I've also been paid for consulting assignments which resulted from the *exposure* I got from those speeches and seminars. Most of my consulting business comes from *inquiries*, and most of them come from people hearing me speak or reading something I've written.

I'm at a stage now where I want to do even more speaking but much less heavy lifting — and that's a pretty good way to describe my consulting activities. Consulting involves long days of meetings and extensive follow-up. Speaking involves showing up on time and delivering a presentation that I can do in my sleep. Beyond that, I often earn more for delivering a 55-minute keynote or a 2-hour seminar than I do for a full day of consulting work, so I think you'll agree that my new business strategy makes a fair amount of sense!

Goals and Process

OK, having established my overall business *strategy*, I've set some overall business *goals*. The primary goal is a revenue goal: $$X00,000 in total revenue for next year, with half of that coming from the speaking component of my business. Taking that another step — by dividing my average speakers' fee into my speaking revenue goal — I've determined that I'll need approximately Y speaking engagements in order to reach that goal. Taking that still one more step — by projecting how many speaking engagements I'll get from current customers — I've determined that I'll need approximately Z new customers in order to reach my goal. All of this will have some bearing on how many *suspects* I'll have to run though my selling *process*.

Now let's consider the specific goal of that selling process, and the best way to express that goal starts with a question: *What exactly do I want these suspects to say yes to?*

The answer is: *Yes, I want to hire you to train and/or motivate my people.*

I don't expect that to happen on my first contact. I do want to engineer a process that gets me there. So, my *strategy* is both consultative and transparent, my *goal* is to get hired, and my *process* has to address all of the obstacles and objections that may stand in my way.

What are those obstacles? The best way to answer that question may be to refer you to another well-known scientific Law: Murphy's Law, which states than *anything which can go wrong, will go wrong.* I'm sure you're heard of Murphy's Law, and maybe also its First Corollary — that *Murphy was an optimist!*

I ran into an interesting translation of Murphy's Law recently, and it came back as *what can go wrong will go wrong.* It strikes me that the best way to predict obstacles and objections — and also the best preventative against having Murphy's Law bite you somewhere unpleasant — is to put a question mark after the first half of that statement: *What can go wrong?* If you do a thorough job of answering that question, you should be able to engineer a solid and effective selling process.

Science, Engineering and Arithmetic

It may not be 100% correct to call Einstein and Newton *scientists.* In fact, much of their work would be labeled more correctly as *mathematics.* Einstein, for example, had to use very complex math to demonstrate many of his theories since practical experiments simply weren't possible. We still can't go fast enough to see any measurable difference of relative time on human aging.

The mathematics of selling are not nearly as complex. In fact, I think selling is governed by pretty simple arithmetic — X sales volume requires Y individual orders which in turn requires Z new customers. We'll talk more about that later on.

For now, a quick story. My wife has told me that when I die, she's going to put these words on my tombstone: *It's all just arithmetic.* I've spoken those words many times, often along with this Dinosaur Wisdom: *Selling is a numbers game!*

I've been told that's a painfully primitive approach to selling in the modern world, but that doesn't make it any less true. And here's something else to consider — I'm not telling you that *numbers* alone will make you successful. What I am telling you is that, regardless of your level of selling skill, the more people you run though your process, the more customers you'll develop and the more money you'll make.

Let's say that you're a rookie in a very tough selling situation, and only 1 out of 100 suspects is going to buy from you. If you start the ball rolling with 25 suspects every week, you'll end up with a new customer just about every month. If you start the ball rolling with 75 suspects every week, you'll end up with 3 new customers in the same timeframe.

Now let's say that you're an experienced salesperson with a success rate of 1 out of 10. If you start the ball rolling with 3 suspects every month, you'll end up with a new customer about once each quarter. If you start the ball rolling with 3 suspects every *week*, you'll end the year with 15-or-so new customers.

Here's another way to look at a selling *process* — as a *selling machine*. Close your eyes and picture a very complex Rube Goldberg device, with all kinds of tracks and belts and moving parts. You put raw material (suspects) into one end of the machine, and you hopefully get finished product (customers) out of the other end. In between are the various steps in the production of a customer *(the process!)* and along the way, a lot of the raw material gets trimmed or cut or damaged or disqualified.

I want to close this chapter with two points: first, that there's a measurable relationship between how much raw material goes into any machine and how much finished product comes out. As noted, we'll talk more about that later on. Second, the great salespeople's *selling machines* are not at all Rube Goldberg-ish — they are well-thought-out processes, and they create new customers as quickly and efficiently as it can possibly be done.

Rube Goldberg

Reuben Garret Lucius Goldberg (1883–1970) was an American cartoonist, sculptor, author, engineer and inventor, best known for a series of cartoons depicting complex devices that perform simple tasks in indirect, convoluted ways. His spirit lives on in the annual National Rube Goldberg Machine Contest, which is hosted by Purdue University. This year's challenge (2010) is to design and build a machine to apply an appropriate amount of hand sanitizer into a hand. Past years' challenges have included putting toothpaste on a toothbrush, putting a stamp on a letter, and two different variations on changing a light bulb. There are both high school and college level competitions, and the rules state that the process must have a minimum of 20 steps, with no maximum number of steps.

You can see some of the results — and some of Goldberg's original cartoons — at www.rubegoldberg.com. I have no information on how many past participants have gone on to successful sales careers.

Suspects, Prospects and Customers

As we discussed earlier, time is money. It's also important to understand that customers are money too. If you're not making enough money, part of your problem is probably the you don't have enough customers! The solution to that, of course, is prospecting for some new ones, but before we get too far into that, let's revisit some terminology I introduced earlier.

There are four kinds of people on the buying side of your personal sales equation: *suspects, prospects, customers* and *maximized customers.* They are suspects when you *think* they might be prospects; they're only prospects when you *know* for sure that they are prospects; you only call them customers when they're actually *buying* from you; and they become maximized customers when you're getting a *maximum share* of their business. (And that, of course, is really the name of the game, to develop and grow customers to their maximum potential!)

Let's take a step backwards in this progression and consider the reason that I think you should only use the word *customer* to describe someone who is actually buying from you. This goes to the issue of what buyers really think about in making a buying decision. I've done a lot of research on buyer behavior over the years, and the research indicates that the single most important factor in most people's buying decision is simply the matter of whether they trust the salesperson or not.

Here's some more Dinosaur Wisdom: *The reason that most of your current customers are buying from you is simply that they trust you. The reason that most of your current prospects are not yet buying from you is simply that they don't yet trust you enough. Your challenge with these people is not to get them to like you more, it's to get them to trust you more.* I think that's such an important understanding that you should never use the word *customer* unless you're talking about someone who has already demonstrated the necessary level of trust. That will — hopefully! — keep you focused on the challenge of *building* trust with everyone else.

Most salespeople make a fundamental mistake in this regard. Sure, developing a new customer is all about developing a relationship, but here's the mistake: the relationship has to be about *trust*, not just about *like*. Does *like* play a part in it? Sure, but I'll explain where *like* fits in a little further along. For now, I hope you'll accept the fact that it takes a leap of faith for most people to place an order with most salespeople. Why? Because unless you actually have the merchandise with you when you make the sale, there are all sorts of possible problems between placing the order and receiving the delivery. That's especially true when you're selling a custom-manufactured product, or any kind of service. They ultimately have to trust you to deliver on your promises.

Promises, Promises

That leads to another important point: The essence of a salesperson's job is to make promises! Think about how many promises you make every day. *I promise that you'll be happy with the quality. I promise that you'll be happy the service. I promise that we'll deliver on time. I promise that the finished product will look exactly like the samples or the pictures or the drawings. I promise that it'll work exactly the way it's supposed to. I promise that it's the right tool for the job!*

Beyond those *overt* promises, think about some of the *implied* promises you make — things you may never actually say but your suspects and prospects and customers may nonetheless hear: *I promise that the people who will manufacture this product or execute this service are well trained and well managed and highly motivated. I promise that we do all of the preventative maintenance on all of our equipment to minimize the chances that one of our machines will break down and cause a problem for you. I promise that we know what we're doing, all the way from the order through to the invoice. I promise that we'll live up to our end of this deal!*

Here's some more Dinosaur Wisdom: *If you can get them to believe your promises, they'll think seriously about maybe buying from you. If you cannot, they will not.*

But My Situation Is Different!

Now, I can hear some of you thinking, "That may be true with some people, but the ones I'm talking to, the decision is more about price than anything else."

OK, here's another way to look at your pool of suspects, prospects, customers and maximized customers. It's been my experience that all buyers fall into one of five categories, and I call them Solids, Liquids, Gases, Players and Price Monsters. *Solids* are completely happy with the status quo, and they're not going to change. (We know there are solids out there, right? Hopefully you know that because you have solids among your own current customers!) *Liquids* are generally happy with the status quo, but they'll talk to you and give some thought to whether you represent something better than what they already have. *Gases* are dissatisfied with what they already have, and many of these people are actively looking to make a change.

Players spread their business around, among a group of trusted suppliers. They're price sensitive to the degree that they'll usually give the order to the supplier in that group who offers the lowest price on any individual product or project, but they won't have the cheapest supplier in town in their group, because if they did, they'd be *Price Monsters*. That's my term for people who make all of their purchasing decisions based on price alone.

So yes, there are *Price Monsters* out there, but they are not the majority! My research indicates that nearly 75% of all buyers make their decisions based primarily on *trust*. So why is there so much talk about price from the buying side? We'll talk more about that when we get to the issue of handling price objections. For now, though, I'd just like you to consider that the *Price Monsters* are the ones who are most likely to talk to you early in the process, since the more salespeople they talk to, the more likely it is that they'll end up with the lowest possible price!

Let's say that you identify 100 suspects, 25 of whom are *Price Monsters*. Let's also say that you'll get to talk with 20 out of that group of 100 within a relatively short timeframe. The concept of even distribution suggests that you'll be talking to 15 trust-oriented buyers and 5 *Price Monsters*, but the concept of even distribution doesn't seem to apply here. It's far more likely that you'll find yourself talking to 17-18 *Price Monsters* and just a couple of trust-oriented buyers.

Do you see how this warped distribution can affect your perception? Do you also accept that it's harder and takes longer to get on the radar of the people you really want as your next customers? It takes patience and a plan — and probably *persistence and creativity* — to accomplish that, and most salespeople never get beyond the initial obstacles.

An Important Distinction

This is a good place to consider the distinction between selling to an established need or to a new opportunity. By *established need*, I mean a situation where your suspect or prospect is already buying your product or service from another supplier. I think this is an important distinction, because more salespeople have been defeated by "We're happy with our current supplier" than by any other objection — including the price objection! I'll tell you how I think you should handle this objection a little farther along, but for right now, let's consider that *Solids, Liquids, Gases, Players* and *Price Monsters* play a little differently if we're talking about selling to a new opportunity — for example, a new technology.

In this case, the *Solids* are the ones who won't consider a new way of doing something, because they're happy with the old way — the status quo. Or, they won't consider being an early adopter of something new and different. You've no doubt heard their battle cry: *If it ain't broke, don't fix it!*

The *Liquids,* on the other hand, will consider something new, although they'll probably still need some convincing. The *Gases* are the ones who are always eager to look at something new and different, which means that it's often easy to get them to talk to you, but not always easy to get them to buy,

The *Players* don't really play in this scenario, at least in the adoption stage. Once a new technology — or product or service — becomes mainstream, they'll probably spread their business around like they do with everything else they buy. And the *Price Monsters* may not have another price to compare yours too if we're talking about a completely new and unique product, service or technology, but they'll try very hard to "negotiate" a lower price than whatever you initially offer them. It may turn out that the only way to get them to buy is at a price level below what you're willing or able to sell at. Here's some more Dinosaur Wisdom: *You can't sell to everyone!*

Bad Attitude?

I've been told that's a bad attitude. "There's always a way," one veteran salesperson told me. "It may take time, and you may have to be really creative, but if you set your mind to it, you can always find a way to make the sale."

What do you think about that? I think there's some truth to the idea, but there's also a huge time management trap. And that ties in to another element of Dinosaur Wisdom: As I just noted, you can't sell to everyone, *but you will probably never run out of people to possibly sell to!*

Note the word "probably." I recognize that there are products and/or services that apply to a very limited target market. But unless you sell one of those, I think you're better off passing on the *solids* in favor of the *liquids* and the *gases* — with one important caveat! If a solid has *huge* volume potential, I would definitely recommend the *persistence and creativity* approach. If we're talking about a minnow rather than a whale, though, I recommend passing and looking for a more likely suspect.

One more important caveat — *persistence* and *creativity* have to go together. Persistence alone is usually counter-productive. While I've heard plenty of success stories from salespeople attributed to pure persistence, I've heard lots more horror stories from buyers about "sales stalkers" who call week after week, month after month, without anything new to say. And when I probe the success stories, I usually find out that there was an element of creativity involved. In other words, persistence/patience *and* a plan!

Good Attitude

OK, you can't sell to everyone, but you'll probably never run out of people to possibly sell to. What I think that means is that you don't have to become *fixated* on any individual suspect or prospect. Ultimately, I don't think you even have to care who your customers are, as long as they're good customers and you have enough of them to make the kind of money you want to make. As I said back on Page 1, I believe in creativity, but I also believe very strongly in not banging my head against a wall!

My attitude toward prospecting has always included doing a lot of it. Beyond that, though, I think prospecting is mostly about looking for people who have a good attitude. *I'll be happy to talk with you* is a good attitude. *If it ain't broke, don't fix it* is a bad attitude. *I see the value in your product or service* is another good attitude. *I'm not willing to pay your price* is another bad attitude. When you think about it, is there anything that's harder to change than another person's attitude? So here's some more Dinosaur Wisdom: *The larger your suspect pool, the less time you should spend on any individual who shows you a bad attitude!*

Fully Qualified Prospects

Remember that they're *suspects* when you think they might be *prospects*. In the early stages of prospecting — which should probably be called *suspecting!* — all you really have to care about is whether someone *looks like* they might be a prospect.

So what does a prospect look like? It's pretty simple really, A *prospect* is an individual or a company or an organization which can meet three criteria. First, they have to buy, want or need exactly what you're trying to sell. Second, they have to buy, want or need enough of it to make pursuing them worthwhile. Third — and this is ultimately the most important consideration — they have to show some interest in buying from you!

Before reading on, stop and think about the people you think of as *prospects* right now. Are they really? And for the moment, let's forget about the biggest issue, whether they have any real interest in buying from you. Do they even buy exactly what you're trying to sell?

What Exactly Do You Sell?

What exactly do you sell? I'm not looking for a metaphysical answer here, but rather just a clear and simple description of your product or service. Maybe the best way to express what I'm looking for is to tell you that *what you sell* can probably be defined on three separate levels: (1) a clear and simple description of your product or service, (2) a description of a *tangible* benefit that's derived from your product or service, and (3) a description of an *intangible* benefit that can be derived from your product or service.

Let's say that you sell insurance. A clear and simple description might be *all types of insurance including auto insurance, life insurance, homeowners' insurance and liability insurance*. A second-level description might be *financial protection*. The third-level description could be *the sense of security that comes along with solid financial protection*. Do you see the difference between the tangible benefit and the intangible benefit? I am hoping to demonstrate the difference between a *thing* and a *feeling*.

Now let's say that you sell for a wholesaler of sunglasses, calling on a wide range of retail stores which sell sunglasses — and probably other things — to consumers. A clear and simple description might be *sunglasses, including a wide range of styles and sizes from all of the major brands*. A second-level description might be *products in high demand, with very good profit margins.* The third level description could be *the status associated with selling all of the major brands or just some of the coolest brands.*

Here's a third example. This time, let's say that you're a retail salesperson in one of those stores, and let's make it a trendy little boutique. A clear and simple description might be *trendsetting clothing and accessories, including sunglasses.* A second-level description, specific to those sunglasses, might be *fashionable eye protection.* The third level description could be *the status associated with wearing one of the coolest brands or styles.*

Here's some more Dinosaur Wisdom: *People don't buy a product or service for its own sake, they buy the benefit it provides.* That can be as tangible as financial security, or as intangible as just feeling really cool in a pair of Oakley sunglasses.

Here's another piece of Dinosaur Wisdom: *The very same product can have a very different benefit, depending on who you're trying to sell it to.* That bit of wisdom that needs to be considered on two separate levels. First — and probably most obvious — is that one individual may value the *fashionable* part more than the *eye protection* part when considering a pair of sunglasses.

Beyond that, though, the benefit may be different based on where in the *distribution chain* you're trying to sell your product or service. If I'm a retailer of sunglasses, for example, I'm probably not in it for the eye protection, I'm in it for the *revenue* I can generate by selling your sunglasses to people who are interested in eye protection — or just in feeling good/looking good in one of the coolest brands or styles. Most purchases are ultimately motivated by WIIFM — *What's In It For Me!* The great salespeople always seem to recognize the benefit that's most important to the buyer — tangible or intangible — and that's the benefit they sell.

We'll talk more later on about how they figure that out. We're also going to talk about the FAB Formula later on — Features, Advantages and Benefits. For now, I just want to stress the importance of communication in the early prospecting stages. Because you can talk yourself right out of an opportunity — or right into trouble! — if you don't communicate *exactly* what you sell.

Out Of An Opportunity

The issues of *jargon* and *communicating exactly what you sell* are very closely related. The mattress company I mentioned in Chapter 2 probably lost sales opportunities by advertising *sleep solutions* rather than mattresses. Here's some more Dinosaur Wisdom: *If they don't know what you sell, they probably won't buy it!*

Here's another example of poor communication. My wife is a teacher and she just transferred to a new school, and I was doing the "What do you do?" conversation with a couple of other significant others at a staff party just before the start of the school year. "I sell office products," one of them said, and another one asked: "What kind of office products?"

"Oh, you know," was the answer. "Pens and paper and staples and rubber bands. Blank CDs and toner cartridges. All the things that make an office run."

The asker seemed ready to let the conversation end, but I jumped in, because it seemed to me that she was disappointed by the salesperson's answer: "Did you have a particular reason for asking about what kind of office products?"

"We had a flood in our conference room," she said. "and we have to replace the rugs, which were matched to the chairs, which are all getting old and ratty anyway, so my boss just told me to start looking into ten new conference chairs. That's one of the million things that's on my desk for Monday morning."

"Hey, I sell office furniture!" the salesperson said. "I can help you with that. Wow, I'm glad I ran into you here!" They quickly made arrangements to get together on Monday, and this 'What do you do?' conversation resulted in a very nice sale for the office products salesperson.

Here's the question, though: What if I hadn't jumped into the conversation? That opportunity might have been lost simply because the salesperson did a less-than-stellar job of explaining exactly what he sold. Remember this bit of Dinosaur Wisdom: *It is not the buyer's responsibility to communicate with the seller, it's the other way around!* Please also remember that many of the people you'll be talking to are *civilians* — people without professional experience with your products and/or services.

In a room full of office products professionals — salespeople and perhaps experienced buyers — everyone in the room would probably know that "all the things that make an office run" would include conference room chairs. Outside of that room, though, a *civilian* might never make the connection.

So here's some more advice: Start thinking about a brief but comprehensive description of *exactly what you sell*, something that will minimize the likelihood of a missed opportunity. I've heard this sort of thing referred to as an *elevator speech* — something that can delivered from start to finish during a 30-second elevator ride.

Make it clear and concise, and here's another little piece of advice: *Make your elevator a jargon-free zone!*

Right Into Trouble

Now let's take a look at how you can talk yourself right into trouble. This relates to another way to look at *exactly what you sell*. On a very basic level, you have a *product line* — which, for now, you can think of as a simple listing of the products and/or services you sell. Beyond that, though, you may also have a *strike zone*, which can be defined as *the elements of your product line that you're best equipped to sell.*

Equipped may have something to do with production equipment — for example, I do a lot of consulting work in the printing industry, and my clients range from big-press commercial printers to small-press quick printers. If you need to print 50,000 catalogs, one of my big press clients has the right tool for the job. If you need 1000 sales flyers, they do not — but one of my quick printer clients does!

Equipped may also have something to do with experience and knowledge — for example, an insurance salesperson who specializes in auto and homeowners' insurance might run into an opportunity to compete for a large, highly specialized liability policy. That kind of insurance might be part of his/her product line, but the question is, will a buyer buy a complex and specialized insurance policy from a salesperson who doesn't have significant and direct experience with that kind of insurance?

Product line is all about *capability,* and for most salespeople, capability is theoretically infinite — consisting of anything a company can produce on its own or outsource from somewhere else. *I don't normally sell that, but I can get it for you!*

Strike zone, on the other hand, is all about *competitive,* and it's an unavoidable fact that you can't be competitive all the way across an infinite product line. If you don't have — or have access to — the right production tools for the job, you may not be *price competitive.* And if you don't have the necessary knowledge and experience tools, you may not be *trust competitive.* Remember, the essence of your job is to make promises, and your success is tied very directly to their willingness to believe (a) that you know what you're talking about, and (b), that you can and will deliver!

Stick To Your Strike Zone!

What's the point of all of this? Simply that in the early stages of trying to build a relationship, you want to *seek out* opportunities to look good and *avoid* opportunities to look bad. That starts with situations where lack of knowledge or lack of experience would put you at a disadvantage. You should avoid those if you can — although let's recognize that sometimes it's simply not possible; for a rookie salesperson, for example, or an experienced salesperson just starting out in a new position, with a new product or service. It's been said that you have to *earn your experience*, and most of the great salespeople suffered some knocks along the way. (Most of them learned pretty quickly, though, and I hope you will too!)

Looking bad in terms of price, though, is a whole different story, and the damage tends to be more permanent. So here's some more Dinosaur Wisdom: *Avoid — like the plague! — any situation where your price is likely to be competitively high when your relationship strength is low.*

With that wisdom in mind, I've made an ironclad rule: *I will consider selling just about anything to a* customer — remember, that means someone who has already demonstrated that they trust you enough to buy from you, and it's probably someone who likes you at least a little bit too! — *but I will not stray from the middle of my* strike zone *with a suspect or a prospect.*

For example, if I were a small-press quick printing salesperson and a suspect or prospect invited me to compete for a project that was out of my strike zone, I would decline, and here's exactly what I'd say: "You know, that's really not the sort of printing we specialize in. If it was a quantity of 1000, I'd have the right tool for the job, but for 50,000 you really need someone who has a bigger press. We're really good at what we do, and I'm never going to ask you to consider me for anything that lies outside of what we're really good at."

Trust Builder

I hope you'll see that this is an opportunity to look *good* in terms of trust, and to avoid looking *bad* in terms of price. Sadly, it's not what usually happens, so let's take a closer look at the more common scenario. The salesperson gets all excited about the chance to quote on a "big" job and either quotes it on the small press — which would be *hugely* inefficient on a project like this — or gets a price from a bigger-press printer, marks it up and quotes that price to the suspect or prospect,. Then the salesperson wonders what the hell happened when the suspect or prospect stops returning phone calls.

Here's what probably happened. The buyer looked at the price, in comparison to one or more competitors for whom that particular project was right down the middle of the strike zone, and said: "Wow, this company is really expensive. I guess I don't want to waste my time on them anymore." The real tragedy, of course, is that the salesperson never gets the chance to compete for orders that he/she would be very competitive on.

The baseball analogy is very apt. Sure, swinging at bad pitches delivers positive results every once in a while, but you'll have a much higher *batting average* if you're patient enough to wait for good pitches to swing at. That takes us back to the first test of a fully qualified prospect: *they buy exactly what you're trying to sell.* The complicating factor is that most suspects will also have needs that are outside of your strike zone.

If *all of* their needs are outside of your strike zone, they're simply not prospects. If *some of* their needs fit your strike zone — and that adds up to enough volume potential to pass the second test for a fully-qualified prospect; *they buy enough of exactly what you want to sell to make pursuing them worthwhile* — then they're two-thirds of the way to being fully qualified. I just hope you'll see that the most important consideration in the early stages of *suspecting* might be to avoid disqualifying yourself! Remember, the third test of a fully qualified prospect is that they show some *real interest in buying from you.* It would be tragic to undermine that interest by putting yourself in a position where your price is competitively high while your relationship strength is low.

Competitive Pricing

All of this raises the question of what it means to be price *competitive* in the first place. That's hard to define, because like beauty and quality and many other things, *competitive* is often in the eye of the beholder. I can tell you this, though, if you quote me a price on something, I tend to assign your quoted price to one of three categories — three *buckets* if you will. The first bucket is *too high*, meaning more than I think it should cost, or more than I want to pay. The second bucket is *too low*, meaning that your price is so low in comparison to others that it scares me. The third bucket is *competitive*, and that tends to be the biggest bucket of the three.

Here's some more Dinosaur Wisdom: *Competitive is not a point, it's a range. And the real artistry in selling is getting the order when your price is on the high end of that range, not at the low end.* Just understand that if you're not in that competitive range — if I put your quote in the *too high* or the *too low* bucket — you're not even in the competition! And if I disqualify you from the first competition you enter, you will probably find yourself *permanently* on the outside looking in!

The Expanding Strike Zone

Here's some more Dinosaur Wisdom, though, which reflects an interesting and important phenomenon: *Your strike zone expands as the relationship grows.* In other words, the more they trust you and the more they like you, the less important price becomes as part of the buying decision.

That makes perfect sense, right? And that's why my ironclad rule lets me consider selling just about anything to a *customer*. Just remember that in the absence of a real relationship, price is about the only factor you'll be judged on. So try not to swing at pitches you have little chance of hitting — and lots of chance of looking bad trying!

Does that mean you'll lose out on those out-of-the-strike-zone opportunities forever? Absolutely not! Let's say that you handle the first opportunity to compete for one those out-of-the-strike-zone orders the way I've suggested, but you continue to work on the relationship, and before too long you get a chance to compete for an order that you are well equipped for. Let's say that you win that order, and you deliver on all of your promises and that leads to another order, and then another — all orders that are right down the middle of your strike zone. After 6 months of that, I can easily see you calling that *customer* and saying: "Do you remember that first order you invited me to quote on, and I told you that it wasn't really in our strike zone? Well, some things have changed since then. We've brought in new equipment, (or perhaps 'we've established a strategic relationship with a new supplier') and I'd like to take a shot at that sort of order if it ever comes around again." You may still be at a pricing disadvantage, but as long as you're in the *competitive* range, you may well have a shot at winning the order.

By the way, if I were in this situation, I would have been looking forward toward that conversation from the day I first declined to quote on the project. My ACT notes would have included the specs of the project, and I would have scheduled a call for 6-8 months out to remind myself that I'd want to have this conversation *if* I'd been successful at winning a few inside-the-strike-zone orders by that time.

Do you see how this fits into our discussion of time management and organization? Remember this piece of Dinosaur Wisdom: *You won't gain new customers from prospecting; you will gain new customers from follow-up.* Follow-up is also a big part of creating *maximized* customers.

Effective Communication

I hope I've impressed you with the importance of effective communication. Too many salespeople talk themselves out of opportunities and/or into trouble on a regular basis — and to this point, I've barely touched on the issue of salespeople who just plain talk too much!

I'll come back to that later. For now, here's an example of another way to *talk yourself out of an opportunity*: I called a landscaping company recently about installing an irrigation system for our lawn. My first question was: "Can you tell me what I need to know about irrigation systems?" From my perspective, all I knew at that point was that I wanted one, and I had a long way to go before I'd be capable of making an intelligent buying decision. In effect, I was providing the salesperson with the perfect opportunity for a consultative sale.

Sadly, the first thing he told me was that I'd need a permit and a separate water meter — "and that'll run you about $1500 before we even start talking about the cost of the system." By *sadly*, I mean *sadly for him*, because the attitude I got from him was "Naw, you don't really want an irrigation system. It's too expensive." I ended the conversation pretty quickly after that, and I think you'll agree that he did a pretty good job of talking himself out of an opportunity.

After I hung up with him, I flashed back on my old friend at Ace Hardware, who probably would have handled this situation differently. "OK," he might have said, "I can help you with that, but let's start here...you don't really want an irrigation system. I think what you really want is a beautiful lawn!"

By stressing the *objective*, he'd have started the process of defending the cost if that became necessary. Sometimes a salesperson's closing position has to be *this is what it will cost to get exactly what you want.* For what it's worth, that's how it ended up with my irrigation system. The whole thing cost more than what I really wanted to spend, but I am 100% happy with the result.

6

The "Prospecting" Stage

I think it's time to start the search for some new customers — not just in terms of the plotline of this book, but because I think the reason you're reading it is that you want to make more money! As we've discussed, *time is money* and *customers are money* too. The arithmetic here is pretty straightforward: *more money* probably requires *more customers*, and *more customers* definitely requires *more prospecting*.

For most of recorded history, *prospecting* hasn't had anything to do with selling. I found an article on Wikipedia which defines the term as *the physical search for minerals, fossils, precious metals or mineral specimens, also known as* fossicking — a term that another Wikipedia article traces to Australia by way of Cornwall, in England. It's easy to see the connection, I think, since the ultimate goal of prospecting is to enrich the prospector.

My Google search also led me to a discussion thread on LinkedIn, which started with a question: "What is *your* definition of prospecting?" There were 37 responses, all of which expressed some variation on the theme of developing new business. The responses ranged from 4 words — "identifying new business opportunities" — to several hundred. (Obviously some people gave more thought to the question than others!)

I have my own definition, of course, and I'll share it with you in just a moment, Before that, though, I'd like you to think about your own definition. What exactly does *prospecting* mean to you, and what does it entail? I think lots of salespeople fail at prospecting because they don't understand exactly what they're doing or why they're doing it. Sure, there's probably at least a vague notion of finding new customers and making more money, but I'm talking about *what* and *why* from an engineering perspective.

By the way, I'll have more to say about LinkedIn a little farther along.

Prospecting Is…

OK, here's my definition: *Prospecting is an activity chain which begins with the identification of suspect companies, and ends with the first substantive conversation with the buyer.* In other words, prospecting is a *stage* in the overall selling process, with a starting point and an end-point of its own. Your overall goal is to create a new customer, of course, but the goal of this *stage* is more modest — the opportunity to have a serious talk with a likely suspect!

Let's talk about that serious talk — that *substantive* conversation. First of all, do you want it to happen face-to-face, or over the phone, or will a dialog via e-mail or voicemail be sufficient? I think the answer to that question depends on the complexity of your product and the logistics of your selling situation, but I hope we can agree on this hierarchy: face-to-face is best, followed by the phone, followed by the sort of "interrupted dialog" that's most likely with e-mail or voicemail. The important thing is that you establish the specific goal of *your* prospecting stage, because your next challenge is to engineer a process that will get you there.

Now, what is the goal of the conversation itself? Again, that may differ depending on the complexity of your product, but unless a *one-call close* is a reasonable expectation — and that rarely happens with anything more complex than a pure impulse sale or a purely price-driven commodity sale — I think your first substantive conversation should be all about *qualifying*. Remember, prospecting starts with *suspects*, which means only that you *think* they might be prospects. Personally, I want to be sure that someone qualifies before I commit myself to the next stage of my selling process. Here's some more Dinosaur Wisdom: *It's pretty easy to sell to a prospect. It's pretty much impossible to sell to a non-prospect.*

Remember my definition of a prospect: (1) they buy, want or need exactly what you sell, (2) they have enough volume potential to make pursuing them worthwhile, and (3) they show real interest in buying from you. Setting the dollar volume issue aside for a moment, if they simply don't buy, want or need what you sell, will you ever sell it to them? How about if they buy lots of it, but they don't have any interest at all in buying it from you? Yes, they may develop a want/need over time, or you may change their minds about buying from you over time, but that doesn't change the fact that they are not fully qualified prospects *right now!*

I think more time is wasted on efforts to sell to non-prospects than on anything else in selling. You avoid that by *qualifying before continuing* to the next stage.

Selling and *Marketing*

I think it's time to draw another distinction — between *selling* and *marketing*. I asked a young salesperson to tell me the difference recently, and she answered: "*Marketing* is like advertising, and *selling* is when you actually call on people."

I asked a veteran salesperson the same question, and he answered: "*Marketing* is *selling* from a distance."

As I thought about that, it occurred to me that the veteran was on the right track, but he had it sort of backwards. I think it would be more accurate to say that *selling* is *marketing* at its *closest point of approach*. The young salesperson was almost on that track, but she seemed to think that *marketing* and *selling* are two different things, and that's not correct.

Here's a better description of the relationship between selling and marketing: *marketing* is the parent discipline and *selling* is one of its children. I like to define marketing as *the broad business discipline by which people and/or organizations get connected to the products and/or services they either desire or require. Selling* is one of the ways the connection can be made, and the key element of *selling* is the *dialog* between seller and buyer.

Advertising is another sub-discipline, and in commerce, it's commonly applied in two ways: *image advertising* to build awareness of a company and/or *product advertising* to build awareness of what the company sells. Note that advertising isn't limited to commerce. We get a lot of political advertising too, sometimes *image oriented* and sometimes *issue oriented.*

Sales promotion is still another sub-discipline; for example, putting something *on sale,* or maybe a buy-one-get-one-free offer. The role of *promotion* is to provide the buyer with an incentive to *buy now.*

In addition to all of that, *marketing* includes several more sub-disciplines: market research, product development, pricing strategy and the whole planning and evaluation cycle. In other words, *marketing* is a parent with a lot of children!

Lead Generation

It's been proven that *advertising* can sell some products and services all by itself; for example, I saw an interesting product in both a magazine ad and a TV commercial one day last week — Nivea Active 3, a combination shampoo, body wash and shaving gel. The very next day, I went into three different drug stores trying to buy it. (Sadly, whoever sells Nivea Active 3 to my local drug stores is lagging behind the marketing curve. *Demand* has been created, but *supply* is not yet in place. That may be a sales problem, or it may be a production or shipping problem. Either way, it's a "lose-lose" situation for both the seller and the buyer.)

Other products and services *cannot* be sold by advertising alone; for example, I got a mailing from Hilton Grand Vacations a couple of weeks ago. They want to sell me a timeshare, and part of their *process* is to get me to visit the property, where I'll enjoy the amenities for a few days at a greatly reduced price, in return for my commitment to attend a 2-hour sales presentation. In other words, they're offering me a *promotion*, not as an incentive to *buy*, but merely to *try*. That's brilliant engineering, but that's not the point I want to make right now.

That point is that one of the *capabilities* of advertising is to provide *sales leads* — in other words, to deliver "qualified" prospects to a salesperson. The only problem with that statement is that they're usually not really qualified prospects, and that takes us to one of the most common complaints I hear from salespeople: "The leads I get are worthless!"

Here's my answer: They're not worthless. They're just *suspects*. If you expect more than that, you're probably setting yourself up for disappointment.

That doesn't mean you should ignore the leads you're given. In fact, it means exactly the opposite. They may not be fully qualified prospects, but they are probably legitimate suspects, and prospecting is an activity chain which begins with the identification of said suspects. Leads which result from advertising or other marketing activities are one of your suspect sources — nothing more, but nothing less.

Inquiries, Tips and Finds

I wrote a column for a printing industry trade magazine nearly 20 years ago, titled "Inquiries, Tips and Finds." The basic idea was that *leads* come in three varieties: *inquiries*, which are generally raw responses to some form of advertising; *tips*, which have been qualified to at least some degree; and *finds*, which are suspects a salesperson digs up on his/her own.

One of my clients is a regular advertiser in a local business journal, and its readers have two ways to respond to most of the ads. The first is to call the advertiser directly, and the second is a "bingo card" they can fill out and mail back to the magazine. The "bingo card" lists all of the advertisers, and readers can check off the ones that they're interested in. The magazine then sends a lead report to the advertiser, with contact information for anyone who has expressed interest in learning more about the company, the product or the service.

When these lead reports arrive, they're given directly to the salesperson, and she's expected to follow up on them in an appropriate manner. I remember her telling me how excited she used to get, until she found out that most of the respondents didn't even remember filling out the card. "The lag time between publishing, reading, responding and reporting pretty much guarantees that these aren't going to be hot leads," she told me, "but eventually I realized that I'm no worse off with these *inquiries* that I am with any other suspect. I just had to learn where they fit in terms of my priorities, and I don't drop what I'm doing to follow up on them anymore."

When a suspect calls in, it's a very different story. Those calls are routed to the owner, and she almost always drops what she's doing to take an "I'd like to get more information" call. I've listened in a few times as she engages a suspect, answering his/her initial questions and asking questions of her own to determine the real level of interest and opportunity. Most of those calls end with a promise to have "the perfect person" call to follow up, and after that, she'll brief the salesperson on what she learned, and they'll discuss what to do next.

"When Martha tells me they're hot, she's usually right, and I close pretty quickly," the salesperson told me. "It makes a world of difference that she's qualified them." So in effect, Martha has had that *first substantive conversation* with the suspect, and she used the opportunity to determine if the suspect was worth turning over to the salesperson for the next stage of the process.

You may not have a *Martha* to do that for you — to provide you with *tips* as opposed to raw *inquiries* — but that just means that you'll have to do the qualifying yourself. Remember, they're *suspects* when you think they might be *prospects*. They're only *prospects* when you *know for sure* that they qualify.

I hope you've recognized, by the way, that my definition of a *prospect* is far more stringent than most people's. There's a lot more to this than simply *thinking* or *wishing* or *hoping* someone might buy what you sell. But that's why *it's pretty easy to sell to a prospect* — remember that Dinosaur Wisdom! — because the heavy lifting is all in the suspecting/prospecting/qualifying stage.

Finds

As noted earlier, *finds* are suspects that you identify on your own. So where do you start looking for them? Here's some more Dinosaur Wisdom: *Your next customer will probably look a lot like a current customer!* I think that means you should start with your current customer list — your own individual list and/or your company's overall list.

If you think about it, a list of current customers is also a collection of *models* for fully qualified prospects. There's something about those people, companies or organizations that causes the *want* or *need* for what you sell. In addition, it causes them to want or need *enough of it* to make pursuing them worthwhile, and to have some real interest in buying it from you. The better you understand all of that, the more accurate you'll be in the "suspecting" stage.

This is more of a *science* activity than an *engineering* challenge, by the way. Remember, scientists observe the world as it is and seek to understand and explain things. The *understand* part is really important! Many salespeople can tell you which markets seem to offer the best opportunity, but they can't tell you *why*. The great salespeople tend to be a lot more scientific in their approach, so they know *why* — and that knowledge also helps them in the later stages of the process.

Situational Differences

I have a nephew who sells endoscopes — medical devices used for looking inside the body. His suspect pool is pretty narrow, consisting of a well-defined list of medical specialties. Your gastroenterologist might buy an endoscope from my nephew, and so might your veterinarian, but your podiatrist would not.

I have another nephew who sells ad specialties — a wide variety of items that can be used to promote a product, a service or a company. His product line ranges from imprinted writing instruments to embroidered apparel to engraved precious metals. His *suspect* pool is huge, but his *prospect* pool is considerably smaller, and at this stage of the game, it's mostly limited by the second qualifying criteria: buying enough of what he sells to make his pursuit worthwhile.

The fundamentals of prospecting are the same for both of my nephews, but there are some situational differences in their *suspecting/prospecting* challenges. Theoretically, both of my nephews could be calling on the same gastroenterologist, for example, and that suspect doctor would definitely meet the second qualifying criteria for Nephew #1 — a state-of-the-art endoscopy system is a $130,000 sale!

For Nephew #2, though, it might be a whole different story. A one-doctor gastroenterology practice might buy small quantities of 2-3 ad specialty items, putting its volume potential in the less-than-$1000 annual range. For my nephew, that's not enough volume to justify the effort it could take to turn that suspect into a customer. On the other hand, a practice with 3-5 doctors could easily have $2500+ potential, and that's his qualifying point — anyone who seems to have that much potential is worth taking a closer look at, and anyone who doesn't is not.

Now remember, he's not limited to a group of medical specialties like Nephew #1 is. His product line has application to almost any kind of business, and his customer list encompasses a wide range of business types. He has established a few pretty good *industry niches*, though, and he has determined his "suspecting" criteria for each of those.

For example, he does a lot of business with professional practices — doctors, dentists, lawyers, accountants, and even a private detective firm — but he won't even call on a practice with less than 3 doctors or dentists, 6 lawyers, or 10 accountants. Experience has taught him that with rare exceptions, it takes that many practitioners to generate enough *want* or *need* for his products to add up to $2500 per year. Trade associations are another one of his niches, and in that market segment, his suspecting threshold is 10 staffers and/or 200 members.

How does he identify professional practices and organizations which fit his targeting criteria? For one thing, he does a lot of *canvassing*, and I'll talk more about that later on. Beyond that, he has found list resources — some that he's had to pay for and others that are available to the public — and even though those lists don't always tell him everything he needs to know, he has a *process* in place to fill in the blanks.

List Resources

I'm feeling generous today — hypothetically at least — so I'm going to buy a list of all of the gastroenterologists in the world and send a copy to each of my nephews. (They're not related, by the way. Nephew #1 in one of my brothers' sons, and Nephew #2 is on my wife's side of the family. They're not even close geographically, but that doesn't matter, since this whole thing is hypothetical anyway.)

Here's what I think Nephew #1 will do with that list. First, he'll cross-reference it to his current database of suspects, prospects and customers, to see if the list contains any doctors doing business in his territory that he doesn't already know about. If it does, he will add them to the database, and schedule a time to start them on the next stage of his selling process, based on his current workload and priorities. The suspect identification stage is already complete, because every gastroenterologist qualifies as a suspect for his product, because they all use endoscopes.

Not every gastroenterologist is a fully qualified prospect, but he's not going to worry about that yet. Remember, they're suspects when you *think* they *might be* prospects. That's the only burden of proof that has to be met at this stage.

Here's what I think Nephew #2 will do with the list. First, just like Nephew #1, he'll cross-reference it to his suspect/prospect/customer database to see if it contains anyone he doesn't already know about. (Nephew #2 uses Microsoft Outlook with Business Contact Manager, but as I said earlier, I don't care which contact management software you use. It's not the brand name that's important here, it's the organizational capability.)

After doing that, I think he'll start Googling the unknown doctors, taking no more than a couple of minutes researching each one. Why such a short time? Because he only needs to answer one question at this point: *How many doctors are there in this doctor's practice?*

For what it's worth, I just Googled my own gastroenterologist, and in about 25 seconds with just three mouse clicks, I found myself looking at a roster of the 14 physicians in his group practice. I would assume that Nephew #2 — or you, for that matter — could have done the same thing in about the same amount of time, and since 14 is greater than 3, that's all it would take for Nephew #2 to know that this medical practice qualifies as a legitimate suspect.

Next Step

OK, assuming that each of my nephews identifies a few legitimate suspects from this list, what's the next thing they need to know? I hope the answer is obvious — it's the name of the buyer!

Interestingly, I asked that question in a recent seminar, and the first answer was: "You need to know if they want to buy what you want to sell!" That's certainly something you do need to know, but aren't you most likely to learn it from the person who makes — or would make — the buying decision? That means the name comes first!

Here's some more Dinosaur Wisdom: *The wrong person often leads you to the wrong result.* That means you don't ask the first person you talk to whether the company or organization would be interested in your product or service. You ask that person *who you need to talk to* about your product or service. And the way you do that has a great deal to do with the level of cooperation you'll get.

In a business-to-business situation, the first person you talk to might be a receptionist, or a secretary, or a clerk, or a manager, or even the owner of the business. In a business-to-consumer situation, it might be the husband or wife or parent or child of the person you ultimately need to talk to. Here's some more Dinosaur Wisdom: *You should always assume that the first person you encounter* is not *the buyer you ultimately need to sell to.* If you end up asking the actual buyer who you need to talk to, the answer will probably be *me.* If you try to sell your product or service to the wrong person, the answer will probably be *no!*

Canvassing

I mentioned that Nephew #2 does a lot of canvassing, and I have encouraged him in that strategy, because his suspect pool is so huge. I would not give the same advice to Nephew #1, because his suspect pool is so narrow. By *canvassing*, I mean simply walking into buildings and offices and speaking to the first person he encounters.

Oh My God, you may be thinking, *he's talking about cold calls!* I guess I am, but I want to make something clear. I am 100% opposed to cold calls — *on the actual buyer!* I am 100% in favor of *cold starts* for research purposes, because the fact of the matter is that you have to start somewhere. And while you can initiate a *prospecting start* in a number of ways, including buying or developing a list and getting busy on the telephone, there's a lot to be said for simply getting out and prowling around in your marketplace.

That may seem primitive — and I should make it clear that I'm talking about business-to-business selling here, not walking into people's houses! — but here's some more Dinosaur Wisdom: *Not every good suspect is easily visible from "list distance."* For many salespeople, there are plenty of what I like to call *hidden treasures* out there, and the only way you'll find them may be by walking in their doors.

What you say when you walk in the door is important, though. Here's what you *do not* say: *"Hey, toots, I want you to do me a favor and drop what you're doing and call the person who buys the stuff I sell here and ask them to drop what they're doing and spend some time talking to me."* Obviously, you would never put it so crassly, but that's pretty much the substance of millions of cold calls every day.

So here are two things to consider: (1) you're not likely to get in to see the buyer on a walk-in cold call, and (2) you don't want to see the buyer anyway! I can see you nodding your head at #1, but maybe shaking your head at #2. After all, didn't I just say something about prospecting being all about getting that first substantive conversation with the buyer?

I did, and I meant it, but one of the issues here is that I don't want to have to start from scratch on that first conversation. So let's consider both challenges, and engineer a strategy that will address both of them. What I say when I walk in the door is: *"Hello, my name is Dave Fellman, and I'm from (your company name). I'd like to send some information about our company in the mail to your company, and I'm hoping you can tell me who to address it to. Who's the person who's most involved in ordering or dealing with (exactly what you sell)?"*

Magic Words

It's been my experience that the magic words here are "in the mail." I have watched thousands of receptionists, secretaries and clerks — let's call them *gatekeepers* — as I've approached them, and I have seen their shields go up as I got in close. I remember one gatekeeper who told me that she could always tell when the person approaching her was a salesperson, and her thought process was: "OK, let's see what sort of a *salesjerk* this one's going to be!"

I have seen the shields go down, though, as I spoke the words "in the mail" — which tells me that you'll often get what you want when what you're asking for is easy rather than hard. Giving you a name is fairly easy. Interrupting that person is hard. (Don't forget, by the way, that most gatekeepers are lower on the food chain than the buyers behind the gate. Which would you rather do, please your superiors or be part of their noise and annoyance?)

Granted, there are gatekeepers who won't cooperate. I once walked into a building in San Francisco with a young salesperson who approached a receptionist just as I've suggested, and this gatekeeper's response was a very brusque: "We don't give out that information." I'll continue that story in a moment, but first, let's talk more about a positive response — for example: "You should address it to John Smith." OK, you've got a name, now what else would you like know before following up with Mr. Smith?

Answering that question really raises two more: (1) "Is he really the right person?" and (2), "Do I really want to pursue this company?" Let's start with the second one. You're talking to this gatekeeper because you've indentified a *suspect* company, and all that means is that they look like they *might* be a prospect. In order to be considered a fully qualified prospect, they still have to pass those three tests. First, they have to buy, need or want exactly what you're trying to sell. Second, they have to buy, need or want enough of it to make pursuing them worthwhile. Third, they have to show some interest in buying from you.

The third test is probably something you'll have to have to take up with the buyer, but many gatekeepers can give you insight into the first two. The best strategy is a pretty simple question: "Can you tell me anything about how much and what kind of (*exactly what you sell*) a company like this uses?" My experience has been that the gatekeeper often knows, and his/her answer will often tell you whether it's worth going to the next step. "Oh we use a lot" would certainly take you there. "We don't use any" or "We get it all from our home office" might not. "I have no idea" would probably leave you somewhat up in the air. As a general rule, I'll choose to err on the side of *inclusion* in situations like this. In other words, if I'm not sure, I'll probably go to the next step. If it's really obvious, though, I'll move on to the next *suspect* in search of more potential.

Quality vs. Quantity

The next step is going to be to send something by mail, or possibly by e-mail. Before I describe that part of the process, though, what if feet-on-the-street *canvassing* isn't practical in your sales situation; for example, because of time and/ or distance constraints, or because of the specific nature of what you sell? In either of those situations, the telephone is probably your best tool for *prospecting starts*, and I would use the same approach: *I'd like to send some information in the mail. Can you tell me who to address it to?*

I still recommend doing this in person, though, if you can, and my reasoning is based on *quality* vs. *quantity*. Sure, you can make a lot more phone calls in an hour than walk-in visits, but can you learn as much that will help you to make an intelligent decision on what to do next?

It's been my experience that you can have a longer conversation with most gatekeepers in person than you can on the telephone. Think about that in terms of the gatekeeper's job description: *answer the phone, route the call, and then get off the phone so you're ready to answer and route the next call.* I've had lots of 3-4 minute canvassing conversations with gatekeepers which took 6-10 minutes to complete because we kept being "interrupted" by those phone calls.

In between calls, though, I was able to ask my questions, and given more time, I was able to learn more. For example: *What exactly does this company do? Is this the home office, or a branch location? Who do you buy (*exactly what I sell*) from right now? When I get to the point of following up on the telephone — after I sent my information in the mail! — is there a particularly good time for me to call? When I get to that point, would I be better off following up by e-mail? If that's the case, can you give me (the buyer)'s e-mail address?*

Put yourself in a gatekeeper's shoes for a moment. Do you really want to answer that many questions on a cold phone call? Granted, a gatekeeper might not really *want to* answer that many questions on a walk-in prospecting call either. I'm just saying that you have a better chance of learning more when you're physically out there.

What Exactly Does This Company Do?

Let's consider this question: Is it important to know the exact nature of a company's business? In some cases, the answer is certainly *yes*. In others, it's probably *no*. If you sell office products, for example — something every business needs! — it's probably not critical information (unless, of course, you're like my Dad, working a couple of specific market niches.) If you sell ad specialties, on the other hand, you probably do want to know the nature of the business, because some business types buy a lot more than others.

The name of the business sometimes tells you all you need to know; for example, event management firms tend to buy a lot of ad specialties, so if the sign on the door of the office says Excelsior Event Management, my nephew could take that as a pretty strong hint that there's a likely suspect on the other side of the door . If the sign on the door said Paul Johnson and Associates, he wouldn't be so sure — but if he were standing outside that door, it would be easy enough to walk in and talk with the gatekeeper!

Here's still another benefit to walking in rather than calling in — *walking in* lets you bring another important set of senses into play. On the phone, you're limited to what you hear. When you're physically out there, you can also learn from what you see. That might include the size and condition of an office or building, the number of cars in the parking lot, the kind of trade magazines in the waiting area. All of this can be helpful in making your *initial qualifying decision* — whether this is a suspect you really want to take to the next step in your selling process.

By the way, W*hat does this company do?* is a question you *never* want to ask a buyer! More on that will follow!

Working A List

The telephonic equivalent of canvassing is *working a list.* As noted, either of my nephews could work with a list of gastroenterologists. Beyond that, a restaurant equipment salesperson might acquire a list of all of the restaurants and caterers and schools and hospitals and nursing homes in an area, knowing that all five categories cook and serve meals, either as their primary business, or as a support element to their business. An insurance salesperson might acquire a list of new businesses or a list of wedding or engagement announcements — all of those being circumstances which suggest new or changing insurance needs.

Now, what does *acquire* mean? Depending on your resources —time, money and possibly helpful uncles — it could mean anything from buying or renting a list from any of a number of commercial sources to building your own list from a variety of "public" sources. In the old days, we often started our business-to-business prospecting with the Yellow Pages and our business-to-consumer prospecting with the white ones. We sometimes went to the library for more specialized business listings, or we scoured the newspapers or visited the local permitting offices looking for leads.

These days, we can do all of that on the Internet. You can go to the websites of any of hundreds of list brokers, define your criteria, pay for your list and download it almost immediately. You can use search engines to identify business types within specific locations — for example, I Googled "nursing homes Cary NC" as I was writing this and came up with 10 listings in less than 10 seconds. Then I went to the Raleigh News & Observer's website and found 12 wedding announcements and 14 engagement announcements within another 10-15 seconds. It really has never been easier for most salespeople to develop a suspect list.

The Chamber List

Having said that, most salespeople still seem to lack direction when it comes to developing a suspect list. I recently spoke with a salesperson who told me that she was gearing up for her annual prospecting effort, because the Chamber of Commerce list would be coming out later in the month. Setting aside the issue that prospecting should be an ongoing activity — *not* limited to one surge of prospecting activity each year! — I have some issues with using any annual list as your main source of leads.

As you probably (hopefully?) know, most Chamber organizations publish a list of their members somewhere near the beginning of each year. In addition, many Chambers and other organizations — including local/regional business publications — publish Top 10/Top 25/Top 50 lists broken down by various business categories. These lists have value, of course, but they also represent a trap for the salespeople who count on them as their sole source of prospecting information and sole trigger for prospecting activity. What does that mean? Let's look at it from the buyer's perspective. All of a sudden, it seems like you're getting calls from a million new salespeople. Why? Because the Chamber list just came out! Do you have time to deal with this onslaught of prospecting activity? In all probability, the answer is *no!*

Still, though, a Chamber or publication list is a legitimate source of suspects. So how do you best use it, without getting lost in that onslaught? Here's some Dinosaur Wisdom: *You're probably better off starting at the end of the list, rather than the beginning!* Experience has shown that very few salespeople will work their way through an entire list, for whatever the reason, so if you start with the smallest companies on a list sorted by sales volume, or start with the Z's rather than the A's on an alphabetical list, you stand to be among the smaller group of salespeople calling on those particular companies.

Now, I should probably mention that starting at the other end is a strategy that quite a few progressive salespeople have already latched on to. How can you stay one step ahead of them? Here's some more Dinosaur Wisdom: *Depending on the size of the list, you may find that the least trampled territory is not at the beginning or the end of the list, but in the middle!*

The Right Person

Regardless of which strategy you choose to find your *finds* — canvassing or working from a list — it's still of the utmost importance to identify the decision-maker. That takes us back to the question of whether the name you are given is really the right person. How do you make sure of that? Again, the best strategy is a pretty simple question: "What is his/her title?"

I promised you earlier that we'd return to the consideration of titles in prospecting, and the basic idea here is that if you know the titles of the people who are your current customers, that tells you what titles to be looking for in your prospecting efforts. If you don't know the exact titles of your current customers, you should start on gaining that information right now! (Remember that *title* is one of the 8 critical database fields we discussed in the chapter on Organization and Time Management!)

Please also remember what I said about using *buyer* as a noun, not a title. As I told one of my sales coaching clients just this morning, Mr. Smith is probably not a (upper-case) Buyer by title. It's much more likely that he's a (lower-case) buyer in his role as the Marketing Manager, or Office Manager or Human Resources Manager or Purchasing Manager.

Knowledge of your *target titles* can also be very important if the gatekeeper doesn't know whose name to give you. Sometimes they need help, or maybe just a little prompting. That may start with the last part of your initial question: "Who's the person most involved in ordering (*exactly what you sell*)?" If the gatekeeper doesn't seem to know, you could prompt him/her by continuing: "I usually find that it's a Marketing title" — or Operations or Human Resources or whatever is most specific to *exactly what you sell*.

Do you see how this works? I hope you also see how this is another reflection of an element of Dinosaur Wisdom that we've already discussed: *Your next good customer will probably look a lot like a current good customer.* That holds true right down to the title of the person who's likely to be the buyer/decision-maker.

Purchasing Titles

Let's consider one specific type of title for a moment — purchasing titles, such as Purchasing Agent, Acquisitions Specialist, Purchasing Manager or Materials Manager. The question is, do you really want to deal with purchasing types? On one hand, they place a lot of orders, for everything ranging from commodity products to highly complex, customized services. On the other hand, though, they tend to be more price driven than the "end users" of those products and services. My attitude has always been that I'll deal with them if I have to, but *only* if I have to!

Back in my restaurant equipment days, I once called on a conference facility and was given the name of a Purchasing Manager. "You know," I said to the gatekeeper, "I usually find that it's not the Purchasing people who really want to talk to me, to learn about new products for the kitchen. I usually find that it's someone *in the kitchen* who's most interested in what these new products can do in terms of efficiency and productivity. Do you have a chef who runs the kitchen, or maybe the title is Kitchen Manager or Food Service Manager?"

The gatekeeper replied: "Oh, I'm sorry. You're in sales, so naturally I thought of our purchasing department. Our chef is…." And that's a reflection of still another element of Dinosaur Wisdom: *Sometimes, all it takes to get what you want is one more question!*

It's not *always* that easy, of course. I remember a gatekeeper who told me: "Bub, if you want to sell to us, you go through Purchasing!" OK, like I said, I'll deal with them if I have to, but I'm always going to ask. And I have had some very satisfactory relationships with purchasing types in the past. Doesn't it make sense, though, to avoid them if you can? Or maybe I should say that another way — doesn't it make sense to get as close to the *owner* of any order as you can? By *owner*, I mean the person who really has something to lose or gain on the back of any order.

Let's say that you're a sign salesperson calling on a retail store, and the order on the table is for a couple of banners that will be part of a big sale. Let's also say that a Purchasing Agent will normally place the order, but the specifications will come from a Merchandising Manager. Which of those two will experience the most pain if the banners are printed wrong or not delivered on time?

Here's some more Dinosaur Wisdom: *People run to pleasure, and from pain.* I'm not sure there's a lot of pleasure connected with buying banners, but I do know there can be a lot of pain!

Now, let's consider still another element Dinosaur Wisdom: *If you are selling to en established need (*as opposed to a new opportunity, a distinction we discussed earlier), *everyone you're not yet selling to already has a supplier for what you'd like to sell them, which means that the decision to start buying from you has to be accompanied by — or preceded by! — the decision to stop buying from that other supplier.*

Why would they stop buying from that other supplier? If it's not for lower prices — pure *Price Monster* behavior, right? — it has to be for greater value, and that means getting *more* for their money or *less* for their money. (I'm talking about *less* pain, of course, and *less* aggravation and *less* time spent dealing with problems caused by a supplier's poor performance.)

The Blame Game

Think about this for a moment: What will the Purchasing Agent say to the Merchandising Manager if the banners for the upcoming sale are printed wrong or delivered late? Probably this: "The sign company screwed up. I got us a great price, but they didn't do what they were supposed to do!" Does the Purchasing Agent suffer if the sale is a flop? Possibly, but probably nowhere near as much as the Merchandising Manager suffers.

Now the critical question: Who gets the next order? It may be a different supplier if the Purchasing Agent places the order, but the decision will probably still be driven by price. It will almost certainly be a different supplier if the Merchandising Manager places the order, and I think the chances are far greater that this buyer's decision will be driven by *value*.

So here's some more Dinosaur Wisdom: *If you can't sell on price, you have to sell on value.* Maybe I should rephrase that and say that if you *don't want to* sell on price, you *absolutely have to* sell on value. And if that's the way you want to sell, you have to be selling to the person who's most likely to appreciate your value!

So Far, So Good

OK, let's get back to the engineering of your prospecting process, and let's consider where we are so far. You have identified a suspect company, and you have identified a buyer. You have made the decision that you would like to talk with this buyer, because so far, it looks like he or she (1) buys exactly what you sell, and (2) buys enough of it to make your pursuit worthwhile. Now the challenge is to arrange that *first substantive conversation*, and among the obstacles you can anticipate are: (1) buyers don't respond well to cold calls, (2) most buyers have a lot of noise in their lives, and (3) most buyers use voicemail to screen out some of that noise. Now think about this — *all of that is why my strategy includes "I want to send some information about our company in the mail to your company" in the first place!* In other words, cold calls don't work, so let's do something to warm up your first contact with the buyer.

We'll get to the *what* in just a moment. Before we do that, let's consider the *how*, or the means of transmittal for this information. What I have in mind could be delivered via traditional mail or e-mail, and I hope you're already thinking that there'll be a phone call somewhere in the future to follow up on whatever information you send. All of that means that I'd like to finish up with the gatekeeper having captured all of the information I'll need to reach out to the buyer and then follow up: physical address, e-mail address, phone number and fax number, and let's not forget the correct spelling of the buyer's name if it's anything that sounds tricky!

Critical Contact Information

Do you recognize that list of essential contact information? As a reminder, here are the 8 essential fields I specified in our discussion about Time/Contact Management:

- Company Name
- Contact Name
- Title
- Physical Address
- E-mail Address
- Telephone Number
- Fax Number
- ID/Status

You have (hopefully) captured the buyer's title earlier in your conversation with the gatekeeper, and the only field left after physical address, e-mail address, telephone number and fax number is ID/Status, and for that I recommend something like "Suspect Worth Taking The Next Step With."

Now, quickly, what document will almost always have all of this information you're looking for right on it? Yes, the buyer's business card! I will *always* ask the gatekeeper if he/she has the buyer's business card handy, and I will always wait patiently if he/she says "No, but I'll run back and get one for you." I've found it interesting that some gatekeepers aren't willing to give you all of the information you ask for, for example, the e-mail address. But they will give you the business card which probably has the e-mail address on it, and many business cards also have direct phone numbers and even cell phone numbers on them. That's not logical, perhaps, but it's illogic that works in our favor.

Now think about this. You can do everything I've just described — this whole interaction with the gatekeeper! — over the telephone, with only one exception: getting the business card. That's one of the key reasons I recommend live canvassing whenever time and distance considerations allow it.

Gatekeeper Objections & Obstacles

Gatekeepers come in all shapes and sizes, and a very wide range in terms of level of cooperation. I've seen guarded and open, cold, warm and hot (yes, that's exactly what I mean!), friendly and hostile. I think I've also heard all of the standard and therefore *predictable* objections and obstacles from gatekeepers. Remember what I said about Murphy's Law, and asking yourself *what can go wrong?* If you do a thorough job of answering that question, you should be able to engineer a solid and effective selling process.

Here are some of the most commons gatekeeper objections and obstacles, and the way that I'd address them:

Obstacle/Objection: "We don't use much/any of (*exactly what you sell.*)"
Response: "That may only be because someone needs to know more about (my product/my service/my company)!

It's important to say this with a smile on your face! It's also important to understand that you're not trying to sell your product or service or company to the gatekeeper, you're only trying to sell *the idea* that he/she should give you the name of the most likely person to have any want, need or interest in what you sell. Remember that you can't sell to everybody. Remember that prospecting is largely about looking for people with a good attitude. Finally, remember that the gatekeeper may in fact be doing you a favor by telling you that you'd really be barking up the wrong tree with this particular company!

Obstacle/Objection: "We get it all from our home office."
Response: "Where is that home office?"

If it's somewhere in your marketing area, go there! If not, you should probably move on to the next suspect. Again, remember that you can't sell to everyone, and some companies do buy most or all of their products and services from long distance. This is a very straightforward qualifying issue. If they don't buy exactly what you sell *locally*, or if they don't buy enough of it *locally* to make pursuing them worthwhile, they're simply not prospects. Period. End of story.

While we're on this subject, here's a trap I've seen more than a few salespeople fall into. The gatekeeper says: "We get it all from the home office." The salesperson says: "How's that working out for you?" The gatekeeper answers that they often have to wait a long time to get what they need. The salesperson sees that as opportunity, and decides to pursue the suspect. I think the value proposition is pretty obvious — *if you buy from me, you won't have that particular pain anymore!*

Unfortunately, some pain just can't be relieved, and here's some more Dinosaur Wisdom: *Pain caused by external suppliers often can be relieved; pain caused by internal bureaucracy most often cannot.* Sure, there are exceptions, but given that your prospecting time is probably limited, I think you're a lot better off swinging at pitches that offer you a greater likelihood of success.

Now, before I get too far off this subject, here's a caveat to that last comment. It's perfectly OK to have a few "speculative" or low percentage possibilities among your active suspects. It's not OK, though, to focus all of your prospecting efforts on that category. Remember that, ultimately, the most important of the three qualifying criteria is that they have real interest in buying from you! *Can't* buy from you is just as big a problem as *won't* buy from you, for whatever the reason — and it may be even a bigger problem if you can't talk to the people who make the ultimate decision.

Obstacle/Objection: "We're happy with our current supplier."
Response: "Who is that?"

It's been my experience that the gatekeeper will often tell you, and when given a name, I will continue: "Oh yeah, they're very good. In fact, they're probably the second best supplier of (exactly what you sell) in the area." Say that with a smile, and you'll probably be rewarded with a smile or giggle, which tells you that they get the joke. Then you can say: "Seriously, they're very good, but do you think your company should ignore the possibility that we're even better?"

Remember, you're *not* trying to sell your products or services to the gatekeeper. You're only trying to sell *the idea* that he/she should give you the name of the buyer, so you can approach that person directly. I've found that a little humor — coupled with pretty sound logic! — will often get you to that objective.

Obstacle/Objection: "He/she doesn't see/take calls from salespeople without an appointment."
Response: "Neither do I. That's why I want to send some information about my company in the mail. I apologize if I didn't make that clear from the beginning."

This is an objection you may never hear if you do a good job with your opening statement. If you do hear it occasionally, just respond as I've suggested above. If you hear it more than just occasionally, though, you're probably *not* doing a good job with your opening statement. If that's the case, you need to practice you approach and delivery.

Obstacle/Objection: "We don't give out that information."
Response: I promised to continue the story about walking into a building in San Francisco, where the salesperson asked for the name of the person she should

address her information to, and was told by the gatekeeper that: "We don't give out that information." The salesperson gave me a "what now?" look, so I stepped forward toward the receptionist and said: "Hey, tell me something, whose stupid idea is that? Did you get that instruction from some moron upstairs, or was it your own stupid idea?"

As you might expect, the gatekeeper was taken aback by my behavior, and the salesperson looked a little freaked-out too, so I took her by the elbow and said: "Come on, we should probably leave now." By the time we reached the street, she was totally freaked-out and screamed "What's wrong with you! Are you X$%X&# crazy?"

"No, I'm not," I answered calmly. "I did that for a very specific reason. I wanted you to know that you didn't do anything wrong in there. In fact, I think you did your best job yet of approaching the gatekeeper and introducing yourself and saying what I want you to say. What she said back to you really was stupid, and unfortunately, you're going to run into stupid people with stupid ideas on a regular basis. What's important is that you move on and say — to yourself! — 'OK, I met a stupid one, so now I'm going in the next door to look for a smarter one.'"

Please understand, I am *not* recommending that you should confront every misguided gatekeeper you meet. And I'm not recommending that you should disqualify every suspect who isn't immediately cooperative. If you don't want to give up on a particular suspect — for example, a company you strongly believe to have whale-sized potential — there are several other ways in which you can probably identify a buyer, starting with an Internet search or a visit to the suspect company's website. Beyond that, you might try calling on the phone at a time when that gatekeeper might not be on duty — early, late or lunchtime. A third possibility — and this is about as devious as I'm willing to be — is to call and ask: "Who do I talk with about getting some pricing from you guys?" That question usually gets me to some sort of sales or customer service person, and at that point, I say: "I'm not 100% sure how I ended up with you, but let me tell you who I am and what I want." It's been my experience that sales and customer service people are usually pretty sympathetic and cooperative in a situation like this.

Here's a variation on that theme. When I call on the phone and get an automated answering system — especially one with the "if you know the extension of the party you're trying to reach" option — I usually punch in 1-0 or

1-0-1 to see what will happen. If that leads to a live person answering the phone, I continue with the "I'm not 100% sure how I ended up with you, but let me tell you who I am and what I want" approach.

Remember, we're just talking about *gatekeeper* obstacles and objections to this point, specifically their unwillingness to give you the name of the buyer. There's a whole other set of *buyer* obstacles and objections on the horizon, and we'll get to those soon. For now, just understand that if you can't get the name, you can't make the sale.

A Little Bit Of Research

As I mentioned earlier, one of the reasons I recommend live canvassing whenever it's possible is the opportunity to bring more of your senses to bear on your prospecting challenges. On the phone, all you can learn is what you hear/what you're told. In person, you can also learn from what you see. Many companies have clues to the nature of their businesses in their lobbies; for example, racks of brochures and other sales literature or copies of trade publications.

Looking forward toward the substantive conversation that's the goal of the prospecting process, I hope you'll see the value of gaining knowledge about the company in advance. Here's another story I promised you earlier. I recently met with an insurance salesperson, and his first question after sitting down in my office was: "So, what does David Fellman & Associates do?" My answer was: "Well, we don't spend much time talking with salespeople who aren't professional enough to do a little research before they come to try to sell us something." Then I got up and pointed to my chair.

"Come around and sit here at my computer," I said. "Find your way to Google. Then search on 'David Fellman & Associates'. OK, now follow that link to davefellman.com. Is there any reason you couldn't have done that somewhere in between setting the appointment and arriving here today?"

I'll have more on the best strategy for your first meeting a little further along. For now, I hope you'll embrace the idea that *knowledge* is a significant selling advantage. That raises a question, though: should you do the research *before* you go out prospecting, or *afterward?*

The answer is: it depends! It depends on whether you are canvassing or working from a list, and if you're canvassing, my advice is to Google afterward. Go out into the marketplace, talk with as many gatekeepers as you can, and then Google the companies/organizations that seem to have prospect potential.

If you're working from a list, Google first to see what you can learn before you call. Many company websites provide a wealth of information, including names and titles of key personnel. In fact, sometimes an Internet search eliminates the need to even talk to the gatekeeper.

One caution, though, it should take *no more than 2-3 minutes* to pre-research any company on the Internet. If you're spending more than that, you're wasting time. Remember, at this stage you're only evaluating the likelihood that a suspect will turn out to be a real prospect. Later on in the process — for example, when you're preparing for a scheduled meeting — you will probably benefit from additional research. For now, though, I want you to do only enough to make a go/no go decision on whether to take the next step with any individual suspect.

The time management considerations here are really pretty straightforward. A 2-3 minute *investment* is appropriate at the suspecting stage. That's all it should take to support a go/no go decision. A 10-15 minute investment might be appropriate at the meeting prep stage, but you don't make that investment until you have scheduled the meeting!

Introductory Letter

Here's some more Dinosaur Wisdom: *Cold is always bad. Warm is always better.* That's half of the reason I recommend sending something through the mail — or via e-mail — in advance of your first phone call to the buyer. Now we get to the *what* to send in the mail. I recommend a short introductory letter, and by short, I mean no more than 3-4 paragraphs. As noted, this should be something that can be transmitted either by traditional mail or by e-mail, and 3-4 paragraphs fits that bill. What exactly should your introductory letter say? I think the best way to answer that question is to explain the thinking behind this specific element of the sales process.

As noted earlier, I don't want to make cold calls, and I do want to build trust, so the thinking behind this strategy is to open a "window of recognition" and then make a promise, which I will keep. So here are the four elements I want to express:

> *I'm interested in you because...* (I've been told that you buy — or possibly want or need or have an application for — exactly what I sell)...

I think you'll be interested in me because… (of that want or need or application)…

So with that in mind, I'm going to call you to set up a meeting…

And, by the way, here's why I think you should take the time to meet with me…

You may be surprised by how little I think this introductory communication should say, but remember, part of the challenge it faces is to get read in the first place, and *short* is good strategy in that regard. If you feel that you need to provide more information about your company, you can certainly include some sort of company brochure with a letter, or a PDF brochure or a link to your website with an e-mail. I would not do that, though. In fact, I wouldn't even enclose my business card with a letter. Less is better, here, and my reasoning goes beyond simply keeping it short so it's more likely to get read. Another part of my thinking is that this whole strategy is really aimed at setting up that *first substantive conversation*. The danger with sending *literature* is that they might actually read it and say to themselves: "OK, I know what this company can do, and I don't need that right now (or I'm happy with my current supplier right now), so I'll just file it away in case I want to call them someday."

Think about this for a moment. The real *solids* are not going to meet with you. The *gases* probably are, but there are probably not enough of them out there to make you rich. The *players* tend to be more like solids than gases, because they already have a group of trusted suppliers. The *price monsters* tend to be more like gases than solids, because the more salespeople they talk to, the more likely it is that they get even lower prices. The *liquids* are the real target of this strategy. In fact, I think the liquids are the ones who *are* most likely to make you rich. Remember what makes a liquid a liquid: they are generally happy with their current supplier or their status quo — which indicates that they buy on trust, not on price — but they'll talk to you and give some thought to whether you're better than what they already have.

You have to help them to decide to talk to you sometimes, though. *That's* what this strategy is all about! Here's some more Dinosaur Wisdom: *The decision to buy from you is way too important to be left up to them!* Think about that for a second. Do you really want to trust them to read your brochure and understand exactly what you and your company and your products and/or services are all about? I don't! I want to talk to them, and I don't want to do anything that might lessen the chances of having that conversation.

OK, so part of the plan here is to open a "window of recognition." Would you agree that getting a letter or e-mail from you — putting your name and your company name in front of them, possibly for the first time — is far less obtrusive than getting a cold phone call? Your intro letter or e-mail also tells them what's going to happen next, and it positions you to make a far warmer follow-up phone call: "Mr. Smith, my name is Dave Fellman, and I'm from David Fellman & Associates. I wrote to you the other day, and I promised that I'd be calling to see if we can set up a meeting. How does that sound to you?"

That's exactly what I'd say, by the way! The key obstacle, after all, is a *lack of interest* in meeting with me, so why not get right to the point? If the answer is: "Yeah, that sounds good," all that's left is to establish a time and place for the meeting. (Sadly, it's not usually that easy, but I'll cover the common objections in just a moment.)

Exact Words

Look back again at the exact words I use: "I wrote to you the other day and *I promised* that I'd be calling." I don't want to make cold calls, and I do want to build trust, so I've *engineered* a strategy in which the phone call is the second communication, and it keeps a promise that was made in the first one. Remember this element of Dinosaur Wisdom: *If you can get them to believe your promises, they'll think seriously about maybe buying from you.* The best way to show them they can believe the *big promises* you'll be making later on is to make *smaller promises* and keep them early on.

Now, look back again at the next to last piece of Dinosaur Wisdom: *The decision to buy from you is way too important to be left up to them!* I'm not willing to assume that my early-stages suspect will connect all the dots here and remember that I made a promise and now I'm keeping it. That's why I'm actually going to say it: "I wrote to you the other day and *I promised* that I'd be calling." I'm trying to plant the seed of the most important sale any salesperson can make in the early stages, and that's when you sell the idea that *when you say something is going to happen, it will happen, period, end of story, and they can take that to the bank!*

Common Obstacles and Objections

We have already considered the most common gatekeeper objections. With one notable exception, I would apply the same strategy to those obstacles and objections if I heard them from the buyer. That exception is to "we're happy with our current supplier," and I'll come back to that in a moment. First, let's consider a few of the other common "O&O's" that are encountered at this stage — where you've identified a buyer and sent out your introductory letter or e-mail, and now you're calling to see if you can set up a meeting.

Remember that *prospecting is an activity chain which begins with the identification of suspect companies, and ends with your first substantive conversation with the buyer.* That will hopefully be in person, although it might be have to accomplished over the telephone. Here's something to think about, though. Obviously, a face-to-face meeting will be scheduled for some time in the future, but what if your circumstance requires that it be a telephone conversation? In other words, are you calling to *schedule* a substantive conversation, or to *have* a substantive conversation?

Here's my answer. I think you have to be *prepared* to have the substantive conversation if the buyer insists on it. Unless that's the case, though, I think you're better off scheduling a time to talk in the (hopefully) near future. Here's my reasoning. This whole process is based on taking things one step at a time, and the first critical step is to show the buyer that he/she can trust you. That's why you send the letter or e-mail that makes the promise! Ideally, you want the buyer to have a little time to reflect on the fact that you made a promise and kept it, *before* you get into a situation where that detail might get lost in a conversation about wants and needs and features and benefits. Most salespeople try to make things happen too fast — remember Einstein's Theory of Special Relativity! Slowing the process down can be a significant differentiating factor.

Maybe it comes down to this. Do you want to rush things, or would you rather have the buyer thinking kindly about you for a few days before you get to the next stage of the process? *I like the way he/she operates — calm and professional and not pushy like so many other salespeople.*

In any event, remember that at this stage of the process, you are mostly trying to sell the idea that the buyer should *meet* with you, and you have to overcome any obstacles to the *meeting* before you can have any hope of *selling.*

Obstacle/Objection: "I'm really busy right now!"

Response: "When would be a better time?"

This is really pretty straightforward in terms of your question, but the buyer's response will tell you something about his/her interest in meeting with you. I have always treated "Call me in a week" — or 2 weeks or 3-4 weeks, anything less than a month! — as an expression of real interest, and my reply would be: "You got it!" Then I'd note the details and schedule the follow-up call in ACT.

Here's a key point: I'm going to start that call by reminding the buyer that I was asked to call at this point in time. "Mr. Smith, this is Dave Fellman from David Fellman & Associates. I hope you'll remember our recent conversation. You asked me to call back around now, and I promised I would, and I hope you'll note that I kept that promise. We were talking about setting up a meeting. How does your schedule look?"

Here's another key point. A lot of salespeople seem to want to push hard at a "soft" obstacle, and that's how I'd characterize "Call me next week." I frequently hear "What day next week?" or "What's the best time to reach you?" or "Can we set a time now for me to call you next week?" You don't need to be that pushy in the face of a positive response, and I think you're a lot better off with "You got it!" and the strategy I described above.

You *should* push hard at a "hard" obstacle, though, and that's how I'd characterize "Call me in 6 months." In my experience, what that usually really means is "I'm not interested and I hope you'll forget about me between now and then!"

Here's how I'd handle that one: "Mr. Smith, I can certainly do that, but while I've got you on the phone, I have one more question. I think I've learned in my travels that when someone says 'call me in 6 months,' there are two possibilities. One is that you really want to meet with me, and 6 months from now is the right time for it to happen. The other, though, is that you really don't want to meet with me, and you're hoping that I'll forget about you between now and then. Here's my question, which of those situations do we have here? And please, don't worry about hurting my feelings. If it's bad news, I can take it!"

I remember a buyer who answered: "Well, if you're sure you can take it…" I laughed, and said "OK, well, thank you for your time." It has always been part of my philosophy that if you're not going to be successful with someone, you're better off knowing that sooner rather than later. I hope you'll understand that as a time management concept, and that you'll relate it to those three tests a suspect has to pass in order to be considered a fully-qualified prospect — specifically the one about showing real interest in buying from you!

I remember another buyer, though, back in my Moore Business Forms days, whose response struck a different chord in me. He said something like: "Your feelings are your business, but I think you understand where I'm coming from." So I said: "I don't get it, why would you *not* want to talk with the representative of a really good printing company?" That took him aback, and then he stuttered something about being happy with his current supplier. OK, that's a whole different objection, and the "second best" strategy might be just the ticket to address it. As promised, though, I'll suggest another approach to this particular objection a little further along.

Here's some more Dinosaur Wisdom: *The first objection is not always the most important objection, or even a real objection.* Challenging each objection as it's thrown at you is analogous to peeling back an onion, and remember, as long as you're still in the competition, you have a chance of winning. Here's some more Dinosaur Wisdom: *There will be times when you simply have nothing to lose by pushing harder.* Even if that strategy doesn't keep you in the competition, it at least lets you feel like you went down swinging. Remember my story about the gatekeeper in San Francisco. You will run into *stupid* out there. Don't let those morons get you down!

While we're on the subject of pushing harder, here's a variation on the strategy for dealing with "I'm really busy right now." Rather than "When would be a better time?" you could also say: "Yeah, me too. In fact, there's no way I can meet with you over the next couple of weeks. I do have some time after that, though, how would (a day and date that far out) work for you?" One of my clients was intrigued with this approach, and he called me after trying it for the first time.

"It was great," he said. "Complete silence, and then she stuttered something like 'OK, I guess that would work.' She probably answered the phone thinking that her time was a lot more important than my time, but I think I established that my time could be valuable to her."

Obstacle/Objection: "I don't need anything right now."
Response: "I think that means that now is the best time for us to talk."
Most salespeople seem to view *immediate need* as their best opportunity. It

probably won't surprise you by now that I view things differently. Remember what it takes to be a fully qualified prospect: (1) they buy, want or need exactly what you're trying to sell, (2) they buy, want or need enough of it to make pursuing them worthwhile, and (3) they show some interest in buying from you. On one hand, I don't care if they need something right now, because unless we're talking about a one-time-only selling situation, it's how much they'll need over the *lifetime of the relationship* that really matters. And on the other hand, I think I'm more likely to win some of that business if I have time to build a relationship — to build some trust! — before they start comparing my prices to my competitors'. If we're talking about selling to an established need, I expect my price to be higher than what they're paying now, or at the very least, not enough lower to win the work strictly on that basis. And I know that in the absence of a solid relationship, (which everyone except the *gases* already has with at least one other supplier, right?) price is all they'll probably measure.

I remember a conversation with a buyer which started out just like I've described above. He said: "I don't need any printing right now." I said: "I think that means that now is the best time for us to talk." He said: "I don't think I understand," so I said: "Well, here's the way I look at it. At this point, you don't know me at all, and you don't have any reason to believe the promises I'm going to have to make to get the order from you when you *do* need something printed. And I don't know enough about your situation to be anything more than an order-taker at that point. If you'll give me the time to start getting to know you and your situation now — when there's no pressure on you to get something ordered, which would probably make it easiest for you to just buy from someone you'd bought from before — maybe I'll be able to suggest a better way of doing it when we get to the point where you do need something, and maybe you'll be more inclined to believe me and believe *in me* when I say 'here's what I think you should do.'"

There was silence on the other end of the line for a moment, and then he said: "You know, that might be the smartest thing a salesman's ever said to me. Let's get together this week." I was very proud of myself that day!

Obstacle/Objection: "We're under contract."
Response: "Can we explore the *length, width* and *height* of that contract?"

The first issue surrounding contracts is that there are basically fours kinds of them: *formal/written, implied, assumed* and *imaginary*. In my experience, there are relatively few *formal/written* contracts in most market segments, and most of the contracts referred to fall into one of the other three categories. Both the *implied* and *assumed* categories reflect the belief that some pricing level is dependent on some level of sales volume, and the *imagined* category is simply a strategy for pushing you away.

The response is still the same, though, and the best question surrounding the *length* of the contract is: "When do the renewal discussions begin?" (From your perspective, the intention is to begin them *now!*)

The best question surrounding the *width* of the contract is: "Does the contract cover (every applicable element of your product line)?" — in other words, don't just ask: "What does the contract cover?" *Prompt* the buyer to make sure he/she fully understands the breadth of your product line, and that you probably have interest in items that aren't covered by the contract, real or otherwise.

The best question surrounding the *height* of the contract is: "Are you completely satisfied with the quality and service you're getting in return for your contract commitment?" Most people tend to look at contract *pricing* as the only binding consideration, and I've had a few conversations with buyers during which their answer indicated that the other supplier had already broken the contract. "Yes, they promised you attractive pricing if you made a commitment to them, but didn't they also promise you a level of quality and service that would meet your needs and make you happy? If they're not giving you that — even if they are giving you the pricing — they're not giving you all that they promised and I think that means the contract is broken!"

Remember, your only objective when faced with any obstacle or objection is to get past it and continue the discussion. *Length, width* and *height* should give you something to work with!

Obstacle/Objection: "Send me some literature and let me look it over."
Response: "I can do that, Mr. Smith, but all that will really do is tell you about my company/products/services. I think it's a lot more important that I learn about *your* needs and wants. Do you see that there's a difference, by the way, between needs and wants? Lots of us can sell you the products and/or services, but I'm trying to be the one who learns how to make your life easier, to be the one who really adds some value."

Remember my definition of prospecting: an activity chain which begins with the identification of suspect companies, and ends with your first substantive conversation with the buyer. Prospecting is all about getting to that conversation! Sending literature is not enough, because *the decision to buy from you is way too important to be left up to them!* The essence of dealing with this obstacle — with most obstacles, in fact! — is to position your goal as a benefit to the buyer.

This approach doesn't always work, by the way. In fact, this may be a good time to tell you that I've never found anything in selling that *does* work every time. My goal here is to give you something to *work with*, a strategic response to a predictable objection. And if it doesn't work, your *Plan B* might be to send the literature that your suspect has asked for. Just don't forget to follow up and ask again for the meeting!

Obstacle/Objection: "I'm happy with my current supplier."

As noted, this is an obstacle/objection that I will approach differently, depending on whether I hear it from a gatekeeper or a buyer. With a gatekeeper, I'll use the "second best" technique I described earlier, and I might try the same technique if I hear "I'm happy with my current supplier" from the buyer on the first phone call after my introductory letter or e-mail. If it doesn't work in that situation, my *Plan B* is what I call the "How Happy" letter.

Let me tell you the story behind this selling tool. One of my printing industry clients called me and described this situation: "I called the suspect to ask for an appointment, after sending out my intro letter, and she said 'I'm very happy with my current supplier, but your timing is good because I always like to get pricing from another company around this time of the year, just to make sure that what I'm paying is competitive.'" My client asked: "How many items are we talking about pricing here?" and the answer was four or five.

"I'm willing to do that," he said, "but I want the opportunity to meet with you and learn more about exactly what you're doing." The suspect agreed, and in the course of that meeting, my client learned that this buyer was an excellent candidate for an online ordering capability which her current supplier didn't offer. When he called me, he said: "I think there's real potential here if I can get her away from that 'happy with my current supplier' mindset."

I put together the "How Happy" letter, which asked the suspect to consider just how happy she was in terms of five specific criteria: quality, service, pricing, general ease of doing business, and innovation/bringing new ideas to the table, each on a scale of 1-20 points. That, of course, adds up to 100 possible points, and the situation I was hoping for was a total score of 90 or below — in other words, less than an "A" grade. As it happened, the final score was 87, and we made our point: "You have *good*, but there is room for improvement. You can have *better*. You should talk to us about that!"

The "How Happy" strategy has worked well for quite a few of my clients, and it has proven to be pretty flexible. It can be delivered by e-mail or traditional mail, and it can also be executed in a face-to-face conversation or over the telephone. I hope you'll see that this is a strategy which *tests* solids to see if they might really be liquids! Remember, the entire objective of prospecting is to get to that first substantive conversation with the buyer. That's all you're trying to sell at this stage of the game!

Voice Mail

OK, now we come to what most salespeople tell me is their greatest source of frustration — voice mail! "They hide behind it," a salesperson told me recently, but I don't think that's true. Voice mail is a tool, and it's a great tool for both the receiver and the caller

Here's what I love about voice mail. It lets people talk to me when I'm not available to talk to them, and vice versa. Let's start with the "talk to me" perspective. My phone rings 30-50 times most days, and the callers range from suspects to prospects to customers to family and friends and finally to people trying to sell me stuff. I would answer all of those calls if I could, but the nature of my work doesn't allow it. When I'm in the office, I spend a significant portion of my time on outbound calls, ranging from prospecting and follow-up calls to the sales coaching and consulting activities I get paid for.

I will occasionally ask someone I'm talking with to hold while I take another call — caller ID is another great tool! — but I try to avoid that unless the "caller waiting" is a very high priority. Everyone else goes to voice mail. When I'm on the road, everyone who calls the office goes to voice mail, and so do most of the people who call my cell phone, since it's consulting or speaking work that takes me on the road, and I apply the same sort of prioritization to the decision on whether to interrupt what I'm doing to take a(nother) call.

I check my voice mail messages frequently, and I apply Stephen Covey's principles to *when or whether* I return the call — urgent and important, important but not urgent, urgent but not important, or neither urgent nor important. So I'm not hiding behind voice mail, I'm using it to help me manage my time! I will call you back quickly if you are urgent and important. I will call you back when you get to the top of my priority list if you are important but not urgent. I may not call you back at all if you are urgent but not important or neither urgent nor important.

Now, do you understand your voice mail challenge a little better? I'm not sure there's much a prospecting salesperson can do to make himself/herself truly urgent, but you damn well need to make yourself seem important!

Vice Versa

From the "vice versa" perspective, I love voice mail because it gives me a way to tell people why I think it's important for them to call me back. And that raises a very key point — some more Dinosaur Wisdom: *When you get connected to voice mail at this stage in the process, your objective is* not *to sell anyone your products and/or services. Your only objective is to get them to call you back!*

So here's what I'd say when the follow-up phone call to my letter or e-mail takes me to voice mail: "Mr. Smith, my name is Dave Fellman, and I'm from David Fellman & Associates. I wrote to you the other day, and I promised that I'd be calling to see if we can set up a meeting. Please give me a call, and let's set up a time to get together. You can reach me at 800-325-9634." (By the way, that's my actual phone number. Don't hesitate to call if you have questions on any of what you're reading here. The way I look at it, having bought this book makes you a customer, and that earns you the right to call me if I haven't explained something clearly enough. Fair warning, though, it also gives me an opportunity to sell you more of my products and/or services!)

Overall Strategy

Did you recognize that voice mail message as being substantially the same as what I'd say if Mr. Smith answered the phone when I called? Remember, this is all part of an overall process which has been engineered to avoid cold calls and to build trust. And that leads to another important point. I know salespeople who won't leave a message, they'll just hang up and call again later and keep on calling in the hope of finally reaching the suspect.

That's a very bad strategy, for two reasons. First, because I know people who never answer their phones. They let voice mail answer every call. That creates a perpetual tail chase, and you can call as many times as you want to but you're still going to get voice mail every time.

The second reason is even more important in terms of the overall process, and I think the best way for me to make this point is to ask this age-old question: *If a tree falls in the woods and there's no one there to hear it, does it really make any noise?*

I'm asking you this as a question of philosophy, of course, not of physics, and the application to prospecting is simply this: If a salesperson makes a promise in a letter or e-mail, but then doesn't leave a message to prove that he/she kept the promise, does that salesperson gain any *trust points* from the exercise? The answer is *probably not.*

Follow-Up Schedule

After leaving my message, I'll give my suspects a day or so to call me back. To be more specific, I'll give them the rest of the day I leave the message and all of the next day, but if they don't return my call, I'm going to call again on the following day. As an example, If I leave my message on Wednesday, I'll give them the rest of Wednesday and all of Thursday before calling again on Friday.

That raises the question of when you should make your first phone call after sending an introductory letter or an e-mail. My feeling is that sooner is much better than later. If I mailed a letter on Monday, for example, and I thought it would be delivered on Tuesday or Wednesday, I would make my first phone call on Wednesday afternoon, or on Thursday at the latest. If I sent an e-mail on Monday, I would make the phone call on Tuesday. Remember, half of the purpose of this introductory letter or e-mail is to open a "window of recognition." By nature, that tends to be a brief window, so you need to act while it's still open. The ideal scenario, in fact, would be (1) the suspect reads the letter, (2) the suspect puts the letter down, and (3) the phone rings and it's you. If I could figure out how to master that timing, I'd be a very happy man!

Now, there is some risk with this *fast-break* strategy, that you'll be calling before your suspect has even seen your letter. That's OK, though, because that situation is easily dealt with. You simply say: "Well, it was a short little letter. Let me tell you very quickly what it said. It said 'I'm interested in you because I've been told that you're the person who buys (exactly what you sell) at your company, and I think you'll be interested in me because we specialize in exactly that. The letter promised that I'd be calling to follow up, and it also mentioned a couple of specific reasons why I think you should take the time to meet with me. Those reasons are... So, what do you think?"

I have had salespeople call me and make reference to letters or literature that I've never seen, and when I tell them that, they almost universally suggest one of two things — either waiting a few days for the Post Office to get its act together, or sending me another copy/package and then calling again. Bad strategy either way! I think you'll agree that getting a suspect on the phone in the first place is a low percentage proposition, and I don't want to have to count on that happening twice in the early stages of prospecting.

I hope you'll also see how one element of this process — a *short* letter — sets up a later element, the ability to say "It was a short little letter. Let me tell you very quickly what it said." I think that brings you pretty close to even with the 1-2-3 ideal scenario I mentioned earlier.

Second Message

So now it's Day 3 after your first voice mail message, and your suspect hasn't returned your phone call. It's time to call again, and if Mr. Smith answers the phone, you should say the same thing you would have said if he had answered your first call: "Mr. Smith, my name is Dave Fellman, and I'm from David Fellman & Associates. I wrote to you the other day, and I promised that I'd be calling to see if we can set up a meeting. How does that sound to you?"

What if you find yourself in voice mail again, though? You can't leave the same voice mail message, because that didn't work the first time. It's time to be more assertive, and here's the way you should look at this situation: You *asked* Mr. Smith to return your call and he didn't do that. Now you have to *tell* him why he should.

I see this as a message in three parts: the first part will identify you, the second part will attempt to grab his attention, and the third part will provide a compelling reason for him to call you back. Here's an example:

"Mr. Smith, my name is Dave Fellman, and I'm from David Fellman & Associates. I wrote to you the other day, and I promised that I'd be calling to see if we can set up a meeting. Please give me a call, and let's set up a time to get together. You can reach me at 800-325-9634. (This, of course, is the part that identifies you.)

"You know, I'm sure you get a lot of calls from salespeople, and I bet that returning all of those calls isn't at the top of your priority list every day. This is a call I think you should return, though, and let me tell you why." (This part will grab many people's attention. It's *not* what they're used to hearing from salespeople. Put a little pause in between your phone number and this part of the message.)

Now we come to the fun part. What would be a truly compelling reason for this suspect to call you back? There's no one-size-fits-all answer to that question, but here are a few possibilities:

> "I think you should call me back because I've been doing this for a long time. In fact, this is my XXth year in this business, and what I think that means to you is XX years of product knowledge. I don't think it's too much of a stretch to think that XX years of specific industry knowledge could be of value to you, and I know that if you talk to some of my current customers — and I'll be happy to put you in touch with a few of them — they'll tell you that's exactly the value I bring to their businesses. They tell me what they're trying to accomplish, and I can usually tell them the best way to go about it. So if that would be of value to you, Mr. Smith, you need to call me at XXX-XXX-XXXX."

I'm sure you'll agree that significant knowledge and experience represent a competitive advantage. But what if you don't have that kind of experience? What if you're on the opposite end of the experience spectrum, just getting started?

> "I think you should call me back because I've been a (exactly what you sell) salesperson for two entire months. That may not sound like something to be bragging about, and there are certainly people with a lot more sales experience than I have, but I'll tell you what I don't think you're going to find. I don't think you're going to find anyone who brings more *enthusiasm* to the job, or someone who has a better understanding of the need to work hard to earn and keep some people's business. If that would be important to you, Mr. Smith, you need to call me at XXX-XXX-XXXX."

Is *enthusiasm* as compelling as *significant experience*? Maybe not, but it might be more compelling than it seems at first glance. I've stressed that, for most people, the buying decision is driven mostly by trust in the salesperson. Now let's talk a little bit about the *not buying* decision — the decision to change suppliers. I've seen research which indicates that about 10% of all people who change suppliers say they did so because of quality problems, and another 10% say they changed because of service failures. (Those are certainly *trust-breakers*, right?) Another 15% say they changed because they found "better" prices, and 5% changed for a variety of miscellaneous reasons. The largest group of all, though — fully 60%! — say they changed suppliers mostly because they didn't feel like the one they'd been buying from really valued their business. Now let's say that you're that inexperienced salesperson, and you're leaving that *enthusiasm and hard work* message on someone's voice mail. If that someone has been feeling underappreciated by his/her current supplier, you may very well get a return phone call.

What vs. Why

I hope you'll see, by the way, that there's a difference between "I'll work very hard to earn and keep your business" and "I don't think you're going to find anyone who has a better understanding of the need to work hard to earn and keep some people's business." The first is a *what* statement; the second adds a *why* component. People generally respond better to the *why* than just the *what*, because the *why* provides a reason to believe that the *what* is likely to happen. Most salespeople never get beyond the superficial; they make *what* statements, but they don't address the *why* or the *how*. The great salespeople know that the *why* and the *how* are what sells the *what*!

Other Possibilities

Here are a couple of other possibilities for the *why* component of your second voice mail message:

> "I think you should call me back because I'm the owner of (your company name), and I don't know about you, but I always like dealing with the owner. I think that can be especially important if you've ever had to deal with late deliveries because your salesperson didn't have the horsepower to get your orders to the front of the line. You won't have that problem dealing with me, so if that's an issue for you — or if you just like the idea of dealing with the owner — give me a call at XXX-XXX-XXXX."

"I think you should call me back because I worked on your side of the desk for X years before taking this job as a salesperson, and I think that means I have a good understanding of both what you need and what you want from a supplier. To give you an example of what I mean, I often needed something delivered by a certain date, but I also wanted to know that my order was on track all through the process so I wouldn't end up with a problem when it was too late to do anything about it. So for me, it's all about communication. If that's what it's about for you, you should return my call at XXX-XXX-XXXX."

"I think you should return my call because I'm more of an idea person than a pure salesperson, and I think it's fair to say that my ideas have saved time, aggravation and even money for my customers. I can prove all that, by the way, with testimonials from those same customers, and if you'd like to talk with some of them yourself, that can be arranged. Please call me at XXX-XXX-XXXX, and we can take the next step."

It's All About You!

Did you notice that all of these messages are about *you*, not about your company? This is an important point, and it relates back to something I said earlier about how most salespeople face two core selling challenges. The first is to sell themselves. The second is to "close the sale" on a product or service. At the prospecting/voice mail stage of selling, you're not anywhere near closing the sale on a specific product or service, so it's all about selling yourself.

Most salespeople do this wrong, and leave messages about their products and/or services and/or companies. Remember, you'll have covered that in your introductory letter or e-mail — 'I'm interested in you because I've been told that you're the person who buys (exactly what you sell) at your company, and I think you'll be interested in me because we specialize in exactly that" — the question before the buyer right now is whether to return your call or not. Not a company's call, *your* call!

Here's another important element of voice mail strategy. You should *always* ask them to call you back. You should *never* say that you'll call again, or even that you'll call again if you don't hear from them. The latter will probably be assumed, and the former just gives them a reason not to call you. Remember that one of the things we're trying to measure is their interest in buying from you, and returning your call would seem to be an expression of interest.

Granted, sometimes they'll call you to tell you that they're *not* interested, but even that has the benefit of giving you closure. As I said earlier, from a time management perspective, if you're not going to succeed with someone, you're better off learning that sooner rather than later. And as I also said earlier, an "I'm not interested" response doesn't have to be the end of the discussion. You still have the option of challenging it, for example: "I appreciate your kindness in making the call, but I still find myself wondering, why would you not want to at least talk with me?"

Grammar/Structure/Scripting

Before we move on from here, please take a look back at the "scripts" I'm suggesting. As I wrote them, I found myself thinking about my 8th Grade English teacher, Miss Anna Collins. She once said something along these lines to me: "David Fellman, I will tolerate some variation from good grammar and sentence structure in the spoken word because it passes through the mind so quickly. The written word, however, has permanence that demands a greater respect for our language. In other words, you bozo, you don't write the way you talk!"

With all due respect to Miss Collins, if we're talking about scripting, you *do* want to write the way you talk! The recipe for effective scripting is to take advantage of the opportunity to think about what you want to say and how you want to sound while you're not under any pressure — like, for example, when you're on one end of a live phone call talking to a person or to his/her voice mail!

How you want to sound is every bit as important as *what you want to say*. You want to sound comfortable and natural — not like a salesrobot reading off a script! So stay away from words that you wouldn't normally use, and don't be afraid of contractions and awkward-looking sentence structure. The best strategy is to write and then practice and then edit and then practice and then practice and practice and then practice some more. When you think you're ready, here's a (hopefully) final step in the scripting process — call home or call your cell phone and leave your scripted voice-mail message on your own voice mail or answering machine. Then listen to it. I think you'll know then if your message is ready for prime time, and if it's not, see edit and practice and practice and practice etc. above.

What Next?

OK, I hope you'll see the *escalation element* of my voice mail strategy. First, you *ask* them to return your call. If that doesn't work, you *tell* them why you think they should. But what if *that* doesn't work? Again, I'll give them the rest of the day of my second message and all of the day after that, but if I don't get a return call, I will call again on the following day. I'm not going to leave a third voice mail message, though. This time, if I don't get to talk to the buyer, I want to talk to the gatekeeper, and here's what I'll say: "My name is Dave Fellman, and I hope you'll remember speaking with me the other day, and by the way, I want to thank you again for giving me Mr. Smith's name as the person who I need to talk to. I wrote to him, just like I promised that I was going to, and I've called a couple of times to follow up on that and left messages and he hasn't returned my call. I'm just wondering, can you tell me if there's a time that I'd be likely to catch him in the office?"

I remember a gatekeeper who told me to call early in the morning. "Anything after 7:30 or 7:45 and you're not going to catch him," she said, "he'll just be caught up in the craziness of the day." I remember another gatekeeper who told me that her boss stayed late every Monday and Wednesday to catch up on paperwork, and that I could probably reach him around 7:00 PM. Still another one told me that the man I'd been calling had been in China for the last two weeks, and wouldn't be returning for another month. That's all good information, right? Sometimes it's not a lack of interest, but more a matter of timing.

Sometimes, though, it is a lack of interest. I remember still another gatekeeper who said: "Let me make sure I understand this. You wrote to him and you've called him twice and he hasn't returned your call?" I answered: "Yes, Ma'am," and then she said: "Well, what're you stupid? He obviously doesn't want to talk to you!" She hung up, and then I hung up, and as I recall, I got up and walked around the office for a couple of minutes before I made my next call. Key point: I *made* my next call, knowing that you can't sell to everyone, and also determined not to let the morons get me down!

Based on what I learn from a gatekeeper, I might schedule another phone attempt, or I might decide to try e-mailing my suspect. *I'm trying hard to connect with you*, I wrote to one recently, *to see if there's a match between your needs and my expertise. Do you have any interest in talking to me?* The suspect wrote back: *Not really.* OK, not the response I was hoping for, but a response nonetheless. So I wrote back to continue the dialog: *I don't get it. Why would you not want to at least talk to me?*

Do you see how the same basic obstacles and objections seem to raise their heads from different places? The good news is, once you develop a response to each objection, you can use it no matter where in the process the objection arises.

Closed-Ended Question

Here's something else to think about. After hearing that story, a recent seminar attendee told me that I set myself up for a negative answer in the way I asked the question. "You asked a closed-ended question," he said, "and you gave the guy an easy way to get rid of you, just by saying 'no.'"

"I look at it a little bit differently," I said. "From my perspective, I gave him any easy way to get us to the next stage of a relationship, just by saying "yes.' But I wasn't afraid of a negative answer, because I have a response ready for that answer, and I'm willing to push him to see if he might not be a little more *liquid* than *solid*." Remember that people are often satisfied with *good*; your challenge — your opportunity! — is to get them thinking about *better*.

Now let's look at how that dialog developed. He didn't respond to my voice mail messages, so I sent him an e-mail. *Do you have any interest in talking to me?* No. *I don't get it, why would you not want to at least talk to me?* I'm happy with my current supplier. *Oh, who are you using?* From there, I might go into my "second best" routine, or I might decide to use the "How Happy" approach.

One of the benefits of an assertive strategy is that it allows you to "peel back the onion" and identify the real obstacle/objection. I hope you also see how this whole prospecting *process* is driven by the overall *goal*. As I wrote earlier, the process itself is nothing more than a plan for dealing with predictable obstacles. I didn't engineer this process by asking myself what should I do first. Instead, I looked at the desired end result — a new customer! — and started working my way backward through the predictable obstacles.

When To Give Up

It's important to remember that you can't sell to everybody, and from a time management perspective, if you're not going to succeed with any individual, you're better off knowing that sooner rather than later. I used the term *fast-break* earlier, and there's another basketball term that's appropriate to this discussion: *full court press*. My prospecting strategy is to throw a lot of interest at each suspect over a short period of time, to see if they return it. If they don't — after a letter or e-mail, two escalating voice mail messages and then a pretty blunt e-mail, all delivered within a pretty brief timeframe — I think you have to accept that this is a person who has no interest in you right now.

The *right now* part is important, because the situation could change. *Solids* can become *liquids* and even *gases*, right? So how do you position yourself for an opportunity if something changes? You *don't* do that by continuing to call until the first note of your voice sounds like, well, whatever noise would make you cringe the most. A much better strategy would be to *retreat and recycle*; in other words, to back off and try again 3 or 4 or 6 months later.

By that time, any number of things might have changed — including the identity of the buyer! Because of that, I would start the process from scratch at that point, going all the way back to a quick Internet search, or to the gate-keeper to ask who you should send your information to. If the name is the same, I would suggest a modified version of the introductory letter or e-mail: *I hope you'll remember me. I wrote to you several months ago to introduce myself. I'm writing again because I'm still interested in you, and I still think you might be interested in me, and as before, I'm going to call on the phone to see if we can set up a meeting.*

Retreat and recycle has proven to be a far better strategy than *persist and annoy.*

Long Messages

I wouldn't be surprised if this thought crossed your mind as you were reading my thoughts on the second voice mail message: "Damn, that's a long message! No one's going to listen to that, they're going to delete you before you're halfway through!"

It's true, many people are going to do just that, but I don't care, because they're not the people I'm talking to. This is another element of the coordinated and engineered *process* I'm trying to teach you, and it takes us back to the introductory letter or e-mail. As I hope you remember, the letter makes a promise — *I'm going to call you to ask for an appointment.* If you look at it from a slightly different perspective, though, that promise might also be seen as a warning — *I'm going to try to get you to buy from me instead of whoever you're buying from now!* The people you're writing to are (hopefully) not idiots. They understand your objective, and it's been my experience that many of them make the decision about whether to meet with you or not right at the point where they read your introductory communication.

I know from experience, in fact, that the majority of people I've written to over the years reacted something like this: *OK, this sales guy wants to come in here and try to convince me to buy from him. I'd rather go to the dentist than let that happen!* I know that's true, because the majority of people I've written to over the years wouldn't take my calls or return my calls. I also know, though, that some of the people I've written to reacted differently. *Oh yeah,* they must have thought, *I want to meet with this guy.* I know that's true, because they took my calls — some even called me before I called them! — and quickly agreed to meet with me.

Here's something else I know. There's a third group, and their reaction goes something like this: *Yes, I should meet with this guy, but I'm really busy (or I don't need anything right now) so I'll put calling him back and meeting with him on the back burner.* Here's what I want you to understand: *These* are the people I'm talking to when I leave that long, second voice mail message. I'm not talking to the people who've already decided that they're not going to meet with me, and I'm not talking to the people who've already decided that they are going to meet with me. I'm talking to the people who might call me back and agree to meet with me — all of this sooner rather than later! — if I give them a good reason why they should.

This is *proven* voice mail strategy, so I hope you'll embrace it. It is not, however, a strategy that guarantees that 10 out of 10 people will call you back. Here's what you can expect, though: it's a strategy that can take you from 1 out of 10 people calling you back to 2 out of 10 or maybe 3 out of 10. And I don't know about you, but 2 out of 10 is a 100% improvement over 1 out of 10, and I'd be pretty happy with that.

Less Talk, More Action

Prospecting is similar to Time Management in that it's the subject of a lot of talk, but often not a lot of action. The real winners in sales have what I like to call a *prospecting attitude,* and that attitude can come from one of three factors. First, a lot of those real winners have a prospecting attitude because they want to make *more money.* Second, most of the real winners have a prospecting attitude because they want to minimize the likelihood of making *less money* — they know that their own *solids* can become *liquids* or *gases,* and that there's no guarantee of keeping a customer forever. Third, there are some among the real winners who have a prospecting attitude mostly because *management wants them to.*

Here's my perspective: I don't care which of these three factors — or which combination — motivates you to have a prospecting attitude, and long as you have one. As we've discussed, time is money, and customers are money too. If you're not making enough money, part of your problem is probably that you don't have enough customers, and the solution to that problem is prospecting for some new ones.

Solids Into Something Else (The Donut Guy's Bad Day!)

Here's a little story to close this chapter. I was out on calls with a young salesperson who brought donuts very regularly to his customers and prospects. On this particular day, he got a "get over here now" call from his #1 customer — something that definitely qualified as *urgent and important* — and we arrived to find the Marketing Manager in tears because the open house event was that evening and the signs and banners were wrong. "Paul," she said, as we walked in, "there's not enough donuts in the world to make up for the pain this is causing me."

Let me rephrase that, with some artistic liberty, but I think you'll understand: "Paul, I have always liked you but I don't think I can trust you anymore." Here's some more Dinosaur Wisdom: *Pain is a pivot point. It makes people think about changing suppliers.* And here's still more: *If you lose their trust, you'll probably lose their business.*

That's how *solids* turn into something else. It's good when it happens to your competitors. It's really, really bad when it happens to you. One of the morals of this story is to stay focused on *trust* — both in your prospecting and in your ongoing dealings with established customers! — and to not ever let yourself think that the *like factor* will be enough.

Here's a second moral to the story, and another piece of Dinosaur Wisdom: *If they have no problems, you may have no opportunity.* So let's use that first substantive conversation — which you've hopefully scheduled now as the end product of your prospecting process — to take the next step toward qualifying a real prospect and maybe turning him/her into a real customer.

7

The First Substantive Conversation

Prospecting is an activity chain which begins with the identification of suspect companies, and ends with the first substantive conversation with the buyer. Scheduling that first substantive conversation is an accomplishment worth celebrating, and the conversation itself is a huge opportunity — but not the opportunity most salespeople seem to think it is. What does that mean? It's an opportunity to learn, not to sell. To *ask*, not to *tell*.

I went out on a first meeting sales call with a young salesperson not too long ago, and the salesperson made his standard presentation—his "spiel" as he referred to it—and then we pretty much left. "How did I do?" he asked me as we walked out of the building.

"Well, that depends on what you were trying to accomplish," I told him. "Were you hoping to educate your suspect or trying to educate yourself?"

"Why would I need to educate myself?" he asked. "I know what we do."

"Sure," I said, "but do you know what he needs? Or more importantly, what he *wants* from a supplier and might not be getting from the company he's buying from now?"

Here's the key point. *Prospecting* ends with your first meeting with the buyer, but the buyer is not a fully qualified *prospect* when that first meeting begins! Even if you're pretty sure of the *want* or *need* or *volume potential* at this point, you can't be sure of the suspect's real interest in buying from you, and it's important to understand that *willing to meet with you* and *ready to buy from you* are two very different things.

If all you're doing is making a "spiel," you are talking but not qualifying, and that represents bad strategy on three separate levels. First, you're putting your cart before your horse in terms of time management. Second, if you're doing all of the talking, the buyer may very well stop listening. And third, I don't care how slick a spiel you've put together, it'll be worthless if you can't give them a good reason to buy from you — a reason that connects to *their* wants and needs, not just yours!

While I'm on the subject of "making a spiel," I should tell you that I always want to smack any salesperson who uses that word, because it's really a derogatory term for what should be a highly professional endeavor. It's bad enough that most of the general public holds the sales profession in such low regard. I hate it when salespeople perpetuate the stereotype with words or actions or attitudes.

Time Management Considerations

OK, let's look first at the time management considerations I just mentioned. Up to this point, you may have spent as much as an hour on the suspect you'll be meeting with. It'll probably seem like more than that because it's been spread out over time, but the cumulative total of all of the prospecting-and-follow-up activities we've discussed should add up to no more than 60 minutes. The first substantive conversation itself might add another 60 minutes, and maybe more depending on travel time. Now let's consider the next stages of pursuit, after your first substantive conversation, which will probably involve further conversations, quoting, research, samples, etc. It could easily take 3-4 more hours of your time to bring this buyer to the point of even *seriously considering* placing an order with you. It could also take the same amount of time to end up with nothing!

I'm willing to invest an hour to see if I can get a meeting with an attractive suspect — and by that, I just mean one who seems to meet the first two qualifying criteria. If that investment pays off, I'm willing to invest another hour or so to confirm #1 and #2, and to explore #3: their level of interest in actually buying from me. If *that* investment pays off, I'll happily commit more time and other resources into developing the prospect.

If not, though, I don't want to invest any more of my time. It's as simple as that. You've probably heard the expression "throwing good money after bad." We've also agreed, I think, that *time is money*. When you put those two things together, I hope you'll see the wisdom in a *progressive investment*; in other words, at each step, you have to decide whether the *next* step is worth taking.

80/20 Situation

Now, how about the possibility that if you're doing all of the talking, the buyer may very well stop listening? Let's consider this application of the 80/20 rule: 80% of all people would rather talk than listen, and only 20% of those people really listen when someone else is talking. We're a pretty self-centered species under the best of circumstances, and the selling situation is further complicated by the individual self interests of the two parties—the seller and the buyer. It's not just friendly conversation, in other words, because there's money involved!

You might think that would make the buyer listen closely, and the truth is that many buyers try. But the sheer volume of statements and promises that most salespeople call a "presentation" pretty quickly overwhelms most buyers, so they start listening defensively or tune out altogether.

I'm sure you've found yourself listening defensively. That's when you start focusing on the things you don't like or believe. "Our product will make your life easier," says the salesperson. "Maybe someone else's life," says that little voice in your head. "My life is different, much more complicated than everyone else's."

I'm sure you've also found yourself *tuning out*. "Our product has a spin ratio of 14:1, a flux capacity of 3000, a 610 hour service cycle and it comes in red, yellow, green, black and brown," says the salesperson. "I need to check up on that proposal for ABC Company," says that little voice in your head, "and a cup of coffee would be really good right now."

If these things happen to you, you have to expect that they happen to others — specifically the people you're trying to sell to. I hope you'll realize that it's critically important to keep your prospects and customers engaged, and that just doesn't happen when the salesperson dominates the conversation.

Need To Know

There's more to it, though, than just keeping them engaged. There are things you really need to know, first in order to decide about taking the next step, and second, in order to know what that next step should be! That is, of course, unless all you want to do is make your spiel and hope for the best.

Think about that for just a moment, because it's all most salespeople do. They deliver a sales presentation which may cover the *what* pretty well — what they hope to sell you — but provides only shallow justification for the *why*. What does that mean? I sat in on a presentation recently which started out with a pretty comprehensive description of the selling company's digital printing capabilities, then the salesperson confidently said: "I'm sure you'll benefit from this. Now, do you have any questions?"

"Yeah," said the buyer. "Exactly why do you think I'm going to benefit?"

"Well," said the salesperson, "lots of other companies have. Digital printing is the future of printing."

"OK," said the buyer. "Let me give that some thought. I'll call you if I need any."

Obviously, "we do digital printing" and "it's the future of printing" didn't hit this buyer's hot buttons. In fact, the salesperson never inquired as to what those hot buttons might be. If she had — and if she'd learned that this buyer had problems or applications that digital printing would address — she'd have been able to say: "Thanks for answering my questions and telling me about those problems you've been having and giving me the opportunity to tell you about a possible solution," or perhaps: "Thanks for answering my questions and telling me about the way you've been doing things and giving me the opportunity to tell you about a possibly better way."

Where would you rather be at the end of your first meeting, where this salesperson was, or where she could have been? I hope I've convinced you that an *interrogatory* approach is much better than a *declaratory* approach at this stage of the game.

What Is The Competition?

Here's something else to think about. In seminars, I often ask this question: "*What* is it that you're competing with when you're trying to develop a new customer?" Most people's first thought is a *who* — another supplier — but *what* is really a more fundamental question. And the answer, as we discussed earlier, is that you're competing with the *status quo*, the way they've *been doing* whatever it is that reflects the intersection between your products and services and capabilities and their wants and/or needs. Remember this Dinosaur Wisdom: *You're always in competition with the current and existing state of affairs as it pertains to your products and/or services.* That may mean another supplier, but it also may mean that they've never purchased a product or service like yours before.

Bottom line: the first meeting/substantive conversation is a great opportunity to explore the *status quo*. And the best possible result would be to find some weakness in the *status quo*, either a problem you can solve, some pain you can relieve, or an opportunity you can help them to capitalize on.

Meeting Length

OK, how do you accomplish that objective? Before we get to that, let me ask you this question: How long do you want your first meeting with a buyer to last? When I ask that in seminars, the answer usually has something to do with "however long they're willing to talk to me." At a recent seminar, one attendee said: "I usually ask for 5-10 minutes, because that's all the time I think most people will give me." Another said: "Yeah, I ask for less and hope they'll give me more." That led me to ask another question: "Who's time is more valuable, yours or theirs?"

"Well, they probably think theirs is," said that first attendee.

"That may be true," I said, "but you have to think *yours* is. And remember, I didn't ask you how long you think they'll give you, I asked you how much time you want!"

If you asked me that question, my answer would be 20-25 minutes. How did I come up with that number? Initially, by scripting and then role-playing a series of questions, and then I confirmed my assumptions by implementing that agenda in the field — lots and lots of times! The way I looked at it, I had the opportunity to design the *perfect sales conversation*. It doesn't always go perfectly, but I know that my preparation has made me a far more effective salesperson.

Will people agree to give you 20-25 minutes, or even longer if your agenda requires it? Yes, they will. Not everyone, perhaps, but I think it's fair to say that most really interested people will commit to the time it takes to do important things right. They may have to be convinced of something's importance, and they may also have to be told how long it will take to do it right. I think both of those things fall into a salesperson's job description!

Here's something else to consider. My neighbor, the owner of a local business, recently asked me this question: "What is it with salespeople? I get all these calls, asking for appointments, and when I ask how long it will take, they say 'Oh, I just need a few minutes of your time.' How the hell important can it be if it's only going to take a few minutes?"

Six Components

I think that *perfect sales conversation* should have five or six components: (1) an opening statement, (2) questions about the company, (3) questions about the individual, (4) questions about the products he/she buys, (5) questions about the status quo, and finally, (6) a mutual decision on what to do next. Numbers 4 and 5 are both important if you are selling to an established need — in other words, when your goal is to displace the current supplier of something the buyer is already buying. Number 4 is probably not necessary if you're selling something that the buyer has never bought before, but the questions about the *status quo* should still be part of your conversation.

Obviously, I think it's important to cover all of the relevant topic areas. Beyond that, I think it's especially important to do it in exactly this order. Why? Because this is another *engineering* exercise. You know the goal, and the best way to reach it is to work backwards through all of the "what can go wrong?" possibilities.

The most predictable obstacle in this first meeting is the distance between two people who don't really know each other very well, a distance which is magnified by the fact that one of them is trying to sell something to the other one. With that in mind, do you think it makes sense to walk in, sit down and start right in with provocative questions? I think it makes far better sense to get the buyer comfortable in talking to you, and experience has shown that most business people love to talk about themselves and their businesses.

Now, I have told you that I want this to be an *interrogatory* meeting, but it's a good idea *not* to open with a question, but rather with an opening statement. For example: "Thanks for meeting with me today. My goal is to learn enough about your business and your situation regarding (your products and/or services) to determine whether I can really be of value to you. I have a bunch of questions I want to ask you, and it generally takes (20-25) minutes to work through my agenda." Now a question: "Does that fit with your schedule?"

Objective and Timeline

The idea here is to establish your agenda and to confirm that you'll have enough time to complete it. Maybe another way to say that is to establish that you're driving this meeting, with both an objective and a timeline. I have occasionally had people tell me that they couldn't or wouldn't give me 20-25 minutes on that particular day, so I would ask them how much time I did have.

If the answer was 15 minutes or longer, I would say: "OK, we'll have to do the express version of my agenda today" and jump right into my first question. With less than the ideal amount of time — but still enough time to cover my agenda adequately — I would simply move the conversation along faster.

If the answer was 14 minutes or less, though, I would ask to reschedule. "That's really not enough time for us to do this right," I would say. "Can we reschedule for a time when you will be able to give me a full 20-25 minutes?"

That might seem like a confrontational strategy, and in truth, that's almost what it is — I say "almost" because I prefer the term *assertive*. Remember, the purpose of this meeting is to *qualify*, and limiting your time is not a good sign in terms of real interest in buying from you. It's been interesting, though, that on most of the occasions where I've had to adopt this strategy, the result was either to reschedule within the next few days, or for the buyer to change his/her position and agree to give me the time I wanted right then and there. As I said earlier, I think people will commit to the time it takes to do important things right. They may have to be convinced of something's importance, and they may also have to be told how long it will take to do it right. Again, both of those things are part of your job description.

I want to stress again, by the way, that this is a *conversation*, not a *presentation*. That's turned out to be good news for many of the reluctant salespeople I've coached over the years. They've had fears about their ability to make a presentation, but far less anxiety about engaging in a conversation.

Isn't it great when the right way is actually easier than the wrong way?

Questions About The Company

Once you've made your opening statement — and dealt with any issues that may have raised — it's time to start the questioning, and as noted, the first area I want to ask about is *the company*. Do me a favor, though, don't come into my office like that insurance salesperson did and ask me what my company does. You *can* know that in advance, and you *should* know that in advance. In fact, doing some research in advance let's you pose your first question in an advantageous manner. I sat in on a meeting not long ago between a sign salesperson and the Marketing Manager for a furniture store, and the salesperson said: "I've seen your ads and I've been to your website, and I know that you carry several of the major brands. Do you have to qualify with those companies to sell their products, or can just anyone open up a store and start selling those brands?"

The Marketing Manager's face lit up. "That's a good question," he said. "Theoretically anyone can buy and sell most of the major brands, but they're all looking for serious dealers who will move a lot of their merchandise." The salesperson picked up on the key word in that answer. "How do you show them that you're serious?" That opened the floodgates, and the Marketing Manager talked for several minutes about his company's culture and attitudes and strategies. He was enjoying himself, and obviously comfortable with the way the conversation was going.

I've had similar success with several variations on that theme:

- "I visited your website, and I noted the list of your current clients. What is it they like most about doing business with you?"
- "Who are your main competitors?" followed by "How do you stand out from them?"
- "From what I can see, you're a leader in your market/industry. Has it been easy to get to that point?"
- "I know A, B and C about your company. What else should I know?"

I hope you'll see how 10-15 minutes of research can drive this part of the questioning process. Remember what I said about pre-approach research earlier, though. In the *suspecting* stages, all you're looking for is enough information to support the decision to take an even closer look at a company. That means 2-3 minutes on a Google search or at their website. You don't do the 10-15 minute research until you're preparing for an actual meeting with the buyer!

How's Business?

Here's a not-so-good opening question: "How's business?" I'm sure it seems like the most natural of questions to ask on a sales call, but you should *never* ask it at the beginning of your first meeting. This is a lesson my Dad taught me many years ago, and here's exactly what he told me: "David, you want to be careful about starting off a conversation with a question to which the answer might be: 'It sucks!' You might never recover from such a negative start!"

Sure, your products and services might help to improve the business, but soft business conditions tend to motivate people toward *not* spending money. And as we've discussed, selling can be strongly affected by time, space and gravity.

Here's some more Dinosaur Wisdom: *If you start your conversation at the bottom of a hole, it'll have to be pushed up out of that hole, with gravity working against you.* If you can avoid the hole in the first place, you're in much better shape!

Transitional Questions

OK, let's go back to the Marketing Manager at the furniture store. He was waxing enthusiastically about his company's culture and attitudes and strategy, and in fact, he probably would have continued talking for at least another 15-20 minutes if the salesperson left it up to him. He didn't, though. After 5-6 minutes, the salesperson stepped into a pause with a *transitional* question: "How long have you been working here?"

I hope you'll see the value of being prepared with a transitional question. That's how you keep the conversation under control in terms of time and agenda. I could actually see the salesperson waiting for an opportunity to *insert* his transitional question into the conversation. He leaned slightly forward about 30 seconds before the opportunity arrived, and the transition was very natural. The buyer was talking about one thing. He finished a sentence and stopped to take a breath. The salesperson asked his transitional question and then the buyer was talking again about another thing.

I think "How long have you been working here?" is also a perfect transitional question. Remember, the purpose of the *questions about the company* was to get the buyer talking, to create a level of comfort. The purpose of the *questions about the individual* stage is partly to build on that comfort level, but also to learn more about the buyer. And this is important, it is *not* to learn whether the buyer is a sports fan or a grandparent or was born and raised in the area.

Granted, there is value in knowing those things, but this is not the time to be asking about them! At this point in the process, what I really want to know is where this buyer fits into the actual buying decision. Can he/she make the decision to change suppliers? Can he/she make even larger decisions about changing the status quo? Remember, you're still *qualifying* here, trying to determine whether to take the next step, and exactly what that next step should be!

Questions About The Individual

The Marketing Manager answered that he'd been with the company for 12 years. The salesperson's follow-up question was: "Have you always been in this position, or have you done other things?" Again, this is an opportunity to learn more about where this individual fits in terms of power and influence on the decision to make major changes. A long time with the company and a pattern of growth within the company would be a pretty positive indicator.

What if the answer had been 12 weeks rather than 12 years? In that case, a good follow-up question might have been: "Where did you work before coming here?" On one hand, a short time with the company might not be as positive an indicator of power and influence, but on the other hand, knowing the buyer's history might provide you with some referral value later on!

And, being new with a company is not always a sign of lack of power and influence. In fact, here's some more Dinosaur Wisdom: *The higher the position, the more likely it is that a "new guy" can make big decisions.* In other words, a new Vice President of Marketing can probably make whatever changes he/she wants to make (at least in terms of the organization's marketing programs); a new Marketing Manager is likely to be more cautious about big changes; a new Marketing Assistant probably can't or won't make anything other than very minor changes to the status quo.

Here's another question I always like to ask during this stage of the conversation: "How much of your time is spent dealing with (your product and/or service or the application for your product and/or service), and is this a part of your job that you enjoy?" I'm hoping, of course, to hear that the buyer spends a lot of time on my product/service/application and absolutely hates every minute of it. That's an expression of *pain,* and weakness in the status quo. Remember this Dinosaur Wisdom: *If they have no problems, you may have no opportunity.* If they do have pain and problems — and you have solutions and pain relief — you're in pretty good shape to change the status quo!

Questions About The Products

OK, as noted, the purpose of these questions about the individual is *not* to learn whether the buyer is a sports fan or a grandparent or was born and raised in the area. It's to learn about power, influence, experience and hopefully to start learning about pain. It is *not* the time to talk about pain relief, though. That comes a little later. First — if we're talking about selling to an existing need! — you want to make sure that this buyer qualifies in terms of buying enough of what you sell to make it worth your while to ease his/her pain in the first place!

That means it's time for the *questions about the products he/she buys*, and again, the best way to move from the *questions about the individual* to this set of questions is with a *transitional question.* Before I suggest the right questions, though, let me tell you about a *wrong* question I observed recently. I was out with a promotional products salesperson (not my nephew!) who said: "So, how much do you spend on promotional products each year?" The buyer was silent for a moment, and then she said: "That strikes me as sort of selfish question. You're really asking me if I'm worth your time, aren't you?"

That shook the salesperson up pretty severely, and he started to sputter something like "No, I would never, I mean I wouldn't, I mean I wasn't trying to insult you…" I finally held my hand out to quiet him, turned back to the buyer, and said: "Yes, that's exactly what we need to learn. Not a very effective way of doing it, though, was it?"

"Not hardly," she said.

"Maybe we could approach this a different way," I said. "Tell us about a typical promotional products order. In fact, can you tell us about your last order? What was it for?"

"Coffee mugs," she said.

"OK, the mug itself, before we even talk about printing on it, would you call it a basic sort of coffee mug?"

"No. In fact, we wanted something special because this was an important event."

"Do you have one of those mugs handy?"

"Yes, I do." She dug in a drawer and handed me the mug, and I handed it over to the salesperson.

"How many of these did you order?" I asked.

"Six dozen," she answered.

"OK," I said to the salesperson. "You can see the mug, and you can see that the logo and text on it were printed in full color, and you know how many she ordered. Ballpark, how much was that order worth?"

"Maybe $5-$6 per mug at that quantity," he answered, "so, probably between $350 - $400, not counting freight."

"Don't worry about freight," I said, "that doesn't have anything to do with what we're trying to accomplish here. We're not quoting, we're learning. Now, ask her if this is the sort of thing she orders regularly, and if so, how many times each year?"

He asked that question, and by now, the buyer was smiling broadly and enjoying being part of the lesson. "We do these events 5-6 times every year. This one was actually smaller than normal. We usually have close to 100 people at our open house events."

"OK," I said to the salesperson. "Let's do the arithmetic. Figure on 5 events a year, and let's figure on 6 dozen mugs for each event, and let's also use the low value for each order. You should always be conservative when you're doing this sort of analysis. I make that $350 times 5, which is at least $1750 worth of a product that's right down the middle of your strike zone. Write that number down." I turned back to the buyer. "Tell us about some of the other promotional products you order?"

She told us about several other items, and I asked the same sort of "how many, how frequently" questions, and walked the salesperson through the same sort of arithmetic. Within a couple of minutes, we had established that this buyer was spending more than $10,000 each year on promotional products that were a perfect fit for the salesperson. In other words, she bought exactly what the salesperson wanted to sell, and she bought enough of it to make pursuing her worthwhile. And all of this was accomplished without asking any selfish questions!

Annual Budget

While I'm on this subject, another variation on the "how much do you spend" theme would be: "What is your annual budget for (exactly what I sell)?" That can be a bad question too, but for a different reason. In this case, the problem is simply that most companies don't have annual budgets for most of what they buy.

The more sophisticated companies might have departmental budgets — a marketing budget for example — but I have very rarely found these budgets broken down to individual line items. Basically, these sophisticated companies buy the products and services they need and pay for them out of the appropriate departmental budget. The less sophisticated companies simply buy what they need and pay for it out of the company checkbook. If there's no money in the budget, or in the checkbook, they stop buying things. (Or else they stop paying for things, and that's a different sort of problem!).

The discussion of budget on an individual project can be a very different story, though. With a promotional product, for example, an understanding of budget is important because there's such a great range of cost on typical items. For example, there are $2 coffee cups and $20 coffee cups, so you should always ask "have you established a budget?" in a situation like that.

The same holds true on any sort design/build project, where the budget will almost certainly effect the design. I remember a sign designer who once told me: "I can design you a $1000 sign, and I can design you a $100,000 sign, but you gotta tell me which one I'm designing, otherwise we're both gonna waste a lot of our time!"

The Artist's Story

Some buyers won't want to tell you about their budget, though, because they're afraid that your price will rise to that level. (Another way to say that, of course, is that they don't fully trust you!) A graphic artist friend of mine once told me a story about meeting an old classmate at a high school reunion. When the classmate learned what the artist was doing, he said: "Man, I have all kinds of trouble with the guy who designs my monthly mailers. Everything's always late, and my printer always has trouble with his files. Would you like to take a look at what I'm doing and give me a proposal?"

The artist said "Sure," and within a few days, the classmate had sent over samples, and the artist was almost ready to offer a proposal. The only thing holding him back was a pricing decision. "I was going back and forth between $500 and $600," he told me. "I'd have been perfectly happy to do these jobs for $500, especially for a friend. But the thing was, this guy wasn't really a friend. In fact, I never really liked him all that much!" They'd set an appointment, though, and on the way over, the artist still hadn't made up his mind how much he was going to ask for.

"I walked into his office," the artist told me, "and before I even sat down, he held out a piece of paper and said 'Listen, I've been uncomfortable about this. I feel like I'm asking you for a favor, and I know that you don't owe me any favors because we were never really that good friends. Anyway, this is what I've been paying, and if you can even get close to that, I'm going to give you the work.'"

The artist looked at the paper and saw that his classmate had been paying close to $900 for the design of his monthly mailers. "I can get close to that," he said. "In fact, I'll do it for exactly the same price."

That's why many people — me included! — won't be eager to tell you what their budget is. It doesn't mean that you shouldn't ask, but I think it does reinforce the important of building trust from the earliest stages of contact!

Questions About The Status Quo

As I wrote earlier, I want my first meeting with a suspect to last 20-25 minutes, and the questioning process to this point generally takes me to about the 18-20 minute mark. By this time, I have (hopefully!) created the willingness to talk to me, and determined that the buyer I'm talking to does, in fact, qualify in terms of my first and second qualifying criteria. Now it's time to transition to the most important element of the conversation — questions about the *status quo*, where I hope to find some weakness that will translate into real interest in saying *no* to the current supplier and saying *yes* to me.

Here's my transitional question: "Who have you been buying all of this from?" Pretty straightforward, right? I have occasionally run into someone who didn't want to tell me, but far more often than not, my straightforward question gets a straightforward answer. "Colter Corporation" was a recent response, and I followed up with this question: "Is there anything that you absolutely hate about doing business with them?"

The buyer I was talking to was a sales/marketing guy, and he looked at me a little funny. "I was taught that the question you should ask is 'What do you like about them?'" he said.

"I was taught the same thing," I replied, "but one day it occurred to me that I was just reinforcing bad behavior by asking that question. I was giving people an opportunity to brag about their current supplier, and that's really not what I wanted to hear." He thought about that for a moment, and then said: "That makes a lot of sense. You don't want me thinking that things are generally good, you want me thinking that things are occasionally bad!"

I couldn't have said that better myself! Now, if you're going to use the word *hate*, please make sure you ask that question with a smile on your face. I hope you'll see how the question could be harsh without the smile, but "gently provocative" with it. If you'd prefer an even gentler approach, I have often phrased the question this way: "Is there anything about your relationship with that other supplier that you would change if you could?"

New Opportunity

Now let's consider the way this conversation should be altered if you're selling to a new opportunity rather than an established need. As I've noted, the *questions about the products* aren't really necessary if the buyer has never bought what you sell before, but you still need to evaluate your product's or service's relevance to this buyer's business or personal challenges. Remember this Dinosaur Wisdom: *You're always in competition with the current and existing state of affairs as it pertains to your products and/or services.*

So the million dollar question in this scenario is: "Is there anything you absolutely hate about the way you do (the thing I think my product or service will do better for you)?" Here's the two million dollar question, though: *Can you ask that question before you evaluate and fully understand the status quo?* I think the answer is *no*, and that means your transitional question should probably be something like this: "How do you do/how do you handle (the thing I think my product or service will do better for you) right now?" From there, you work your way to questioning the buyer's level of satisfaction.

In either of these scenarios, any answer to the big money question — other than "nothing" — shines a light on a weakness in the status quo. I've been told that the happiest moment in selling is when you get the order, but I'm not so sure about that. For me, the happiest moments were usually when I learned that I did have the solution to a real problem or relief for real pain. The closing stage was often anticlimactic, and that relates back to some Dinosaur Wisdom I introduced earlier: *It's pretty easy to sell to a prospect. It's pretty much impossible to sell to a non-prospect.* That's why the first meeting/substantive conversation should be all about qualifying. It's the end of the prospecting stage, and hopefully the beginning of the *convincing stage* — but beyond that, it's the heart of the *opportunity stage*.

What Next?

I'll come back to a "nothing" answer to your big money question in just a moment. For right now, the question is, what do you do with a more useful answer; for example, an indication of quality problems with a current supplier? I'd like you to think about two possibilities. The first is to immediately address the problem and state your solution. The second is to pack up and leave. My preference? To pack up and leave!

Now obviously, I wouldn't just pack up and leave without explanation. Here's exactly what I would say: "This has been great. I feel like I've learned a lot about your situation, your needs and your wants. What I'd like to do next is to think about what you've told me, and do some research (or gather up some samples, or put together some case studies, or talk to my technical people — something that indicates detailed preparation for the next step), and then I'd like to come back and tell you *exactly* how I think we can improve on your current situation. How does your schedule look for (tomorrow/the next few days/early next week)?"

I have left a lot of first meetings with a second meeting scheduled, which satisfies the final component of my *perfect sales conversation* — a mutual decision on what to do next. I hope you'll also see how that strategy addresses a very common selling problem. "I can get appointments," I hear frequently, "and I go in and make my presentation. But then I don't know what to do next. I don't have a good reason to get back in front of them." I would submit that you'd have a good *reason* — simply because you want to continue building a relationship because you want to sell them something! What you wouldn't have is a specific *purpose*, so doesn't it make sense to build that into your overall selling process?

Let's look at this strategy from the buyer's side, too. I have had more than a few buyers tell me that, if they're lucky enough to encounter a salesperson who asks good questions in the first place, they can usually be pretty sure that the "dog-and-pony-show" is coming right on the heels of the questions. I think this strategy offers you an opportunity to be different, and that leads to some more Dinosaur Wisdom: *Showing that you're* different *is a very good first step toward showing that you're* better. Beyond that, I really like the idea that this strategy gives you time to prepare for and personalize your eventual proposal.

I can't prove this equation, but I think it's pretty likely that you'll be at least 10% better in the presentation stage if you give yourself time to prepare, and they'll be at least 20% more receptive if your proposal is built specifically for them. Like I say, I can't prove the equation, but I think you'll be at least 30% more likely to turn a suspect into a customer using this approach.

My Cousin Vanna

Beyond that arithmetic, I don't think you can overemphasize the importance of being different. I have a cousin who is the Director of Marketing for a small manufacturing company located in the Deep South. I've only seen her a few times in my life, but one of those times was a family wedding just a few years ago, and we were seated at the same table. As often happens in "distant relative" situations, we ended up talking mostly about our work, and she told me a few horror stories about salespeople she has known.

In turn, I told her some of the strategies I teach, and when I described this "let me think about what I've learned and prepare a proposal" strategy, she said: "Gawleeeeee" — honestly, a very Deep Southern drawl! — "the whole concept of a salesman who wants to think before he talks is a revolutionary concept as far as I'm concerned!"

"I Wouldn't Change Anything"

That takes us back to the buyer who says "nothing" when you ask if there's anything they'd change about the status quo. I'm sometimes tempted to ask: "Well, why did you agree to meet with me in the first place?" Seriously, with the exception of purchasing titles and/or others who are *price monsters*, the decision to take the time to meet with you probably indicates that they're hoping to find something better than what they've got.

So what does it mean when your first meeting ends up at the "nothing" stage? I need to answer that question with a question. Have you ever been told that you should never take sales rejection personally? I suspect that you have, and it's certainly true in the early stages of selling. For example, if you identify a buyer and send an introductory letter or e-mail and then end up leaving several voice mail messages without any response, you shouldn't take that personally because that buyer doesn't know you well enough to reject you as a person! That sort of rejection is just part of the numbers game.

I think hearing "nothing" in a face-to-face meeting is a different story, though. In fact, if you really want to be a great salesperson, I think you have to accept that what "nothing" really means in this situation is "I'm not impressed with you" — and that's a rejection you should probably take seriously.

I say *probably* because there is still a *numbers game* consideration here. The more people you talk to, the more likely it is that you'll find yourself talking to some real morons, and as I wrote earlier, I don't want you to let the morons get you down. Here's some more Dinosaur Wisdom, though: *When the non-morons aren't impressed with you, you have to be concerned and ask: "What went wrong?"*

Debriefing

At the very least, you should ask yourself that question when you get back to the car after a face-to-face meeting, or after you hang up from a telephone conversation. I'm a strong believer in *debriefing* every sales call to evaluate what went right and what could have gone better. The question I often ask myself is: "If I had that to do over again, what would I do differently?"

But why not ask "what went wrong?" before you get back to the car or hang up the phone? Why not ask the person who really knows exactly how/where you failed? I mentioned that I'm sometimes tempted to ask: "Well, why did you agree to meet with me in the first place?" but I have rarely asked that question — partially because it might seem confrontational, but mostly because the answer isn't really important. If I'm going to risk being confrontational — and again, I prefer the term *assertive* — I want to gain knowledge that can really help me. I think this would be a better question: "Where did I lose you?"

I had to ask that question recently, and the buyer said: "Huh?" I said: "I'm pretty sure you agreed to meet with me because you were hoping that I'd have something better than what you have now. I'm also pretty sure that I do, based on the answers you gave me to my earlier questions. But when we got to the point where you wouldn't change anything even if you could, I have to think that you're basically not very impressed with me. I think I might be asking you for a second chance here, and it would help to know exactly where I lost you?"

I can't guarantee you that you'll get a second chance — I did in this recent situation, I didn't in many others — but I think I can guarantee you that not asking the question leaves you nowhere. If nothing else, a situation like this is an opportunity to learn from failure. If you do get a second chance, it's an opportunity to learn from success.

The Quote Game

Now it's time to consider whether getting something to quote on at your first meeting is a good thing or not. For many salespeople, that seems to be the whole goal of prospecting, but you already know that I think differently. It's not having something to quote on today that makes someone a good prospect, it's having significant and regular need for what you sell. Remember, even if they do buy exactly what you want to sell, if they don't buy enough of it to make pursuing them worthwhile, they don't qualify as a prospect!

The third qualifier, of course, is showing some interest in buying from you. Is asking for a quote a real indication of interest? Interest in seeing your prices? Yes. Interest in actually buying from you? No. So let's not treat getting something to quote on as a major victory! In fact, let's recognize that there are three major pitfalls in playing the quote game. The first one concerns your strike zone. The second and third are matters of time management.

As I wrote earlier, I'll consider quoting on just about anything with a *customer*, but I won't jeopardize a fledging relationship with a *suspect* or a *prospect* by quoting on something that's not right down the middle of my strike zone. You're far better off declining to quote than quoting a price that's not even remotely competitive.

As for time management, the first issue is really simple. It's a waste of time to compete for an order that doesn't exist! Many buyers will ask you to quote on something they bought previously, or to prepare a matrix of pricing on multiple items and multiple quantities they might buy in the future. Experience has shown that both of these situations usually turn into time wasters. The matrix pricing exercise in particular is a loser's game.

Why? Well, consider what usually happens after the salesperson spends all that time to put the pricing together. The salesperson calls to follow up, and the buyer says: "I haven't had time to look it all over yet." A week later? Same story. A month later? Same story again. Think about this, if it takes a salesperson an hour to put all of the pricing together, it will take the buyer at least twice that long to pull out old invoices and do a serious comparison of prices. Are they going to do that? Lots of unhappy and frustrating experience says *no*!

Just Being Cooperative

Here's something else to think about. I was out on a sales call with a young printing salesperson a few years ago, and we were meeting with a Marketing Manager. Within seconds of getting the "polite pleasantries" out of the way, this buyer picked an inch-thick file folder off of his desk and handed it across to the salesperson. "Here's all my stuff," he said, "if you'd like to give me quotes on it."

"Thank you very much," she said. "I'll get right back to the shop and get started."

"The hell you will," I said, reaching out my hand. "Here, give me that!"

I opened the folder, and it was immediately apparent that some of the printed pieces inside it were nowhere near this particular printing company's strike zone. "Some of this is nowhere near our strike zone," I said. "Do you mind if we pass on those items?"

"No, of course not," he said.

I continued to look through the folder, and picked out three pieces that would probably fit within the strike zone, depending only on the quantities ordered. "These three here," I said, "look like they'd fit us pretty well, depending on the quantities. How many of these do you generally order at a time?"

The answer indicated a very good fit, so now I asked: "Do you expect to be ordering any one of these in the near future?" I handed him all three, and he pulled one out and said: "I'll probably need to order this one within the next couple of weeks."

"So how about if we just give you a price on this item," I said. "It'll be a live quote on a live job, and I think that will tell you where we are in terms of pricing."

"Sounds good to me," he said.

A few minutes later, as we were standing to leave, I said: "You know, it occurs to me that it must have taken a fair amount of your time to put that whole file folder together. I'm curious, why did you do it?"

"Oh," he said, "I was just trying to be cooperative."

I hope you can read that code and understand what this buyer was saying. Just to make sure, though, I'm going to explain it to you. This was a guy who'd met recently with a couple of other printing salespeople, and both of them asked him for samples of all of his printing to quote on. He thought that's what we wanted too! He had no *need* to see comparative pricing. In fact, he was happy in the end to only have to look at one live quote. I think there are a lot of buyers like this guy out there, because I *know* that there are a lot of salespeople whose only semblance of a plan is to ask for stuff to quote on.

While I'm on this subject, I received a post card from an insurance company recently which offered me a "free" quote on my car insurance. I guess I'm wondering if anyone would find a great deal of value in a free quote. I think they all know that quotes are free and come with no obligation. I think they also know that many salespeople have nothing more to sell than the possibility of low prices.

Matrix Pricing

Here's one more thought on the subject of matrix pricing. It's probably a different story if this request for pricing is part of an annual process. There are companies who evaluate vendors and pricing on a yearly basis and make their buying decisions for the following year based on these evaluations. Sometimes formal contracts are involved, but more frequently it's just a decision to use a certain supplier for certain kinds of work. The main difference between this situation and the "here's all my stuff if you'd like to quote on it" situation is that multiple vendors will be submitting their pricing at the same time. That makes the comparison a lot easier for the buyer, since no searching through old invoices is involved.

Does that make it good strategy to compete for business in this way? Maybe. The bidding process suggests that the decision is going to be made mostly on price, but I've never had any problem with a customer whose definition of *low enough* prices is consistent with my definition of *high enough* prices. I'm more likely to get excited about a situation like this if I've determined — through my questioning process — that the buyer has some level of dissatisfaction with the status quo. If he/she bought cheap last time and was disappointed, the chances are at least slightly better that the next decision won't be made on the basis of price alone.

Real Opportunity?

OK, let's go back to the buyer who invites you to quote on a single item at your first meeting. If it's a real opportunity to compete for an order, then you probably want to take it. If it's just a price comparison, though, I think you don't want to play. So, how do you determine whether you're being asked to quote on a real order? The best strategy is a simple question: "When will you need this to be (delivered/installed/completed)?" If the answer is anything other than firm — next week, the end of the month, before an event, a specific date, etc. — you're probably looking at a price comparison situation.

Here's how you might address that situation: "Mr. Jones, I suspect that you're just asking for a price on this to get some idea of where my pricing will fall. Wouldn't it be better, though, to wait until you have a live project to quote on? I'll be happy to give you a quote then, and I think that will tell you more about our pricing than asking for a quote I'm never going to have to honor. Hey, if I were really unscrupulous, I could give you a really low quote on this thing just to make myself look good!" Last time I had that conversation with a buyer, he said: "I never really thought about that. I'm glad you're not that kind of salesperson." (Do you think I might have scored some *trust points* there?)

Here's another possibility: "Mr. Jones, are you just trying to do something nice for me here? I'm sure you know that a lot of salespeople get excited when they get something to quote on, and if that's the case, I want you to know that I appreciate the gesture. I'm a different kind of salesperson, though, and I'm already excited about you because it looks like your needs match our capabilities very well. When do you expect to have one of those needs again?"

Linear Time Management

As mentioned, there are two time management issues surrounding the quote game. The second one takes us to what I call *linear* time management. The opposite of *block* time management — making the best use of the hours of each day — *linear* time management is all about managing the time it takes to build a relationship. With apologies to Sir Isaac Newton, the First Law of Linear Time Management states that *the longer you can go without talking about price, the better off you are.* The Second Law of Linear Time Management states that *trust takes time to build.* The Third Law of Linear Time Management states that *the more trust you build, the less price matters.*

Do you see how these laws apply to your sales situation? I have actually declined to quote on real projects that were well within my strike zone at the first meeting, and I remember once telling a buyer that it was too early for us to be talking about price. "What do you mean?" he asked. "Well," I answered, "you've told me that you've had quality problems with your current supplier, and I'm sort of anticipating that my price — which will include the solution to those problems! — is going to be higher than what you've been paying. We've only spent about 25 minutes together, though, and you can't possibly trust me enough yet to know that, number one, I do have the solution, and number two, my price will represent a great value for you. I'd like to spend more time building that trust before I ask you to make a buying decision. Among other things, I'd like to invite you to visit our plant and take a tour and see how we do things, and actually meet some of the people who are responsible for our quality control."

His answer: "How fast can we make those things happen? I'm feeling more and more like I can trust you every minute!"

The First Meeting — Closing Thoughts

I read something early in my career that has always stuck with me. *Of all things that ultimately get sold,* it said, *1% get sold on the first sales contact, 2% get sold on the second sales contact, 3% get sold on the third sales contact, 4% get sold on the fourth sales contact, 8% get sold on the fifth sales contact, and the remaining 82% get sold on the sixth sales contact or beyond.* Now, do I believe that anyone knows the exact percentages? No way! But I do believe that those percentages tend to prove the Second Law of Linear Time Management — that *trust takes time to build!*

That's not to say that you'll need to hold six face-to-face meetings before you get an order — although you may need that many or more. I think the best interpretation is that it's almost certainly going to take six or more *touches* to get to the point where a buyer will think seriously about buying from you, and with that in mind, I hope you'll see how a big part of your challenge is simply to *get to six!*

Looking back at the whole prospecting process —and remember that I define prospecting as *an activity chain which begins with the identification of suspect companies and ends with the first substantive conversation with the buyer* — I hope you'll see how the first meeting might actually be the third, fourth or fifth *touch*.

It's a *building* process, and the first substantive conversation is a *part* of that process, not the culmination. I hope you'll consider it good news that most of your competitors see a first meeting as an opportunity — maybe even an obligation! — to shoot off all of their big sales and marketing guns. They'll always struggle with what to do next.

You, on the other hand, will be positioned for the next step — a very solid next step; a specific proposal on how you believe that you can improve on the status quo. Beyond that, after multiple touches, each of which added something to the relationship you're trying to build, the buyer is a lot more likely to believe the promises you're about to make than he/she would have been any earlier in the process. Best of all, after an *interrogatory* first meeting, your proposal and those promises can be directed specifically at the buyer's hot buttons.

Now, doesn't that sound like a plan?

Preparing and Presenting Your Proposal

As we've discussed, prospecting is an activity chain which begins with the identification of suspect companies, and ends with your first substantive conversation with the buyer. That first meeting/substantive conversation represents the end of the *prospecting stage* and the beginning of the *convincing stage*, but more importantly, it's the heart of the *opportunity stage*. In other words, it's all about asking questions to identify real opportunity — either an outright problem to which you have a solution, or some other opportunity to reduce pain or improve on the way they've been doing things.

You will hopefully leave your first meeting with a second meeting scheduled. You may even leave your first meeting with a live project to compete for. Either way, you'll now face the challenge of preparing for your second meeting. Hold on to your hat, because we're finally getting to the point where you're going to do some selling!

It's All Selling

I hope you read that last sentence with a wry smile on your face, because I wrote it with one on mine. I've met salespeople who've told me that this is what selling is all about — "on the mound, prepared to pitch" as one old-timer once expressed it. I approve of the *prepared* part, but I think *pitch* belongs with *spiel* in a salesperson's vocabulary. I also think it's *all* selling, from identifying suspects to setting up meetings to learning about their wants and needs to convincing them to buy from you. The convincing stage is exactly that, another stage in the process.

Before we leave *pitch*, though, let's go back to another baseball analogy for just a moment. As I've written, you're at a stage in the process where you have to be especially careful to stay within your *strike zone*. Remember what I said about the most common result of failure to do that. The salesperson gets all excited about the chance to quote on a "big" job, gets a price (internally or from a trade supplier), marks it up and quotes that price to the buyer, and then wonders what the hell happened when the buyer stops returning phone calls. What probably happened was that the buyer looked at the price — in comparison to one or more competitors for whom that particular project was right down the middle of the strike zone — and said: "Wow, this company is really expensive. I guess I don't want to waste my time on them anymore." That's why I'll talk about just about anything with a *customer*, but I won't jeopardize a relationship with a *suspect* or a *prospect* on a project that's not right down the middle of *my* strike zone.

Here's the thing, though, are you pitching or batting? Which is a better analogy for selling? Setting aside my dislike for the terminology, the *presenting* part is more similar to pitching that batting, but the *strike zone* part is definitely a batting analogy. Yes, the pitcher has to put the ball in the strike zone, but the batter decides whether to swing at it. The salesperson makes the offer, but the buyer decides whether to accept it — that is, until we get to the negotiation stage where the buyer may make a counteroffer that the salesperson has to decide on. Damn, this analogy business can get confusing! But it all sort of works if I can get you to take *pitch* out of your vocabulary. Professional salespeople don't make pitches or spiels, they make presentations — better still, they present *proposals*!

Now wait a minute, am I suggesting a *formal* proposal for every prospect? Yes, I think I am, but let's tie that into where I think you are in the selling process. You identified a suspect company, and then you identified a decision-maker. You gained commitment for a meeting — telephone or face-to-face — and during that meeting you learned something about the buyer's needs and wants. You confirmed that he/she buys enough of what you want to sell to make your pursuit worthwhile, and you also identified some weakness in the status quo which you think will translate into real interest in buying from you. We're not talking about making proposals on cold calls here, this *prospect* has been vetted and qualified!

Differentiation Strategy

A *proposal strategy* is another way in which you can differentiate yourself from your competitors — and especially from the current supplier! Think about your dealings with your own current customers. Isn't it fair to say that things get casual over time? If you were on the outside looking into those relationships, would you choose *casual* or more *formal* as a means to break in? I think it makes sense to be the *opposite* of the current supplier in this regard. Not *cold*, by any means, but not presuming a high level of *warmth* either. *Professional* and *businesslike* are two terms that seem appropriate. *Attentive to detail* is another appropriate phrase.

OK, here are the key issues that surround preparing and presenting a proposal. First is your transmittal strategy; in other words, how do you want to put your proposal in their hands? Second is the issue of packaging your proposal; what materials go into it and how are they all held together? Third is the issue of what comes next if they don't say *yes* to what you're proposing.

Transmittal Strategy

I hope you'll agree that the best case scenario for any proposal is for you to present it face-to-face. Time and distance don't always allow that, but it should always be your preference. Unfortunately, it's not always *their* preference, and many buyers — especially the ones who offer you something to quote on at the first meeting — are going to tell you to simply send them your quote, by mail, fax or e-mail.

What should you do then? Here's my recommendation: "I can do that, Mr. Jones, but I don't really want to. I think it's important that I present this to you face-to-face. I've been mostly interested in learning about you so far, and what I've learned will be reflected in my proposal. I haven't taken a lot of our time together talking about me or my company, and there are things I want you to know about us before you make a decision. You also might have questions, and I want to be right here to answer them. That's all part of my approach to customer service!"

Again, the key here is to position your best case scenario as a benefit to the buyer. I can't promise you that everyone will see it your way, but my experience has been that many people will stop and think about what you're asking for and agree that it's a good idea. Remember what I said earlier about people spending the time it takes to do something right. Sometimes, they just have to be told how long it will take, or what constitutes *right*. I've had many people say "OK, that makes sense" and agree to a face-to-face presentation, even after being pretty firm about just mailing/faxing/e-mailing my quote.

Leverage

Here's another key point. Before you put your proposal in their hands, you have some leverage. Once you mail/fax/e-mail or otherwise submit your quote or proposal, you no longer have that leverage. To put that another way, you have the leverage when you have something they want. Once they have it, they have the leverage *in addition to* what they wanted in the first place.

The classic result of this loss of leverage can be seen in my previous example of violating the strike zone, where the buyer looks at the quote and says: "Wow, this company is really expensive. I guess I don't want to waste my time on them anymore." As noted, that usually translates into the buyer no longer returning phone calls or responding to e-mails.

So what if the buyer says *no* again, even though you still have that leverage? Now you have a choice to make, and one possibility is simply to decline to participate. I have done that in the past, my thought process being that the presentation was essential to any hope of turning the suspect/prospect/buyer into a customer. I think you understand that some time and effort are going to go into your proposal, and from a time management perspective, I don't want to spend that time if there's not a reasonable chance of success.

OK, how do you decline? It's easier than you might think. "Mr. Jones," you might say, "I hope you won't take this the wrong way, but I'm not willing to do that. I think I can provide you with real value (or a solution to your problem or an even better way of doing something), but I'm not willing to just send you my proposal and hope for the best. I want the chance to *sell* you on doing business with me, and if you're not willing to give me the time I need to do that, we're probably not all that good a match for each other."

Like I said, I have done this before, and the response has typically fallen into one of three categories. I've had people say "I understand," shake my hand, and that was that. I've had people throw me out of their offices. I've also had people say "Gee, if it's really that important to you..." and then we set up an appointment.

Assertiveness Pays

The lesson? It usually pays to be assertive! In the first example, I minimized the time I spent on a situation which I felt had a low probability of success. (Do you remember what I've said, by the way, about the wisdom of making a *progressive investment* in terms of your prospecting time? At every step, you have to make a decision about taking the next step.) In the third example, I got exactly what I wanted *because of* my assertiveness. In the second example, well, that's the risk you take with an assertive strategy. It's going to rub some people the wrong way. Consider this, though, the second example is probably also a time management victory, minimizing the time spent chasing a low probability of success. I'm willing to risk the occasional alienation in pursuit of my goals.

Now, does that mean you should you always take a hard line in this sort of situation? No, it doesn't. I'm presenting that as an option, and sometimes it's the right option, but there have also been times when I mailed/faxed/e-mailed my proposal and did the best I could in terms of follow up. I had some successes with that strategy, but far more successes when I was able to present my proposal face-to-face.

Bottom line, I think you should at least try once to get people to change their minds if they're not initially willing to schedule the meeting you want. If they still resist, then ask yourself just how good an opportunity you think you're looking at. The better the opportunity — in terms of potential return on the investment of time and energy you're contemplating — the more likely it is that you should mail/fax/e-mail your proposal and then do the best you can in terms of follow up. I want you to be assertive, but I also want you to see the wisdom in retreating and living to fight another day. Here's some more Dinosaur Wisdom: *In selling, it's entirely possible to lose a battle but win a war — or the other way around!*

Packaging Strategy

When I think *proposal*, I'm thinking about a document, and when I think *presenting your proposal*, I'm thinking that the document is both the proposal and the anchor of your presentation. In other words, you present a proposal by walking the buyer through the document and explaining the key points, and then you leave the document behind. You do not simply read the document — they could do that for themselves! — but you use it as a tool to help you cover the important points. You also use this presentation as an opportunity to solicit and answer questions — more on that will follow.

First, though, let me back up and discuss the term *document*. It might be more accurate to describe what I have in mind as a *collection* of documents. They could be *packaged* in a simple file folder, a printed presentation folder, bound into a book or even stuffed into a box for your presentation. The size/shape/weight of the component documents will probably determine the best type of packaging.

For the sake of discussion, let's say you'll be using a printed presentation folder for your proposals. It might have a photo of your product on the outside, or perhaps photos of your plant or of previous projects. It might just have your logo on the outside. No matter what you have printed on your folder, I would expect it to have a pocket or pockets on the inside to hold your component documents in place, and most "pocket folders" also include slots to hold your business card. OK, I'm sure you can picture what I'm talking about. Now let's talk about what goes in the pockets.

The first item should be a cover letter, something that says "thank you for the opportunity to present this proposal and here's what you'll find inside." Another term that could be used to describe this particular component document would be *executive summary.* The purpose of this component is threefold: first, to express your appreciation for the opportunity; second, to demonstrate that you understand the project; and third, to introduce the reasons you think they should buy it from you.

What comes next? Well, that depends on what you're trying to sell them, and more importantly, what weaknesses you've identified in the status quo. I don't think you'll ever be able to create a "one-size-fits-all" proposal package, but if we do this right, most of your future proposals can be created from "off-the-shelf" components. In other words, something that works in one proposal will probably also work in others that address the same products/services/issues, so start building a library of the various samples and documents that you use.

Proposal Scenario

OK, here's a scenario, drawn from my printing industry experience. You had a first meeting with a buyer who prints and distributes a monthly newsletter. She's had some minor quality issues with her current printer, and some major service issues. A recent newsletter was 3 days late coming out of the printshop, and that meant it missed it's scheduled slot at the mailshop (a completely different company), and ended up going into the mail 6 days after the desired publication date. Because of that, attendance was very light at an event this particular newsletter was promoting.

In addition to telling you about these problems, the buyer has given you the specs on the newsletter and invited you to quote on the printing. Though she didn't specifically ask or offer, you also want to compete for the mailing part of the project, since your company is well-equipped to handle that as well.

If I were building this proposal, the cover letter would be followed in the "line-up" in the presentation folder by 2-3 samples of very similar newsletters. *Very similar* is important here, because the purpose of these samples is to show the buyer that you have specific experience with exactly what he needs. If his newsletter is 2-color, for example, I would not show him 4-color samples, because that's not *exactly* what he needs. If his newsletter is 8½" x 11", I would not show him any other size because that's not *exactly* what he needs. (OK, I might include one 4-color, larger format newsletter to illustrate that capability, but it would be the last one I showed him, and I would specifically explain that I brought this one along only to show that we can handle full color and larger formats, but I understand that his current need is more like my other samples.)

Show & Tell

Please note my use of the word *show*. I would not hand the buyer(s) my proposal, because I want to maintain control of the meeting. Picture me sitting across the desk with the proposal package turned toward the buyer(s), but with me handing each component over as I'm ready to talk about it. Please also note my use of the term *buyer(s)*. If I was expecting to meet with one person, I would bring two complete proposal packages — as a rule of thumb, always one more than I think I'll need. So picture me handing each component document across as I'm ready to talk about it, and then passing the presentation folder itself across at the end of my presentation. Remember, you want the buyer listening to you, not reading ahead in your proposal.

After showing the samples — and explaining my purpose: "These are to show you that we have experience with newsletters very much like yours" — I would address the minor quality issues. "You told me that you've had some quality problems in the past. Having looked at these samples, would you say they represent a level of quality that would satisfy you?"

Hopefully the answer will be *yes*. (I hope you realize that if the answer is *no*, you are probably out of luck with this buyer.) Now, wouldn't it be interesting to hand over a document which describes your quality control procedures. "These are our quality control procedures," you could say. "The samples show you that we're capable of the quality you're looking for. This is how we insure that every newsletter we ever print for you will look every bit as good as these samples!"

Do you have this sort of document? If not, I recommend that you start working on one. This is what I mean by creating a library of the various samples and documents that can be part of your proposals.

One-Two Punch

I hope you see the value, by the way, in presenting samples and then quality control as a one-two punch. Most salespeople proudly show samples of their products thinking they represent *proof* of quality. I hope you know better! As a starting point, you know that you (or somebody, at least) hand picks those samples, right? And all those beautiful hand-picked samples really *prove* is that the people who produced them are *capable* of that level of quality. The samples themselves don't say anything about *consistent* quality, and that's the sale you have to make.

When it's appropriate to be talking about quality in the first place, you're probably talking to someone who has been disappointed in the quality they've been getting — and they probably saw beautiful samples from the people who sold them crappy product. It's critically important to understand the importance of building trust here.

Remember, it's not the quality problem itself that causes a relationship to fail, it's the effect of that problem on the trust level. It's the same thing with service problems, not a late delivery which ends the relationship, but the effect of that late delivery on the trust level. Don't ever forget that it's all about trust! And don't ever forget that unhappy customers are the least trusting. (Are you familiar with the expression "once burned, twice shy?") It is good for you if they're some else's unhappy customer — *gases*, right? — but you still have the challenge of convincing them that they can trust *you*!

Samples

Let's talk some more about samples, and what they can and can't do for you. First of all, samples aren't always about quality, sometimes they're simply meant to suggest an idea. Keep in mind, though, that unless you say otherwise, most people will view anything you show them as representative of the quality they'll get from you.

I was out on a sales call with a promotional products salesperson recently (again, not my nephew!) and the salesperson pulled a couple of really ugly imprinted tote bags out of a sample case. I could see the buyer handling them with distaste while the salesperson talked about using tote bags to gain visibility at an upcoming trade show. I stopped him and said: "We're not trying to sell you on *those* tote bags.

They're just to make sure you understand the basic concept. We're thinking of a much higher quality bag and much, much more attractive graphics for your application."

"That's good," the buyer replied. "I thought you were telling me that you liked these bags, and that, quite frankly, had me doubting that you have any clue about what we're all about."

Samples can show people what you think quality looks like, but remember, they can't prove *consistent* quality all by themselves. That's why it's important to be able to talk about *quality control!* Samples can also show people the breadth of your product line, and they probably do that more effectively than spoken or written words. As the old saying goes, a picture is worth a thousand words, and a touchable sample might be worth two thousand words.

For what it's worth, I've had more success in my career using samples to show customers *what else* they could buy from me than showing suspects or prospects what I hoped to sell them. (More on selling more to your current customers will follow!)

Here's a third capability of samples that many salespeople don't seem to understand, and it's especially relevant to companies which produce "extras" of live projects specifically for sample use. Every one of those samples has a *testimonial* value; in other words, it identifies a company that trusts you to handle some or all of (exactly what you sell). I always tried to use samples that were produced for companies who were well known for their own high quality and service standards. The psychology I was looking for was "if they're good enough for those guys, they'll be good enough for me." (Again, I hope you'll see the value of creating that library of samples and documents that can be part of your proposals.)

Back To The Package

OK, what comes next in this proposal? Remember, the scenario involves some minor quality issues and some major service issues, and the samples and quality control document were meant to address the quality issues. Now how can you provide some *evidence* that you won't cause the same sort of late delivery problems as their current supplier? On one hand, you can talk about your commitment to service and even tell people how you'll work overtime to make sure their orders are delivered on time, but nothing sells service more effectively than the words of people who have trusted you and found you to be worthy of that trust.

Do you have testimonial letters from satisfied customers? Do you have letters which specifically praise your service performance? If you do, I'd suggest including them in this proposal, and making plenty of copies for use in future proposals. If not, you probably want to ask some of your happy customers for testimonials — we'll talk more about *that* later on!

As we just discussed, your samples have testimonial value too, and it goes beyond simple testimony to your quality. When dealing with service issues, you still want to show samples that identify companies who are well known for their high standards, but especially companies like that who have done business with you for a while. I remember a presentation where I was doing just that, and the particular company had been my company's customer for more than 10 years.

"I'm curious," I said. "When you look at this sample, what jumps out at you?" I was hoping the buyer was going to say: "Well, it's beautiful work, and I know that ABC Company is known for their very high standards." Instead, she said: "I'd be happy with that quality."

So I said: "I was hoping what you were going to say was that in addition to the quality, you know that ABC Company has very high standards for quality and service."

"I guess they do," she said.

"OK," I continued, "now I want to tell you that we've been doing business with ABC Company for more than 10 years, and I'm wondering what *that* says to you?"

"That they like you?" she replied.

"Well, I guess they do," I said. "But what I was hoping you were going to say was that to keep their business for more than 10 years, it must have more to do with *that they trust us*. We must have met or exceeded their quality and service expectations for all that time, and I hope you'll treat that as evidence that we'll do the same for you!"

Now a key point. She smiled, but didn't say anything else, so I said: "I guess I need to ask you, do you take that as evidence that we'll do the same for you? Am I making progress toward convincing you to buy from me?"

Assertive Questions

Can you see yourself asking those questions, those *assertive* questions? I hope so. It's been my experience that most salespeople leave their meetings without really knowing what — if anything — they accomplished. I sometimes refer to that condition as being a *prisoner of hope*. "Yeah, the meeting went pretty well" is what most salespeople say to their boss, or a coworker, or whomever. "I think she likes me. We seemed to get along pretty well. I think I might get the order." It's important that you *confirm* your accomplishment, and we'll talk more about that in just a moment.

Before that, though, let's fill out the proposal package. We already have a cover letter, samples and other testimonial materials, and the document describing your quality control procedures. Since you would also want to compete for the mailing component of the newsletter project in this scenario, I think some information about your mailing capabilities and services should also be included.

What Else?

Now, what else could add to this *body of evidence* that you can be trusted to keep your promises? How about some information about the people who will be helping you to do that? I like to say that *everybody sells* in most companies, and what I mean by that is that everyone in the organization fits into one of two categories: promise-makers or promise-keepers. As the salesperson, you are probably the primary promise-maker — and that means you're the one who bears the greatest burden of trust! So let me ask you this, is it generally easier to believe an individual, or a part of a team?

Many salespeople talk about their team, but very few succeed at bringing the team to life. How about a document, then, with photos and short bios of your teammates? "At this point," you might say, "I'd like to introduce you to some of the other people who will be working on your project." It's been my experience that learning about these people — and their qualifications! — can have a great deal of convincing value.

Beyond that, I can think of a few other things that might have value to your proposal. Are you a minority-owned or woman-owned business? If so, some documentation of that status might be appropriate. Are you a "green" business? Same story. How about an equipment or capabilities list, or a list of current customers, or even your credit application? These are all things that might add to the *body of evidence* and/or support your proposal in some other way.

Foundation First

OK, here's a question for you. Have you noticed that we've gone this far into preparing and presenting a newsletter printing and mailing proposal, and we haven't even talked about the price yet? Most salespeople make the classic mistake of leading with their price, and that often results in "sticker shock" — the buyer is so alarmed by the price that he/she tunes out everything else. My recommendation is to leave the price for last, and the justification for that strategy is tied to another question: What's the difference between a quote and a proposal?

From my perspective, a *quote* is simply a number: "This is how much I want to charge you for this product/service/order." A *proposal* takes you into another area completely: "This is why I think you should buy it from me!" Ultimately, you have to show them that number, but doesn't it make sense to do that *after* telling them why they should buy it from you rather than before? This may sound crazy, but here's what you want them thinking as you present your samples, your quality control story, your testimonials and your team story: *"Gee, this is probably going to cost more than I was hoping it was going to cost!"*

Now, this is less of an issue if your prices are always on the low side of the competitive range. But I'm guessing that, simply because you're reading this, you'd like to figure out how to sell more when you're on the high side of the competitive range.

Here's an observation that I think is worth sharing. When I'm teaching a seminar, I'm usually pretty sure that all of the people in the room fall into that "high-side" category, hoping to sell greater value at premium prices. The other side of that coin is the people whose only semblance of a marketing plan is to quote really low prices. The people in the room tend to be "high-siders" through the process of elimination — because the "low-ballers" don't come to seminars in the first place! I'm not as sure with a $30 book as I am with a $500 seminar, but I still think you're likely to be interested in defending your prices against those "low-ballers" — in fact, against anyone whose prices are lower than yours.

They say the best defense is a good offense, and that's exactly what I'm talking about here. So here's some more Dinosaur Wisdom: *Establish the value and then show them the price* is a much better strategy than *show them the price and then try to convince them of the value.* Another way to say that might be *build the foundation first.*

Asking For The Order

I read once that a proposal is like climbing up a hill, and the *peak* of the proposal is when you ask for the order. That sounds hard to me, so here's another way to look at it. A great proposal is like rolling a ball *down* a hill, and you ask for the order at the bottom where the momentum is greatest. Doesn't that sound easier?

Unfortunately, it's not a perfect analogy, because uphill or down, it's a mistake to ask for the order at the end of your proposal. It's much better strategy to ask for the order *a little bit at a time* all the way though your presentation. What I'm talking about now is called *trial closing*, and it's been pretty well proven that this is the best way to present a proposal. Why? Because the shortest distance between any two points is a straight line.

Think about that. Point A is the product or service or idea that you're trying to sell. Point B is the buyer's agreement. Now doesn't it make sense that the closer you stay to the straight line between those points, the more likely it is — and the faster! — you'll get where you're hoping to go? The challenge, of course, is staying close to the line, especially when there may be three separate but interrelated things going on: (1) you don't fully understand their problem, (2) they don't fully understand your solution, and (3) you very often won't have their complete attention.

Let's go back to the proposal scenario I've just presented. The buyer has had minor quality issues, and I addressed that with samples and my quality control document. As I presented the samples, I would be sure to ask whether they represent a level of quality that would satisfy the buyer. Think about how far behind the eight-ball I'd be if I didn't ask, and the buyer was thinking: "My God, these are ugly samples!" I'd follow the samples with my quality control story, and now he/she would be thinking: "Great, they have procedures in place to insure that I'll always get this *low level* of quality. No thanks!" I hope you see how that interchange would be taking me *perpendicular* to the straight line — very much the wrong direction!

In that scenario, I don't want to move on to the quality control story until I determine that the quality would be acceptable. And then I don't want to move on to my next selling challenge until I confirm that the combination of samples and quality control has convinced the buyer that he/she will not have those same quality problems with me. This trial closing question is pretty straightforward: "Have I convinced you that you won't have the quality problems with me that you're experienced with the other supplier?"

If the answer is *yes*, that means you're moving along the straight line and you can continue to the next element of your proposal. If the answer in *no*, you better deal with that before moving on! Again, the best way to do that probably starts with a question: "Where *exactly* have I missed the target?"

Do you see, by the way, that it's good strategy to accept the responsibility for miscommunication here? The issue may not be your solution to their problem, it may only be that they don't fully understand your solution, or you didn't have their complete attention. In either of those cases, you don't have to change your proposal as much as restate it.

Still, they didn't get it the first time, so you face two challenges when you're in this situation. First, you have to make sure that they *do* get it before you move on. Otherwise, the answer to you final closing question is almost certain to be *no*. Second, it's best to do that without alienating or insulting them.

Remember this Dinosaur Wisdom: *It is not the buyer's responsibility to communicate with the seller, it's the other way around.* A miscommunication may not be your *fault*, but communication is ultimately your *responsibility*.

With all that in mind, I hope you see the importance of balancing the *statements* in your proposal with trial closing questions. As a rule of thumb, I try never to *state* more than 2-3 things in a presentation without asking a trial closing question. For example: *Are you with me so far? Do you agree with that? Does this all make sense so far? Am I on the right track? Does is sound like we're getting to the solution to your problem? Does that sound better than the way you've been doing that?*

Bottom line: trial closing questions keep you from getting too far off track, to the point where the buyer completely tunes you out! Trial closing questions can bring you back toward that straight line that represents the shortest distance to the sale you're trying to make.

Closing Stage

OK, we're now at the point where you have presented your proposal, right down to your quote on the newsletter printing and mailing project. I would expect there to have been some miscommunication along the way, but let's say that your trial closing questions alerted you to those issues, and allowed you to bring the conversation back on track. The buyer says he's convinced that he'll get better quality from you and better service from you and an all-around better deal from you — as far as you've gone so far. He still hasn't told you you're getting the order, though, so what comes next? Asking for the order! "Based on all we've discussed," you might say, "do I get the order?"

Obviously the answer we're hoping for is an enthusiastic *yes!* But what if it's not? What if, instead, the answer is: "Well, we still have to consider some other proposals." The typical salesperson's response would be: "When do you expect to make your decision?" — but you already know that I don't want you to be a "typical" salesperson! Instead, I'd like to see you ask a much more assertive question: "Based on all we've discussed, is there any reason that you would *not* give me the order?"

Obviously the answer we're now hoping for is an enthusiastic *no!* And if that's what you hear, your next question might be: "OK then, if you were me, what would you do next to keep this ball rolling?" I've had a lot of success with that question in my own career, and I've found that a person who is really interested in working with you will probably give you an honest — and helpful! — answer. From that point, you follow up in the way they suggested and you probably get the order.

What if the answer is *yes*, though — *yes I do have some problem with giving you the order!* This may surprise you, but I would consider that almost as desirable an answer as the *no* in this situation. Why? Because knowing that I might not get the order gives me the opportunity to ask *why* — in effect, the final close turns back into a trial close situation — and more importantly, asking *why* opens up the possibility of changing the buyer's mind *before* he/she makes a final decision.

Don't Get Defensive!

I would probably use the same probing question here that I suggested earlier — "Where *exactly* have I missed the target?" — for exactly the same reason. I don't want to be confrontational, but I do want to be assertive. And then, after asking, it's important to listen closely to the answer. Closely but not *defensively*. What does that mean? There's a tendency to treat a conversation like this as criticism. After all, you just asked where you failed. It's a good idea to listen, and then count to three, and only then respond.

It's been my experience that their *problems* at this point generally fall into one of four areas: (1) they didn't understand something that you said; (2) they didn't agree with something you said; (3) they've decided that they don't like you; or (4) they're just not sure they can trust you. I hope you see how an effective trial closing strategy will protect you from #2, and we talked earlier about how to respond when you run into #3 (the "where did I lose you" conversation we discussed in the last chapter). As for #1 and #4, again, the trial closing strategy is intended to minimize or avoid these problems, but you can't always count on communicating *completely* and *effectively*.

With situation #1, it might be appropriate to "re-explain" the point they missed, but it might also be a better idea to retreat and continue your convincing process at another time. I think the deciding factor should be where you think you stand in terms of #4. If the situation is adequate trust but miscommunication of part of your proposal, I would jump right back in try to "re-explain." If the situation involved *inadequate* trust, though — either coupled with something they didn't understand or as the main issue all by itself, I would retreat and consider what is almost certain to be a longer-term challenge.

Will someone tell you flat out that they don't trust you? Probably not, but I've been in situations where I sensed that was the problem — or where I *knew* it was the problem through a process of elimination. If you're sure it's not 1, 2 or 3, then it has to be 4! So how to you establish a *strategic retreat* in a situation like this? "Here's what I think," you might say. "I'm pretty confident that I have a solution to your problem (or relief for your pain, or an improvement on the way you've been doing things). Beyond that, though, I think you're not sure that you can trust me — not that you think I'm dishonest or anything, but you're just not sure I can or will keep all the promises I'm making. I'm not sure what I should do next, so maybe the best thing for me to do would be to ask you what you would do if you were me." (Again, I love that strategy!) "How do I gain your trust?"

Don't expect an easy answer, or one that suggests a short-term challenge. The most common response, in my experience, has been: "You'll have to give me time!" You can do that, of course, but you also have to think about whether *giving them time* fits into your own time management agenda. As I've written, I believe that your best time management strategy is a *progressive investment* of your time.

That doesn't mean just giving up on anyone who asks for more time, but it does mean that you have to consider the likelihood that *more time* will result in success. I have evaluated some situations as having a very low likelihood of success, and therefore being a very poor use of my time. Remember this Dinosaur Wisdom: *You can't sell to everybody, but you'll never run out of people to sell to.* You can run out of selling time, though, so it's important not to spend it unwisely.

SPMP

It's also important to understand that trust *can* be built over time. That's more likely to happen with a plan, though, than with the purely random follow-up approach that most salespeople employ. I refer to this sort of plan as an SPMP — Specific Prospect Marketing Plan — and your starting point for any SPMP should probably be this question: "How long should I give myself to get this guy to the next level?" (I'm using "guy" in its non-gender-specific form, by the way, even though I'm not sure it really has one. That's what you do when you like alliteration but you don't want to risk alienating any of your readers by using the term "gal.")

For the sake of discussion, let's stick with the newsletter scenario, and say that you'll give yourself a couple of months to build a level of trust that will get you serious consideration for this prospect's business. Now **STOP** and look at that last sentence! Are we really talking about a fully qualified *prospect* here? I don't think so. Remember, the third and ultimately most important qualifying criteria is that they *show some real interest in buying from you.*

At this point, I think this individual is still a suspect, albeit two-thirds of the way qualified. (Hopefully you wouldn't have gone to the effort of putting together a proposal for someone if you weren't very confident that they qualified in terms of buying enough of exactly what you sell to make pursuing them worthwhile!)

OK, what can you do over a two-month timeframe to build trust? Obviously, this SPMP should involve numerous contacts, but it's very important not to cross the line from *professional* to *pest.* You do that with creativity, and with a light touch!

How many contacts? I would probably be thinking about a 5-6 touch program, starting with an e-mail the following day: "Thank you for spending some time with me yesterday. I understand that you're not ready to do business with me yet, but I really feel that I can be of value to you, so I don't want to give up. I want to stay in touch, but I promise not to be one of those 'stalker' salespeople who soon becomes a pest. Keep your eyes on your mailbox and inbox for some things I want to send you. Hopefully I can convince you that you can trust me to be your newsletter supplier."

Two weeks after that, I might put some more samples into an envelope with a short note: "Mr. Jones, here are some more samples of recent newsletter projects. I think the most important thing about them is that they're repeat orders. In fact, we've been printing and mailing the newsletter for (XYZ Associates) for more than (X) years. Would they keep sending us the orders if we weren't meeting or exceeding their expectations? I don't think so, and I hope you'll see that as evidence that you might be able to trust (me/us) in the same way. Thank you for your consideration!"

Continuing With The Plan

Two weeks later I would send an e-mail with my quality control document attached: "Mr. Jones, we may have gone over this last month when I presented my proposal, but I wanted to put it in front of you again because I think that our quality control is one of the most important added-values I can provide to you. Quality doesn't just happen here, we *make it happen*, and I think that means you can trust us to make it happen for you."

Two weeks later, another e-mail: "Mr. Jones, after sending you more samples, and then writing about our quality control procedures, I got to thinking that what I've sent represents pretty solid evidence, but you've still only heard it from me! Would you be willing to give two of my current customers a call? I've asked them both if they'd be willing to talk to you and give you a first-hand assessment of what it's been like to do business with (me/us). Here are the names and phone numbers…" Obviously you'll want to clear this strategy with the customers involved, but I have usually found my good customers to be willing to help me out.

Two weeks later I might drop off a dozen doughnuts, with a note attached: "Mr. Jones, I hope you'll have found my strategy over the last couple of months to be appropriate and effective. You told me that I needed to give you some time, and I have tried to stay somewhere near the front of your mind without becoming a pest. The donuts are my way of saying 'thank you' for indulging me in that strategy, but there's still one more part to my plan. I'm going to be calling you over the next few days to see if the strategy worked, and if you're ready to take the next step toward actually doing business together. Please be expecting my call."

Commitment Call

A few days later: "Mr. Jones, this is Dave Fellman from Dave's Printing. Did you enjoy the donuts? (Hopefully the answer is "yes" and "thank you.") Well, like I wrote in that note, this is the last stage of my plan, calling to see if my strategy worked and if you're ready to take the next step. Can we schedule an appointment to talk some more about your newsletter?"

What if you find yourself talking to voice mail on this call? "Mr. Jones, this is

Dave Fellman from Dave's Printing. I hope you enjoyed the donuts, and like I wrote in the note that accompanied them, this is the last stage of my plan, calling to see if my strategy over the last couple of months has worked and if you're ready to take the next step. I'd like to schedule an appointment to talk some more about your newsletter. Please call me at XXX-XXX-XXXX and let's set up a time to get together."

What Comes Next?

OK, we're obviously hoping for a positive response, but what if it's not, or what if you don't get a return call after leaving a voice mail message? Just as in the earlier "suspecting" stages, you now have a choice to make, and your options include (1) giving up, (2) pushing harder, (3) another strategic retreat and (4) just trying again later. There's a significant difference between #3 and #4, but I'll get to that in a moment. For now, I want to consider the choice between #1 and #2.

More than anything else, this is a time management decision, and it revolves around two statements: (1) "I can't spend any more time on this person/company because they're not worth it" and (2) "I can't spend any more time on this person/ company even though they are worth it!" The issue is the size of the opportunity, and if we're talking about a small opportunity coupled with a difficult selling challenge, I think you should give up and move on to another opportunity. If we're talking about a large opportunity and a difficult selling challenge — and what I really mean is a selling challenge that still seems highly difficult even after you've taken a couple of good shots at it! — your best decision might be to "go for broke" and push right now. That might involve an e-mail or a voice mail message that goes something like this: "Mr. Jones, you're really missing the boat here. I *know* that I have something that you need, and I *know* that I can improve your situation. It might take a leap of faith on your part, but I think you really need to give me a chance!"

When should you employ this strategy? It's really simple. Only when you have a lot to gain and nothing to lose. This is an "all in with a short stack and a drawing hand" move (if you're not a poker player, think *desperation* and you won't be far off), and the most likely result is to alienate the buyer forever. Again, though, if your only other option is to give up, it might be worth a try.

The potential downside to this strategy is if the buyer starts telling everyone he/ she knows what a jerk you are, so you have to evaluate the likelihood that will happen. In my experience, people don't do that as often as most salespeople think. They're way too busy to launch smear campaigns against every salesjerk they encounter. In fact, most of the times when I've encountered objectionable behavior on the part of a salesperson trying to sell something to me, I just thought "What a jerk!" and went back to what I was doing before the incident. (A related note: People don't share positive experiences with salespeople as often as salespeople think they do either.)

OK, you might "go for broke" if the only other choice is to give up, but is that your only other choice? Don't forget about #3 and #4, another "strategic retreat" or just trying again later. I wrote earlier that there's a significant difference between the two, and it's the element of making/revising your plan to try to add something new to the relationship or body of evidence you're trying to build. Remember what I wrote earlier about *creativity* combined with a light touch.

So when should you employ the "just try again" strategy? NEVER! Sadly, that's all most salespeople do. They call and they call and then they wait a while and then call and then call again. I call that *blind persistence*, and I hope you'll bring more than that to the table! Here's some more Dinosaur Wisdom: *Blind persistence tends to cause deafness.* In other words, buyers usually tune blindly persistent salespeople out pretty completely.

Another SPMP Application

Here's another SPMP application — the situation where you have a first meeting with a suspect but he/she is not willing to schedule a second meeting. Again, the starting point for your SPMP is the question: "How long should I give myself to get this guy to the next level?" You might adopt a two-month plan like the one I just described, or you might also recognize that you're facing a longer-term challenge and allow yourself six months. With a six-month SPMP, it might be more appropriate to have the "touches" a month apart as opposed to 2 weeks apart. Just as in putting together a proposal, there's no one-size-fits-all strategy that's likely to work for you.

Just as with the proposal, though, every "touch" and/or document you develop will probably have application to other SPMPs. I love the idea that you'll soon have a large collection of tools at your disposal, and that eventually, putting together a proposal or crafting an SPMP will be mostly a matter of assembling proven tools from your toolbox.

Preparing and Presenting Your Proposal — Closing Thoughts

I've tried hard to convince you that the best selling happens when you propose a solution to a real problem, or relief for real pain, or maybe just a little bit better way of doing something — an improvement on the status quo. It's important, though, to propose the *right* solution or the *right* pain relief or the *right* way to improve on the status quo. In my experience, many salespeople propose *their* solution, which is not necessarily the right solution.

Step 1, then, is to identify the pain, problem or opportunity — and that's why the questions precede the proposal! Step 2 is to propose the right pain relief, solution or strategy. Step 2 requires significant product knowledge, and I want you to remember that there are two kinds of product knowledge that are important to a salesperson: *technical* product knowledge and *applications* product knowledge.

Here's some more Dinosaur Wisdom: *The result of the right solution is usually a happy customer. The result of the wrong solution may still be a sale, but probably never another one!*

9
Price Objections: The Art of Negotiation

"All that sounds easy," a young salesperson said to me. "I can put a proposal together and I can present it and now I know how to deal with the situation where they're not ready to commit yet. The one I have real trouble with is when they tell me my price is too high."

"Do you hear that a lot?" I asked.

"Let's just say that it's a special occasion when I don't," he replied.

OK, I think we've uncovered a fundamental truth here. In selling, you are going to face frequent price objections. Why? The answer to that question reflects some more Dinosaur Wisdom: *No one wants to pay more than they have to for anything.* The core of your price objection strategy, then, probably has to address that *have to.*

A Pricing Exercise

Here's an exercise that I think will help you to understand this issue. I need to buy batteries, and my Sunday paper featured ad inserts from Target, Best Buy, Home Depot, Office Depot and Office Max, all of which are within easy driving distance from my home. All of them have advertised specials on Duracell batteries, with Target, Best Buy, Home Depot and Office Depot selling them for $3.69 and Office Max selling them for $3.49. None of these stores is any more or less convenient than another, and I think you'll agree that I don't *have to* spend $3.69 for Duracell batteries since Office Max will sell them to me for $3.49.

Target's ad gave me something else to think about, though. They sell a house brand for $3.29. Now I have to ask myself if Target brand batteries are as good as

Duracell batteries. If they are — if I trust them to be! — I don't even have to pay $3.49 for batteries. I think it's telling, though, that so many people buy the "name" brands instead of the "house" brands.

But let's go back to the "name" brand for a minute. With the price of gas at close to $3.00 per gallon (I paid $2.94 the day I wrote this), how much distance differential would make $3.69 batteries a better deal for me than $3.49 batteries? That depends on what kind of car I drive, of course, and what sort of gas mileage I get, but I'm sure you understand that *distance is money* in this equation, and considering what else I might have to do today, *time is money* too. I might *have to* spend $3.69 on batteries to avoid spending $.41 on gasoline, or spending an additional 15 minutes of my time on this particular purchase.

Lowest Possible Price

Here's a quick question. What percentage of all things that are purchased do you think get purchased at the lowest possible price? When I ask that question in seminars, the first person to answer usually says something like 60% or 70%, but the later (and more thoughtful?) answers are always much lower. I usually end up saying that I won't argue with any number between 5% and 15%, because I'm pretty sure the answer is in that range.

OK, now *why* are the vast majority of all of these things purchased at something higher than the lowest possible price? Quite a few factors figure into this, starting with *value*. It has been proven in the marketplace that people will pay more when they feel that they're getting more for their money.

Another key factor, though, is *access* to the lowest possible price. Some buyers simply don't know who has the lowest prices on any given product or service — either who is best equipped to produce the product or execute the service, or who's willing to sell it at the lowest profit margin. They may buy from whoever has the lowest price among the suppliers they do know, but remember, the question addressed the lowest *possible* price. (Also remember that I just described *Player* behavior, as in *Solids, Liquids, Gases, Players* and *Price Monsters*.)

They may also buy from whoever they like the most, which is a good thing when we're talking about a customer, but probably not such a good thing if we're talking about a suspect or a prospect. There's no question that the *like factor* has a value, but just remember that it's a *relative* value. I'll spend $.20 more for my batteries just because I like Target better than Office Max, but if we're talking about 20 *dollars* that's a completely different story. And don't ever forget that the *trust factor* trumps the *like factor.* If I don't trust the quality of the batteries, I'm not going to buy Target's house brand no matter how much I like shopping in their stores.

Convenience Factor

The *convenience factor* has a role to play in this decision too. Some buyers simply do whatever's the easiest thing for them to do, and this is another example of something that's a good thing when we're talking about a customer, but definitely not such a good thing if we're talking about a suspect or a prospect. Remember this Dinosaur Wisdom: *You're always in competition with the current and existing state of affairs as it pertains to your products and/or services. .*

Ultimately the *why* isn't what's important here, though, it's the knowledge that price isn't the absolute driving force in most people's buying decisions. Once you know that, you can take a far more enlightened approach to dealing with price objections. Or maybe I should say that a different way — *until* you know that, you'll be a hopeless underdog in any price objection situation.

Here's something else that's important. Batteries and *exactly what you sell* may be completely different animals. That's especially true if you sell a *service,* or a *custom manufactured product* — both of which add another whole level of complexity to the buying decision.

Maybe I should say that in a different way. Many buyers think of many products and services as *commodities*, and you can't let them do that. If the product is exactly the same, the buyer has to look for reasons *not to* buy it from whoever sells it at the lowest price. Yes, the *like factor* and the *convenience factor* are in play here, but the *risk factor* that's inherent in any non-commodity purchase can be a far more significant selling asset for you. More on that will follow!

Anticipation

No one wants to pay more than they *have to* for anything. Because of that, great salespeople anticipate price objections. "I know it's coming," one top performer once told me, "so I start looking for my leverage very early in the selling process. They're going to ask me for a lower price, and I'm going to have to give them a good reason why they can't have it!"

I've observed three distinct ways in which salespeople address price objections. The first is to lower their prices. I don't recommend this, but I think you know that it's happening every day. (You may even be doing it yourself, in which case, I want you to stop it! — unless there's a very good *strategic* reason for an aggressive pricing strategy, and we'll talk more about that a little farther along.) The second most common strategy seems to be the take-it-or-leave it approach, and I don't recommend that either.

Fortunately, there's a third approach, and this is one that I do recommend. I think the best way to handle a price objection is simply to tell them why you think they should buy from you anyway, even though your price is higher than what others may be offering them. "Oh yeah," I can hear some of you thinking. "That sounds really simple!" OK, maybe *simply* was not the best choice of words, but the strategy really is pretty straightforward, and it all goes back to the questioning stage. Here's some more Dinosaur Wisdom: *If you find some weakness in the status quo, that can be presented as a good reason for* having to *pay more than they really want to, or more than they did the last time, or more than some other competitor is willing to sell your product or service for.*

Key Concept

Now here's a key concept: If the price objection comes up *after* you've presented the sort of proposal I described in the previous chapter, you have already told them why you think they should buy from you, even at a higher price point than what they've paid previously or what they've been offered. You may only need to repeat what you've already told them, perhaps with some amplification or clarification of some of the key points.

Let's go back to that proposal scenario. You had a first meeting with a buyer who prints and distributes a monthly newsletter. She had some minor quality issues with her current printer, and some major service issues. You addressed the quality issues with the one-two punch of relevant samples followed by your quality control documents, and you addressed the service issues with testimonials from current customers. At the end of your proposal, though — or perhaps a week after your proposal, after receiving quotes from several other suppliers — the price objection surfaces. "Your price is on the high side of the quotes we've received," is what the buyer might say.

"Ms. Jones," you might say. "I want to go back to the part of my proposal where I described our quality control procedures, and I want to ask you if the name Philip Crosby means anything to you?" Assuming that the answer will be *no*, you could continue: "He wrote a book in 1979 called 'Quality Is Free,' and I'd like you to consider that it was a catchy title, but it's not really true. Quality is not free, because *quality control* is not free, because it takes time — and training and management! — to ensure that quality happens. You told me about the quality issues that you've had, and my price includes all of the quality control steps it really takes to make sure that you don't have those problems again!" *(Crosby, Philip, 1979. Quality is Free. New York: McGraw-Hill. ISBN 0-07-014512-1)*

Remember, no one wants to pay more than they *have to*. Your challenge is to convince the buyer that your price represents the lowest possible cost of getting exactly what she wants. Here's another way to look at this: Your challenge is often to bring the buyer to the realization that "you bought cheap last time and you got exactly what you paid for!" I'm sure you'll see how this can be a touchy subject, and how it's better to build your case without offending your counterpart, but I've been in situations where I've had to use pretty much those exact words!

A Recent Situation

I was involved in a situation with one of my printing clients recently where the previous quality problem was poor registration on a two-color print job. What that means is that the two colors were supposed to meet but not touch, but over a run of 5000 pieces, about a third of them had a significant gap where the colors didn't meet, and another third had a significant stain where the two colors overlapped. My client's price was about 10% higher (about $60) than the previous printer had charged.

"You're 10% higher," the buyer said.

"That doesn't surprise me," my client answered. "Let me tell you how I came up with my price. You told me about the quality problem, so I priced this job to make sure that the same thing wouldn't happen. Do you mind if I turn this into a little lesson in the graphic arts?"

The buyer was willing, so my client continued: "Our press has a maximum rated speed of 11,000 sheets per hour. The other printer has a similar press, and I'm guessing that they estimated and then ran the job at the maximum speed. I estimated the job with the press running at 8000 sheets per hour, though, because that does two things that specifically address the registration problem. First, we have better control of the position of each sheet at a little bit slower speed, and second, even if we do lose the exact registration, fewer 'bad' sheets will get through the press before we catch the problem. The downside of doing it this way is that the job is on press longer, so that raises your price a little bit, but do you see how the way I did this will solve your problem?"

"That makes perfect sense," was the buyer's reply — and hopefully you just learned something about printing in addition to something about selling!

Civilians

Don't ever forget that most of the people you're selling to are *civilians*. They can compare numbers, but they probably don't understand what goes into the numbers. They are (hopefully!) not idiots, though, and many of them will respond well to the level of explanation you can provide. Most salespeople don't provide enough explanation, and more importantly, they don't provide enough *evidence* to support their claims. I once listened in as another printing salesperson dealt with a similar quality scenario. The buyer said: "Your price is quite a bit higher."

"Yeah, but you're going to get a lot better quality from me," the salesperson replied.

"How do I know that?" the buyer asked.

"Because I'm standing here telling you!" the salesperson answered. "I promise you that you'll be happy with our quality. Just give me a chance to show you what we can do!"

Who would be more likely to gain *your* trust, the first salesperson or the second?

Strong Teammates

In the last chapter, I suggested that you develop a document which features photos and short bios of the key people in your organization. Many salespeople talk about the strength of their team, but they don't take that to the next level. I watched a great example of using team strength as a justification for higher prices 8-10 years ago, with a very talented salesperson from a printing company on the West Coast. When faced with a price objection from a very high-potential prospect, she said: "I'd like to tell you about the man who's going to actually print this order if you award it to us," she said. "His name is Minh, and he owned a little printshop in South Vietnam in the late 60's and early 70's. When Saigon fell in 1975, he and his family got out with not much more than the clothes they were wearing, and they made their way to the US, where he came to work for us 22 years ago."

"In those 22 years," she continued, "he's been to specialized training twice — in fact, he's been trained by the people who actually built our two printing presses. He also teaches printing at a vocational school two nights a week. But the thing I most wanted to tell you about was how he makes time on just about every shift to take some part of the press apart and clean it with a set of precision brushes he bought with his own money. I know that our owner has tried to pay him back for those brushes, but Minh always says 'no, you pay me very well, I can afford to bring my own tools, and it makes me happy to keep these machines in good running order.'"

"The 'pay me well' part is important," she continued, "because I know we pay Minh a lot more than most printing companies pay their press operators. Although it would probably be more correct to say that our customers pay Minh, because his higher-than-average salary is one of the reasons that our prices are usually higher-than-average."

"So it comes down to this," she concluded. "Do you want Minh running the press that prints your order, or are you willing to take a chance that our competitors' press operators will give you the same level of quality and service and attention to detail? I'm not at all ashamed to ask you to pay for Minh — and he's just one example of the way we've built our staff. You can always pay less for less. I'm hoping that you'll see the wisdom of paying more for more."

On this particular day, she got the order, and I congratulated her on her strategy. "It's not always that easy," she said. "There are people who don't want to pay for Minh — there are people who don't want to pay for anything! — but that's OK, because they're not the people we want as our customers. My boss told me very early in my career that I must sell the company, not the printing."

I would add this to what her boss told her. Before you can effectively sell the company, you have to know that the benefit you're trying to sell matches up to an area of concern on the part of the buyer. What if quality was not an issue for this particular buyer? What if he'd never had a problem with the quality he'd been buying at lower prices? Would there be any good reason to pay more for Minh in that scenario?

Another Story

I don't think so, and here's another story to illustrate that point. I was on the way to an appointment with another printing salesperson and I asked him to brief me on his goal and his plan for the meeting. "This is an ad agency that specializes in fundraising clients," he told me, "and I've been collecting samples of mail I've been getting from their clients. Some of it is really ugly printing, and I'm going to put that stuff side-by-side with samples of our printing, and I'm going to try to sell him on the idea that he'll get much better quality for probably not a whole lot more money by going with us!"

I was pretty sure there was a flaw in his reasoning, but I decided not to bring it up at that point. And the way things worked out, it was the prospect who pointed out that flaw. Here's what happened. The salesperson made his presentation, and he asked the first part of his closing question: "Do you agree that our quality is far superior to what you've been buying?"

"Both of youse," the buyer said — perhaps I should mention that we were in northern New Jersey, and that's *exactly* what he said — "come with me!"

We walked out of his office and down the hall and into the "bullpen" where three graphic artists worked at drawing tables. (This was back in the days before artists worked on computers. More evidence that I am, in fact, a dinosaur!) He picked up an artboard from one of those tables and carried it over to a copy machine sitting on a table along the wall. He lifted up the rubber cover and put the artboard on the glass, closed the cover and pressed the start button, and then the copier sort of wheezed into action.

I love telling this part of the story, because all of this occurred 20+ years ago, and the copy machine was probably 15 years old even then. It was the kind where the whole box moved backward on the scanning cycle, and then forward on the printing cycle, and as all of that was happening, the buyer lifted the cover, removed the artboard and walked it back over to the drawing table. By the time he came back, the copy had reached the exit tray, and then he took it and put it on the glass and made a copy of the copy. Then he took *that* copy and repeated the process, finally handing the third copy — which represented a fourth-generation reproduction of the original — to the salesperson. "This is what I gave the other printer for artwork," he said. "Do you understand now why the quality isn't up to your standards?"

"I understand *that*," the salesperson said, "but I don't understand why you *did* that!"

(Just to make sure that you understand, the buyer took an original and placed in on a *photo*copy machine, a different technology than today's digital scanners and copiers. The *photo*copier basically took a picture of the original, then printed that picture to the electrostatically charged drum of the copier, which pulled oppositely-charged toner to the drum, and then deposited that toner to a sheet of paper. At each of the four steps in that process, some resolution was lost, so from original to copy to copy to copy, the end result would have been *fuzzy* enough to produce pretty poor quality printing.)

"Here's what you need to understand," the buyer said. "We're in the business of asking people to give their hard-earned money to our charities. We want them to think that the money actually goes to the charities. We don't want them to think that we spend more of the money on printing than we do on the causes they're trying to support, so we want it to look like we found the dirt-cheapest printer on the planet to do the work."

"You guys in the printing industry," he continued, "are so concerned with your 'reputation for quality' that if we don't consciously degrade the artwork, you're going to 'fix' it and charge us even more for that. I made it clear when I gave the guy the artwork that this was exactly how I wanted the final product to look!"

I could see the dawn of understanding in the salesperson's eyes, and that ties into a question I've asked many times in seminars: *If they're happy with the quality they're getting, no matter how bad it may be, should they spend more to get better quality from you?* The answer, nine times out of ten, is *no*!

Value Objections

But…how about that other time? I was out on a call with a promotional products salesperson who had picked up an imprinted pen while making her "prospecting start" on an interior design firm. The pen was both cheap and poorly printed, and the salesperson asked: "Doesn't this bother you?" We were meeting with the office manager, and her answer was: "No, they're just pens!"

"Do you give them out to customers?" the salesperson asked. "Because if you do, they're not just pens, they're part of your image!"

This was one of those happy days when circumstance breaks just right for a salesperson, because as she was making that statement, one of the principals of the firm walked into the elegant conference room where we were meeting with the office manager. "I'm going to need this room in about 15 minutes," he said. "What's part of our image?"

"These pens," said the salesperson, "and if you don't mind my saying so, I don't think these pens belong in this room. I think the room and the pens say two different things about your company. The room says the right things but the pens let you down."

"Lemme see," he said, and looked the pen over. "OK, the printing's not very good. Our logo looks like crap. Is that what you're talking about?"

"Only partly," said the salesperson. "The printing certainly isn't doing you any favors, but I think the bigger issue is that the pen looks somewhere between cheap and boring. I could find you a much more interesting pen in pretty much the same price range, but I think you'd be much better served by something classier, which does mean more expensive."

I thought we might be getting close to a danger zone, so I piped in at that point. "I think all that Claire is saying is that you went to obvious expense on this room, and the whole nature of your business is artistic and image-oriented. Part of what we think we can do for you is to help you use our products to your greatest benefit."

"Let me ask you this," I continued, "how many of these did you order?" The principal looked at the office manager who said, "500 I think."

"OK, a pen like this in that quantity, you probably spent something like $400 on the whole order. Now, how many projects do you work on in a typical year?" The office manager looked at the principal, who said, "We start two or three new projects each month. We probably pitch twice that many."

"So if you pitch 50 projects each year," I said (while biting my tongue to keep from smacking him for using the term *pitch*), "for the same $400 you spent on these pens, you could give everyone you pitch to an $8 pen rather than a $.69 pen, and we can show you some really cool imprinted pens in the $8 price range. Now the question is, would an $8 pen help you to close any more deals? What do you think?"

"Well," he answered, "if it helped us to close even one more deal it would be a hell of an investment! And you're right on target about our business being artistic and image-oriented. Marian (to the office manager), I like what I'm hearing from these folks, but you'll need to find someplace else to continue your conversation. But go ahead and buy us a few hundred nicer pens."

Here's some more Dinosaur Wisdom: *Sometimes a price objection is not really about price, it's really about* value.

Budget Considerations

Here's some more Dinosaur Wisdom: *Sometimes a price objection isn't about price or value, it's about* budget. Consider these two statements: (1) "Your price is too high. I got 10 quotes on this project, and yours is the highest." (2) "Your price is too high. I budgeted $300 for this project, and you're asking me for $400."

I hope you'll agree that those are two different statements, reflecting two very different objections. I wrote earlier about a classic mistake many salespeople make: attempting to qualify prospects by asking them what their annual budget might be. As I wrote back then, the problem is that few companies actually have budgets for individual products or services.

As I also wrote back then, the discussion of budget on an individual project is a different story, especially if we're talking about a service or any sort of design/build project. You should always ask "have you established a budget?" in that situation. With some products, an understanding of budget is important because there's such a great range of cost on typical items — $.69 pens and $8 pens are a very good example. The same holds true on any sort of design/build project, where the budget will almost certainly effect the design. Remember what a sign designer once told me: "I can design you a $1000 sign, and I can design you a $100,000 sign, but you gotta tell me which one I'm designing, otherwise we're both gonna waste a lot of our time."

So hopefully, you've had some discussion about budget before you get to the price objection stage — at least on a service or a design/build project. If not, though — or if you run into a price objection on an order when everyone was quoting on the same set of specifications — it might be appropriate to ask whether the objection is based on comparative quotes, or on a budget figure.

"I hear you saying that my price is too high," you might say, "but I need to understand whether you're talking about 'too high' compared to what other suppliers have quoted you, or 'too high' in regard to your budget."

Negotiation Strategy

I haven't used the term yet, but what we've really been talking about is *negotiation*, and I have two important concepts here for your consideration. First, you should treat negotiation as inevitable. As I wrote earlier, great salespeople anticipate price objections. "I know it's coming," that top performer once told me, "so I start looking for my leverage very early in the selling process. They're going to ask me for a lower price, and I'm going to have to give them a good reason why they can't have it!" I think you should expect to hear price objections, and you should hear them simply as the signal for the start of a negotiation.

Unfortunately, most buyers don't hear them the same way. I speak occasionally to groups of buyers, and I remember one conversation that took place in Atlanta some years ago. I was talking about the inevitability of price objections, and how I teach salespeople to respond.

"We don't signal the start of the negotiation," one of the buyers said. "The first move in any negotiation is when the salesperson quotes a price."

"No," I replied, "that's just the salesperson telling you how much it's going to get exactly what you want. There's no need for negotiation unless you complain about the price."

"Yeah, well answer me this," he said. "How come every time I complain about the price, the price comes down?" I didn't have a clever answer for that one!

Here's some more Dinosaur Wisdom: *Most buyers don't trust most sellers, especially in regard to pricing.* They think your initial quote reflects your best case scenario, but it's probably not a scenario you're going to stick to. Experience has shown most buyers that most sellers will lower their price when faced with a price objection.

Buyer Training

In fact, there's more to this than experience. Buyers are actually taught to raise price objections. There are hundreds if not thousands of negotiation seminars held every year, but it's interesting that other than in their literature, those seminars don't really use the word *negotiation*. The word they use is *intimidation*, and they teach that you can almost always *intimidate* a salesperson into lowering a price. All you usually have to do is to threaten to not buy whatever they're selling at the price they're hoping to sell it for.

What usually happens when that happens? Most salespeople start backing up as quickly as they can! Yes, the price is usually lowered whenever a price objection is raised, and that's another part of the reason that great salespeople treat price objections as inevitable. This takes us back to our discussion of B.F. Skinner and behavioral psychology — *any behavior which is rewarded will likely be repeated! Positive reinforcement* occurs when a behavior is followed by a favorable stimulus, and the buyer stands to gain two favorable stimuli in this situation. First is the element of *saving money*. Second is the element of *winning* the negotiation. When you put all of that together, you should never be surprised by a price objection.

Does that mean you should start backing up as quickly as you can when it happens? Absolutely not! It means that you should decline to be intimidated and accept the invitation to negotiate, and that leads us to some more Dinosaur Wisdom: *When a negotiation begins, there are actually three things up for negotiation —*

Value, Cost and *Price.* Of equal importance, that's exactly the order in which you should address these three elements. You should first attempt to negotiate *value.* If that doesn't work, Plan B should be to negotiate *cost.* If that too fails, you still have Plan C, which is to negotiate the *price* — but let's not go there until after you've attempted the other two elements!

Value, Cost & Price

Negotiating *value* is all about telling them why you think they should buy from you anyway, even though your price is higher than a competitor's. As we've discussed, the key to this strategy is to convince them that you represent greater value, either *more* for their money or *less* for their money — more value or less pain or less risk of pain. As we've also discussed, it's critically important that whatever *more* or *less* you're stressing is directly relevant to their wants and needs.

If they're not buying the value, Plan B is to look at the cost elements and see if you can find a way to bring the price down by bringing the cost down. A successful cost negotiation represents a classic win-win situation. They get what they want (a lower price) and you get what you want (a solid profit!) When price goes down because cost goes down, profit is preserved.

But what if they're not buying Plan B either? What if the only way you'll get the order is to lower your price without a corresponding cost reduction? Obviously, that's not a win-win scenario, unless getting the order at a reduced profit level is enough of a win for you. So let's explore that. Are there situations where it's really a good business decision to forego profit in search of volume?

Sure there are. I can think of two right away. But before we talk about them, let's recognize that most "negotiated" price reductions derive from weakness, not from strength. In other words, they're not good business decisions, they're poor business decisions — panic decisions! As I think we've agreed, most salespeople start backing up as quickly as they can when a price objection is raised. But you're not going to be "most salespeople" anymore, right? You're not going to lower your price unless there's a good business reason to do so, and you're *absolutely* not going to lower your price unless Plan A and Plan B have both failed to work for you!

Underutilized Capacity

OK, back to situations where lowering the price might be a good business decision. How about this one: you're the owner of a small manufacturing company and you have 15 employees standing around in your production area, looking at machines rather than producing product. In other words, business is slow, and you have underutilized capacity, and you have the opportunity to lower a price and win an order or a contract that you wouldn't get otherwise. I have no problem with doing that, but there are a couple of important caveats — first, be very careful about lowering your pricing *standards* with established customers!

I was involved in a situation a few years ago where a manufacturer reacted to a soft sales cycle by lowering his prices across the board. He won a few orders that he wouldn't have won from prospects, and from *players* among his customers — remember that *players* are the ones who spread their work out among a group of trusted suppliers, usually giving the job to whoever among that group has the lowest price on any individual project — but he also lost revenue on jobs he would have gotten anyway from his *solid* customers.

That wasn't the worst part, though. As the soft cycle receded, he raised his prices back up to normal levels and encountered resistance from some of those *solids*. "How come my price went up?" was the flavor of 3-4 phone calls over a two-week period. "They didn't really go up, they just went back to the normal level," was his answer. "Look," said one customer, "I like doing business with you and I value your quality and service, but if you were willing to sell to me at lower prices last week, I'm going to insist that you sell to me at those same prices this week and next week and every week. I've never questioned your prices before, but now I'm starting to wonder if you've been taking advantage of me!"

Legitimate Argument

Is that a completely rational argument? No, it is not. In fact, it runs counter to the law of supply and demand which is one of the foundation blocks of all commerce. Still, though, it's a *legitimate* argument. After all, if you were willing to sell it to me for $X last week, why wouldn't you be willing to sell it for the same amount this week? Did your costs go up? Did the overall supply of whatever you sell go down? No, what happened was that you set a lower *value* on your product and service. It's been said that the whole economy is a buyer's market, because supply in just about all segments exceeds demand. But that doesn't mean buyers set the prices. Sellers still set the prices, and that means they establish a value for their products and services. Any time you reduce a price — even if it's for a good reason! — you are resetting the value. It's usually easy to reset from high to low. It's usually hard —

and sometimes *very* hard — to reset from low to high.

Beyond all of that, rational or not, this is *not* an argument I want to have with any of my customers, especially one of my *solids*!

Here's the second caveat to this strategy. The decision to lower prices to fill underutilized capacity is an owner/senior manager decision, not a salesperson decision. What I mean is that I want you to tell me if you think you have a customer or prospect who will give us more business if we lower our prices, but then I want you get out of the way. I don't want you spending significant time on that customer or prospect. I do want you spending the vast majority of your time finding and developing customers who will give us plenty of work *without* having to lower our prices. And I don't want a salesperson working for me who seeks the easy way every time — lowering prices rather than negotiating value and/or cost effectively. In other words, I don't want you to *settle* for *price monsters*, and I especially don't want you coming to me *every single time* looking for discounts so you can get orders.

A Foot In The Door

Here's another situation where lowering your price might be a good business decision. Big company. Buys a lot of exactly what you to sell. Has some issues with the status quo. But, doesn't quite believe yet in your value proposition. To put that another way, a prospect you feel will pay for the value you can provide once you prove that it's really there.

I have no problem with lowering your price to get your foot in a door like that, but again, there are a couple of important caveats. The first one is that this strategy works best when it's clearly stated to the buyer. Otherwise, you may be perceived as a "lowballer" — an unkind term for a salesperson who comes in low to get a foot in the door and then "sneaks" the prices up later on. In my own selling career, I've had more than a few conversations that went something like this:

"I really believe that we're worth more than your current supplier, but I recognize that you're not convinced yet. You probably need to see it with your own eyes! OK, I want to ask you to give us a try so we can show you the difference, and I know that we can't ask you to pay a premium price in order to see what we can do, so we're willing to be pretty aggressive on this order. In fact, if you're willing, we'll match the lowest price you have in order to give you a good reason to give us a try."

"But, I want to make sure you understand right from the start that we intend to raise our prices after this demonstration, and we're going into this thinking that you'll happily pay those prices after you've seen first-hand what we can do. We're also going into this knowing that you won't pay those prices if you don't see a difference, so I guess what I'm proposing is an experiment. What do you think?"

Please note that this is a statement followed by a closing question. You *always* need to ask for the order!

Something In Return

Here's the second caveat. A *price* negotiation cannot be considered successful unless you get something significant in return for anything/everything you give up. Getting the order may qualify — especially if we're talking about a capacity-based decision or a getting-your-foot-in-the-door situation — but the great salespeople often manage to get even more than that!

Here's a story to illustrate that point. A young salesperson in California had a situation where she had quoted three projects with a buyer, and each time he told her that he'd love to give her a try, but her price was a little too high. On the fourth project, he called her on the phone and said: "Listen, like I've been saying, I'd love to give you a try, but I'm not going to pay extra to do that. But here's what I am willing to do. I'll tell you what my lowest price is, and if you can match it, I'll give you the order."

I think it's worth mentioning that this young salesperson is *extremely* attractive. That gives her an advantage that I never had in my selling career. I have cautioned her several times not to depend on her looks, and not to trade on her looks either. (Please remember that statement when you read "A Feminist Perspective On Selling" later on.)

Anyway, she went to her boss and said: "I think this is one of those situations that Fellman talks about, where I just haven't convinced him of our value yet, and he's going to have to see it with his own eyes. I understand that he wouldn't be a very good customer for us at this price level, so I'm prepared to walk away from this if one job doesn't convince him that we're worth more than what he's been paying."

Largely based on that understanding, her boss decided to support the experiment — although I think it also had some bearing on the situation that I was going to be out there in just a few days to work with this company's sales team. And as things worked out, the salesperson set up a meeting with the buyer for the first day I was out there.

As we were driving to the meeting, I asked her to brief me on the situation, her objective and her plan. After hearing all of that, I asked her this question: "Is there anything about this particular guy that you would change if you could?" She laughed, because she knows very well where the question comes from, and said: "I would make him return my phone calls promptly. He's not very good at that."

"Tell you what," I said, "when we get in there, let me lead. I know he's your prospect, and you have a pretty good plan, but I think I can show you something." She agreed, and after getting the "polite pleasantries" out of the way, I said this to her prospect: "It's our understanding that if we match the price, we get the order, and in fact, we leave here today with the purchase order. Is that a fair statement of where you stand?"

Commitment

When I tell this story in seminars, I always ask the attendees if they understand why I asked this question at the beginning of the conversation. The answer is that I wanted to make sure that he was ready to commit before we made the price concession. And it was interesting to see by his body language that he may have spoken the words to the salesperson — and I absolutely believe that he did! — but the synapses in his brain hadn't quite clicked together to seal that commitment. Be that as it may, I asked him straight out, and he committed. Then I said: "OK, we are willing to do that, but there's one caveat. There's one thing we want you to agree to in return."

Now his body language indicated concern. "I don't think you're going to find this too burdensome," I continued. "All we want you to agree to is to return Maria's calls more promptly any time that she calls you, within the day, or no later than the next morning."

There was silence in the room for a couple of beats, then he made a sort of half-snorting, half-laughing sound. "That's what you want from me?" he asked. "What do I gain by making that promise?"

Maria jumped in at that point. "Here's the thing," she said. "This is not just about this order for me. I'm trying to build a relationship — a partnership! — that benefits both of us. I know that you're busy, and you have a million things on your mind every day, but I need access to you in order to be really valuable to you."

He thought about that for a couple of beats, and then he said: "That makes sense. OK, I agree."

Ten or fifteen minutes later, Maria and I were walking to her car with the purchase order in hand. "How do you feel?" I asked her. "I feel really good," she answered. "Yeah," I said, "we walked out of there with a very nice order."

"That's only half of what I'm feeling good about," she said, "and in fact, it's the small half. The big half, the thing I really feel good about, is that we won."

R-E-S-P-E-C-T!

Again, when I tell this story in seminars, I always ask the attendees if they understand what we won. Sometimes that question is met with blank looks, in which case I continue: "Aretha Franklin could tell you. R-E-S-P-E-C-T!" We showed the buyer that we were willing to work with him, but that he had to work with us in return.

Interestingly, he has turned into a pretty good customer, but Maria has told me that he still reverts to form every once in a while. "Every 4-5 orders," she told me, "he'll ask me if I can help him out on the price. And probably 4 times out of 5 I'll tell him no. Not long ago, I said: 'Hey Terry, how long have we known each other? I know that you want my best price the first time, and that's what I'm giving you.' He seems satisfied with that. But every once in a while, I'll agree to reduce a price a little in return for some concession on his part. I've gotten more time from him on what started out being 'hot rush' jobs a couple of times, and I've gotten some pretty good referrals from him in return for small price concessions."

Here's an example of one of those referrals. Terry was the chairperson of a local business group, and he set up a lunch for Maria with three other members of that group — two of whom she'd been pursuing for months without any success. He did that in return for a 10% discount on a $350 order.

The point is this: If you're really committed to negotiating — not just backing up as fast as you can and lowering your price whenever you're faced with a price objection! — you can win in a lot of different ways. You can win by convincing your counterpart that he/she will get more — or less! — from you, justifying a higher price. That's a successful negotiation of *value*. You can win by changing the specs of the order, reducing the price but preserving the profit margin. That's a successful negotiation of *cost*. And you can win by getting something significant in return for anything you give up in terms of profit margin. That's a successful negotiation of *price*. The great salespeople seem to win pretty regularly on all three levels.

Worst Case Scenario

OK, let's go back to the idea that great salespeople anticipate price objections and prepare in advance for the negotiation stage. In a *suspect/prospect* situation, that means asking assertive and provocative questions to (hopefully) identify some level of dissatisfaction with the status quo. It has been proven in the marketplace that you can defend a higher price when it provides pain relief, or contains the solution to a problem, or reflects a better way of doing something.

How about a *customer* situation, though, when the status quo is (hopefully) your friend? It's not uncommon to face price pressure from even loyal and satisfied customers — after all, your competitors are almost certainly quoting them lower prices than you are, and making them wonder if they have to pay your prices to get what they want. (Note that *have to* again!) How do you prepare yourself for *that* negotiation?

I've had lots of success asking my customers about the *Worst Case Scenario* as I've taken the specs on the project: "What's the worst thing that could happen with this project, the nightmare scenario that might keep you awake at night as we get close to the due date? And how bad would that be if it actually happened? For your team/company/organization? For you as an individual?" In other words: *What could go wrong here and how bad would it hurt?*

The idea behind this strategy is to get the *risk factor* on the table. In anticipation of some competitor(s) offering lower prices than I do, I want to be able to point to the *possible pain points* and say (1) that I/we understand the pain potential, and (2) that my price includes all of the safeguards against that possibility becoming a reality.

This is another reflection of some Dinosaur Wisdom we talked about earlier: that *the decision about whether to buy from you is far too important to be left up to them!* Most salespeople seem content in a belief that their customers will automatically remember and appreciate great quality and service. Interestingly, they seem to believe that even after seeing it disproved time and time again! On one hand, I hear salespeople complaining that there's no loyalty anymore, but on the other hand, I don't see them reinforcing the connection between performance and loyalty.

The core message is this: *I make it my business to know what could go wrong, and then I build in the necessary safeguards — not the 'lower-the-price' shortcuts! You can always buy cheap, but can you always buy that?*

Insurance

Here's another way to express that core message: *My price may be higher, but it includes insurance against the Worst Case Scenario.* None of us really likes *writing* checks to our insurers — car, home, life, whatever — but we love *getting* checks if something happens and we have to file a claim. Most people are risk-averse to at least some degree, but if they aren't thinking about the risk, there's nothing to be averse from!

Here's some more Dinosaur Wisdom: *He/She who puts the risk on the table usually benefits the most from its power.* In other words, we want them to know that bad things can happen, and then we want them to know that those things are *less likely* to happen if they buy from us!

Trust and Respect

As we've discussed, negotiating *value* is all about telling them why you think they should buy from you anyway, even though your price is higher than a competitor's. If they're not buying that, Plan B is to look at the cost elements and see if you can find a way to bring the price down by bringing the cost down. If that doesn't work either, we're down to Plan C, and negotiating *price* is about getting something significant in return for anything you give up. When you get down to Plan C, though, please don't lose sight of the importance of preserving trust and respect.

Think about that for a moment. Trust and respect together are important because you don't want to have to negotiate the price on every single order. Trust is even more important alone, though, because as I think we've agreed, trust is the single most important factor in most people's buying decision.

If you quote me a price and then reduce it at the slightest sign of price resistance, how can I ever again trust your asking price — or any other promise you make? Remember this Dinosaur Wisdom: *Most buyers don't trust most sellers, especially in regard to pricing.* They think your initial quote reflects your best case scenario, but it's probably not a scenario you're going to stick to. And if you don't stick on price, will you or can you stick on quality and service and all the rest?

You can either be trusted, or you can't. If you convince me that you can, you have a very good chance of getting at least some of my business. If you show me that you can't — and remember, actions speak much louder than words! — you'll probably always be on the outside looking in.

An Alternate Strategy

I am a very strong believer in *assertive* negotiation, but I think it's worth presenting you with an alternate strategy. And this strategy, like a lot of my sales philosophy, can be expressed in a story. I had a suspect who was very willing to meet with me, and at that first meeting, we got along pretty well and he gave me a project to quote on. I didn't win the order, though, and he told me that my price was quite a bit higher than the other bidder.

"OK," I said. "I'm disappointed that I didn't get the order, of course, but I've learned over the years that it's pretty rare to get the first order I quote. The way it usually works—at least for me—is that I'll start winning orders when I gain a better understanding of your needs and expectations, and when you gain greater confidence in me. Let's keep working at that."

I spoke with him twice more before the next quote opportunity, and I learned quite a bit more about his status quo. I also shared a few marketing ideas with him, and referred him to a colleague of mine who had some interest in one of his products. I didn't win the next project, though, although he did tell me that my price was a little closer.

I spoke with him several more times before the next quote opportunity, trying each time to bring a little value in addition to expanding our personal relationship. But I didn't win the third project either. "Keep sharpening your pencil," he told me. "You're not all that far off."

A month later, I won my first order from him. "I knew you'd figure out the pricing thing," he told me. "You were right in line this time." But here's the thing. *I didn't change my pricing level from the first quote to the fourth one. All four quotes were at our full-margin price.* What changed was the value he placed on our relationship, and because I raised that value, I didn't have to lower my price.

Does that contradict the idea that trust is the critical factor? Not at all, because people don't buy from people they don't trust, no matter how much they like them. (If you think about it, isn't it hard to like someone you don't trust in the first place?) I think the moral of this story is that *time* can work for you too, sometimes just as effectively as an assertive negotiating strategy — as long as you work at building trust and adding value during that time.

Here's some more math that I can't prove, but that I think is pretty accurate.

- You have a 30%-35% chance of winning some business when you approach a negotiation as I have just suggested: value, cost and price — especially when you approached the first meeting as I have suggested and identified some weakness in the status quo.
- You have a 10%-15% chance of winning some business if you undertake the time + trust +value alternate strategy; on the high side if you "click" with the buyer, on the low side even if you don't.
- You have 5% or less chance of winning some business if all you've got going for you is blind persistence.

I hope you'll bring more than blind persistence to the table, and beyond that, I hope you won't be satisfied with the 10%-15% strategy. If you can improve your negotiation skills — even a small improvement in attitude and strategy! — you can make a lot more money.

Pet Snakes — A Story For Business Owners

We know there are *price monsters* in the marketplace, and I hope you've accepted the wisdom of letting someone else sell to and service them. From a time management perspective, you're unlikely to gain a good return on your investment with a price monster. But, they might be of value to your company under very specific circumstances. I'm talking about a buyer with a consistent flow of work that fits your company's capabilities very well, and who is willing to put your company on the "quote list" for all of those projects.

You might think I'm leading toward a "making it up on volume" strategy, but that's not where I'm going with this. I'm thinking more of a "faucet" strategy, and by that I mean quoting all of the projects, but adjusting the price levels depending on how much capacity you may want or need to fill. If things are slow and you want the work, even at low profit margins, you quote low prices. If you are busy and don't want the work at low profit margins, you quote higher prices. I have a client who has embraced this strategy, and he thinks of the two hard-core *price monsters* he deals with as "pet snakes."

"I don't really like them," he once said, "but they're handy to have around sometimes. The estimates are very straightforward, so it's not like we're spending a lot of time on them, win or lose. And while we give them good service on the orders we go after, we don't give them the same sort of *customer care* that we apply to our higher-value customers."

He set up a meeting with one of those "pet snakes" when I made an on-site consulting visit to his company a couple of years ago. It turned out to be the first time the buyer and my client had actually met. "I've been looking forward to meeting you," the buyer said, "cause I've wanted to see what the craziest person on the planet actually looks like."

"What do you mean crazy?" my client asked.

"Well, your pricing is crazy," the buyer said. "Sometimes you're right where you need to be and sometimes you're completely out of the ballpark. I've always wondered if you're a drinking man. That might explain it."

I could see something change in my client's face. "No, it's not drinking," he said, "it's something far more sinister than that."

"Huh?" said the buyer.

"Here's the thing," said my client. "You're what we call a *price monster*, and we can't be consistently profitable at the prices you're willing to pay. If we're slow, I'm happy enough to have the work at those prices, but when we're busy, I don't want to push high-margin work off my equipment to run your low-margin work. The way I look at it, we just sort of keep you around like a pet snake in a cage for when we want some of your work."

I saw something change in the buyer's face then. "I'm not sure I like that," he said.

"I'm not sure I care," said my client. At this point, it seemed like a good time for me to get more involved in the conversation.

"Before you two boys start beating on each other," I said, "let's take a step back and look at the situation. Bob (the buyer), are you satisfied with the quality and service you're getting from Steve (the seller)?"

"Yes," he said. "In fact, up until a minute ago I would have said he was probably the best supplier I deal with."

"So his strategy isn't really hurting you," I said, "and it is in fact helping you. When he wants the work, you get the benefit of dealing with a really good company. He probably makes your life easier in that regard."

"OK," he said grudgingly, "I'll give you that, but I still don't like the idea that I'm being used."

"You're not using him?" I asked. "Seriously, you only buy from him when he has the lowest prices. If you ask me, you're both using each other, and I don't see anything wrong with that. You're getting his level of quality and service at a much lower price than anyone else is when he has capacity he needs filled, and while you're not making him rich, you're at least covering some of his overhead when things are slow. You both benefit! This is a good relationship! And now Steve is going to apologize for possibly being a little too brusque, aren't you Steve?"

By the time we left, 15 minutes later, Bob and Steve had discovered that they belonged to the same health club (Steve noticed an imprinted gym bag in the corner of Bob's office), and that both used to run until their knees and ankles started getting sore. They shook hands a lot more warmly that you might have expected considering the level of stress in the early stages of the meeting. Now, when Bob sends in an order, it's often accompanied by a little gentle ribbing. Steve forwarded me an e-mail in which Bob wrote: "Sorry to hear that things are slow again over there. Don't worry, they'll be better soon, and you can put me back in my cage."

Our Prices Are Too High — A Story For Salespeople

"I'm prospecting like crazy," a salesperson told me, "and people really like me. They all tell me that they'd like to do business with me, but our prices are too high."

"No they're not," I said. "There's nothing wrong with your prices, there's something wrong with your prospects."

"What the hell does that mean?" the salesperson asked.

"What was the total sales volume of your company last year?" I asked in return. The salesperson didn't know, so I told him to find out and then call me back. "Almost $3,000,000," was the eventual answer.

"OK," I said, "that means your prices were perfectly fine for almost $3,000,000 worth of buyers. Go find some new prospects like them. Don't complain about your prices, or the people who *won't* pay your prices. Get back out there and find the people who *will*!"

Remember that the buying side of the world you live and work in is populated by *solids, liquids, gases, players* and *price monsters*. And remember what I wrote earlier about how *price monsters* are the ones who are most likely to talk to you early in the process, since the more salespeople they talk to, the more likely it is that they'll end up with the lowest possible price. Don't be fooled into thinking that price is everything to everybody, and don't *settle* for such shallow prospects. There are value-oriented buyers out there, and they're a lot more likely to pay your prices — especially if you do a good job in identifying their needs and wants and creating an opportunity to convince them that you're better than their status quo.

Price Objections — Final Thoughts

How much should any product or service cost? I've seen a wide range of pricing research, both formal and informal, and both large scale and small. All of this research makes it obvious that different companies and different salespeople place different value on their products and services. In every market I've ever been in, there are suppliers and salespeople who charge premium prices, and also suppliers and salespeople whose only semblance of a marketing plan seems to be offering really low prices. All of those people and organizations get orders, but there's a very direct correlation between premium pricing and profit leadership.

The profit leaders tend to ask *"why do they charge* such low prices?" The low-price sellers tend to ask *"how can they charge* such high prices?" I think the answer to that question can be expressed by a formula: $.V_i = P_p - BD$

The left side of this equation (pronounced point-vee-sub-eye) refers to the Initial Point of Value, which defines the price that the buyer would most like to pay— typically the lowest price being offered on that product or service in the marketplace. According to the formula, the Initial Point of Value is equal to a Premium Price (pee-sub-pee) minus any Benefit Differential.

It might be better to express that a little differently. We could also say that the Benefit Differential — the "more for your money" factor that is usually connected to quality, service and/or relationship — added to the Initial Point of Value equals the Premium Price that can be charged for any particular product or service. In other words, when you give them more, you can charge them more! (As we've discussed, you can also charge them more when you give them *less* — less risk and/or less pain.)

The key, of course, is to communicate that Benefit Differential. The people who do that tend to be both the sales and profit leaders. Here's some more Dinosaur Wisdom, though: *The buyer defines the benefit, not the salesperson!* Or to state that another way, a benefit is only a benefit if the buyer thinks it's a benefit.

The world is full of salespeople who spout benefits that don't resonate with buyers, and that doesn't provide much of a foundation for dealing with the nearly-inevitable price objection. And that takes us back to an element of strategy we've already discussed. The first meeting/substantive conversation between the seller and the buyer represents the end of the *prospecting stage* and the beginning of the *convincing stage,* but most importantly, it is the heart of the *opportunity stage.* The first meeting is all about asking questions to identify real opportunity — either an outright problem to which you have a solution, or some other opportunity to reduce pain or improve on the way they've been doing things. In other words, it's all about figuring out what you're going to talk about when they tell you that your price is too high!

Great salespeople anticipate price objections, and they start looking for *leverage* very early in the selling process. Starting right now, that's something you will share with the greatest of salespeople. Right?

10
Dealing With Customers

As we've discussed, there are four kinds of people on the buying side of your personal sales equation: *suspects, prospects, customers* and *maximized customers.* Now let's tie that into the rest of the selling process I've been writing about.

You're going to evaluate lots of *suspects,* some who will cooperate with the process and many who won't. That's OK, though, because you know that you can't sell to everyone. I hope you also know that it takes relatively few *yes's* to make a good living at what you do — as long as you're willing to look at enough suspects to make the *numbers game* work for you!

The evaluation of lots of suspects will lead you to the qualification of a smaller number of *prospects.* That means you *know* — not just think or hope! — that they (1) buy exactly what you're trying to sell, (2) buy enough of it to make pursuing them worthwhile, and (3) have some real interest in buying from you. You learn/confirm all of that at your first meeting, which represents the end of the *prospecting stage,* the beginning of the *convincing stage,* and the heart of the *opportunity stage.*

Remember, the goal of the first meeting is *not* to make a presentation, but to identify the buyer's *hot buttons* and to help you to shape a *proposal* for solving a problem, relieving some pain or providing some other improvement on the status quo. When you present that proposal, you'll be telling the buyer why you think he/she should buy from you.

Sometimes it works like a charm — suspect > meeting > prospect > proposal > order > *customer.* More often, there are obstacles involved, and the opportunity to apply negotiation skills and strategy. But for most salespeople, someone, at least some of the time, says *yes* and becomes an actual customer. And that is something to be celebrated!

Not Quite!

Let's not get crazy just yet, though, because a *first-time* customer is not the same as a *full-fledged* customer. A first order is not a lifetime contract. The only statement a first-time customer is making is "*I now trust you enough to give you a chance!*"

That means two things. First, unless what you sell is a one-time sale with no further opportunity, it means you have a *customer maximization* challenge/ opportunity in front of you. Second — and more immediately! — it means that you have a *customer satisfaction* challenge in front of you. Or to put that a little differently, if I give you a chance and you perform to my satisfaction, I'll probably give you another chance. If not, probably not!

What that means is that extra care should be taken with the first order(s) from any new customer. For the salesperson, that means checking and double-checking to make sure that all of the "i's" are dotted and all of the "t's" are crossed. But let's make this clear, it is *not** your job to babysit every order through the production/ execution/delivery process!

Please note the asterisk. What I'm trying to say is that it's not your job to babysit every order through the production/execution/delivery process unless it specifically *is* your job. I know of some companies where the salesperson is expected to do just that, and I'm not just talking about one-man or one-woman shops here. I also know many salespeople, though, who spend more time babysitting than they do selling — not because it's part of their job description, but because they have control issues, or simply because they'd rather do "inside work" than prospect for more new business.

I've never completely understood the latter situation, but then, I think the best thing about a sales position is the opportunity to make money. I've always taken *time is money* pretty seriously, and in fact, I've occasionally rebelled against things that took up my time without making me any money. The way I look at it, a little extra time and attention to the first order(s) from a new customer represents a good investment, especially considering the time and effort I've already invested in developing that customer. Once I get a customer to the point where he/she has developed what I call a *buying habit*, though, I want minimal involvement in the orders themselves, so I can spend maximum time on *maximization* activities, and on developing new customers and making even more money!

Control Issues

As for control issues, I've probably heard some variation of *"If I don't do it, it won't get done right or on time"* about a million times. Sadly, sometimes I've been forced to agree with that situation analysis. More often, though, it's been more of a justification for staying inside rather than going back outside. This may shock you, but if you really can't trust the people you work with to carry their share of the load, I think you should quit your job and go looking for a better bunch of co-workers. Before you do that, though, I think you should take a good, long look in the mirror and ask yourself whether you're part of the solution or part of the problem.

Here's some more Dinosaur Wisdom: *As a salesperson, you should view yourself as having two customers, an* external *customer and an* internal *customer.* The *external* customer is the person who gives you the order. The *internal* customer is the person you give that order to — the next person in line in the *workflow* that ends with a finished product. Your job is to provide all of the information that your *internal* customer needs in order to make your *external* customer happy. In other words, you're not the "boss" of the order, you're its *facilitator*, with responsibilities to everyone else who'll be involved in the workflow/production process. If you do that well, there'll be *less need* for you to babysit, and *more time* for you to make real money.

Communication Failures

I hope you'll accept that as a fact, and while we're on that subject, I seem to have three categories of "facts" in my own life. First are the things that I know to be true, and I can prove them. Second are the things that I know I don't know. Third are some things that I know to be true, even though I can't actually prove them. Here's one of the things that falls into the third category — the "fact" that the vast majority of all problems which occur between sellers and buyers *originate* at the point where the specifications of the order are being transmitted between the seller and the buyer. *Transmit* means to *communicate*, and it's not important what mode(s) of communication are involved — spoken words, written words, smoke signals or anything else — what's important is that most of the problems are caused by *communications failures.*

Please think back on this Dinosaur Wisdom: *It is not the buyer's responsibility to communicate with the seller, it's the other way around.* Please also remember that I've referred to buyers as *civilians*; in other words, not *experts* on our products and

services and processes and technologies like we're supposed to be. It is important
— and especially so when we're talking about the first order(s) from a new customer
— that communication occurs, and it's your responsibility to make that happen. So
dot the "i's" and cross the "t's" and *communicate* all of the necessary details
between your external *and* internal customers!

By the way, I think one of those details should be that this *is* a new customer. Your
support people won't necessarily know that, nor will any external suppliers. To me, it
just makes sense to let everyone in the workflow know if a particular order is of
greater-than-normal importance. The same would hold true for the first order(s) after
a quality or service problem with an established customer.

He Didn't Say

Here's a story that comes from my first career, as a restaurant manager. (As I
mentioned earlier, I worked my way through college with a succession of restaurant
jobs, everything from dishwasher to short-order cook. I graduated from the
University of New Hampshire in 1973, with a degree in English Literature, and if you
have one of those, you probably know how little it really qualifies you to do in the
real world. I decided to stay with restaurants, and within a few years, I was the
manager of what was arguably the best restaurant in Buffalo, NY, a steakhouse called
The Crouching Lion.)

The story concerns a rookie waiter, who turned in an order without specifying how
a steak was to be cooked — rare, medium, well-done, etc. The broiler cook reached
out and grabbed the waiter's shirt with his long tongs and asked: "How do you want
this sirloin cooked?" The waiter answered: "I don't know. He didn't say."

The broiler cook reached out again with the tongs, and this time grabbed the
waiter by the ear: "He doesn't have to say, you jackass. You're supposed to ask!"

Remember, it is not the buyer's responsibility to communicate with the seller, it's
the other way around.

Buy Time

Here's a suggestion that might help you to eliminate some quality or service
problems in the future — always try to *buy time* on any order. By that, I mean don't
be so quick to commit to the *shortest* possible delivery time, always try for the
longest turnaround that will still meet your customer's needs.

I was involved in a situation recently where the customer asked: "When can I get this?" The company's "standard" turnaround time for an order like the one we were talking about was three working days, so the salesperson said: "I can have them for you three days after you approve the purchase order."

A better strategy would have been to ask: "When do you *need* them?" — and since I was there, that was my contribution to the conversation. "Three days will be fine," the buyer said. "In fact, anytime before the end of next week will be fine."

The salesperson probably heard "When can I get this" as an expression of urgency. As it turned out, it was simply an expression of interest — a question, in other words. And from the day of the question (a Tuesday, in the morning) to the end of the next week gave the company almost nine full working days to fill the order and satisfy the customer.

As we were leaving, I said to the salesperson: "If he has nine days, we want all nine days, because the more time you have on any individual order, the more likely it is that you'll have happy customers at the end of it." The salesperson countered by asking if it wouldn't be better to push the order through the process at the "normal" pace. "That way," he said. "I won't have to worry about the order being late. Get it done, deliver it early, everybody's happy."

"Well how about this," I asked. "What if he'd said he needed the order by the end of *this* week. That makes it a rush job, right? Something that has to move faster than the normal pace. What would you have said to him then?"

"I'd have told him that I have to check with my operations manager," he answered.

"OK," I said, "then maybe you run into a situation where the operations manager says *no*, because he has another order on the schedule that has to be delivered on Friday, and there's not enough time to complete both of them. But what if that other job was scheduled for Friday, even though it really wasn't *needed* until the end of next week. If he knew that, he could stick your rush order in *ahead* of that one, and the company could end up with two happy customers. You didn't hear what I said, I think. The more time you can buy on any individual order, the more likely it is that you'll have happy *customers* — plural! — in the end."

Three Situations

I hope you'll make *buying time* part of your SOP — <u>S</u>tandard <u>O</u>perating <u>P</u>rocedure. And I think you'll find that you'll run into three situations: (1) they need it faster than your normal turnaround, (2) their need is consistent with your normal turnaround, or (3) they have more time than you need for a normal turnaround. In the first situation, it should be obvious that you have to check with whoever you have to check with before you can commit to a rush order. And you have to understand that, as much as you may want the order, there may be other considerations which make it impossible to meet your suspect/prospect/customer's needs.

I've been in situations where time itself was the obstacle; for example, a printing project requiring 22 hours of production time that my customer wanted to order at the end of the business day for delivery first thing the next morning. I've also been in situations where there was enough time to complete the order, but something more important would have to be bumped in order to make that happen. Life would certainly be easier for all concerned if people didn't leave things for the last minute!

By the way, I hope you were thinking: "Well, how about a partial delivery?" as you read about the situation where time itself was the obstacle. In that particular case, it wasn't an option, but there have been quite a few times in my career when it was.

Normal Turnaround

The *normal turnaround* and *plenty of time* situations provide you with significant opportunity — although two different kinds of opportunity. You'll read about a *plenty of time* situation in a moment (No Problem: Part 1). Right now, I want to focus on the *normal turnaround* scenario, because that's where the greatest opportunity to *buy time* can probably be found.

So here's the scenario: the buyer asks "When can I have this?" and the salesperson asks "When do you need it?" and the answer is exactly the same as the normal turnaround. (For the sake of discussion, let's make that three days from the signed purchase order.) The typical salesperson would probably say "No Problem!"

Here's what an atypical salesperson might say: "I can probably do that, but if it turns out that I need an additional day or two, would that work for you?" *Buy time*, right? That answer might be *no*, but if it's not, I think you want all the time you can get on any order — or to put that another way, I think you want to provide the *production/fulfillment side* of the order with as much time as you can!

I'm pretty sure you've noticed that people often tell a supplier that they have less time than they really do. Do you know why they do that? Probably because they don't fully trust the supplier to deliver on time! So they build themselves a little cushion, and I don't think they think about whether that cushion might affect the profitability of the supplier.

It can, though, and I think it's a salesperson's responsibility to represent his or her company and/or his or her suppliers with an eye toward that profit. This is another example of *time is money* — in this case the *scheduling flexibility* created by a salesperson *buying time* can have significant value.

A Very Atypical Salesperson

OK, an atypical salesperson would ask if another day or two would be possible. Let's say the answer was *sure*. What would *you* say next? Most salespeople would probably say something like: "Thank you, we'll try to get it to you on the day you really want it, and only use the extra days if we really need them."

A *very* atypical salesperson would ask one more question: "One day or two days?"

Here's the point I'm trying to make. The great salespeople don't leave anything to chance. They dot all the "i's" and cross all the "t's" and if there's ever any ambiguity — like one day vs. two days — they get down to the brass tacks! Then they can go back to production or to their supplier and say: "He wants this on Thursday but he doesn't *need* it until Friday. I bought us a day, but that's all the flexibility I could get."

Do you see how that information can be important in terms of production scheduling for maximum profit? I think it's a lot more common, though, for salespeople to lie to the system — if the buyer wants it on Thursday, to tell production/fulfillment that he needs it on *Wednesday*. That's a typical salesperson's way of building in a little cushion, but think about what happens when both the buyer and the salesperson are lying to the system. On one hand, the buyer may have a better chance of satisfaction via an early delivery, and that would certainly benefit the salesperson as well. On the other hand, the *company* might lose the opportunity to fit in a legitimate rush job, and that might penalize another customer and another salesperson.

The moral of this story is twofold: *buy time* and *be honest*. It's been my experience that production — and suppliers — take good care of the salespeople who do both of those things. It has also been my experience that ownership/management takes good care of the salespeople who represent the company well, and here's what *that* means: It is *always* your job to be the advocate of the *customer* to the *company* — in other words, to communicate your customer's needs to your company. It is also your job, though, to be the advocate of your company to the customer, and that sometimes involves being the bearer of unpleasant news. Great salespeople are honest. Period. End of story.

This might be a good time to revisit something I wrote earlier about great salespeople. It's not one big thing that makes them great; it's that they master the *little things* that can make *big differences*.

No Problem: Part 1

I don't know about you, but every time a salesperson says "No Problem!" I start to get worried. More often than not, it seems, some problem does develop, and I don't end up getting what I was hoping to get. I remember an experience, though, when a salesperson used a different strategy. It was a situation where what I was asking for was very reasonable, and there was plenty of time to get it done, and I think 99% of the salespeople in the world would have said "No Problem!".

"I'm 90% sure we can do that," is what this salesperson said. "But let me check to make 100% sure, and if I see any problem, I'll call you before the end of the day."

At around 4:00 PM, my phone rang, and it was the salesperson. "Mr. Fellman," he said, "I promised I'd call if I found any problem with getting you what you want when you want it. I checked with my people, and unless something completely unforeseen comes up, we'll have it to you then. And in fact, if it turns out that we can get it there sooner, will you be ready to take it?"

Think about what transpired here. First, the salesperson differentiated himself by not giving me a shallow, typical, salesperson response. Second, he implied that I'd only hear from him if there was a problem, but then he called anyway to confirm that everything looked good. Third, he qualified his response by saying "unless anything completely unforeseen comes up." Fourth, he presented an early delivery as a possibility without making a commitment to it, setting up the situation where he could "under-promise then over-perform."

Fifth, the last thing he said to me was: "OK, Mr. Fellman, don't hesitate to call me if you have any questions between now and then, and you can be sure I'll be calling you if anything unforeseen comes up." As it turned out, he didn't have to call me with bad news, though he did call me the day after the delivery to make sure that I was happy.

To me, that's a story about six little things that added up to one big thing—a happy customer!

No Problem: Part 2

While I'm on this subject, I'd like to recommend that you take that phrase "No Problem" and remove it completely from your vocabulary. OK, maybe I'm nitpicking again, but "No Problem" has become such a common part of our vernacular that I'm pretty sure I hear it 40-50 times a day, usually as a response to "Thank You!"

Now, think about exactly what you're saying if a customer says "Thank You" and you answer "No Problem" — *"I was willing to do this thing for you because it didn't inconvenience me at all!"* Is that really the message you're hoping to communicate? The proper response, I think, is "You're welcome" or maybe better still: *"You're very welcome and I was happy to do it for you because I appreciate your business!"*

Little things *can* make big differences. And remember, they often define the difference between *good* and *great*

Customer Maximization

OK, I think we agree that it's a good idea to take extra care with the first order(s) from a new customer. I hope we also agree that it's a good idea to *buy time* whenever you can. The combination of those two activities should go a long way toward meeting your immediate customer satisfaction challenge, hopefully resulting in that *buying habit* I wrote about earlier.

But building a *buying habit* is not the same as creating a *maximized customer.* That only happens when you're getting a maximum share of that customer's business, and that may mean covering a much larger portion of your overall product line than the original order(s). Here's an example of what I mean. My nephew, the promotional products salesperson, recently opened a new account with an order for 1000 imprinted pens, and a couple of weeks later, there was a second order for three dozen coffee mugs. So far, so good, but we're still nowhere near complete coverage of his overall product line.

Now, without a great deal of additional effort he might get the next order for pens or coffee mugs or anything similar, but I know he both *wants* and *has* the opportunity to get a lot more than that! First a question, though — and this may seem like it's coming out of left field, but really it is not. Here's the question: *Who is your best customer?*

Best Customer

When I ask that question in seminars, the first response is usually something like "the one who gives me the most business" or "they're all important" or "the one I'm talking to now" or "the one I'm talking to next" — some general description of what it might mean to be someone's best customer. That's not the answer I'm looking for, though, so I specify that I'm not asking for a general description, I'm asking who *specifically* is your best customer.

"Tell you what, " I often say, "if you'll indulge me for a little bit, what I'd like you to do is close your eyes and *visualize* your best customer, standing on a pedestal." I let that go on for a moment, and then I say: "OK, open your eyes, and tell me who's standing there."

The last time I did that, the first person to answer said: "Microsoft." There were a few oohs and ahhs in the room, and one person spoke up and said: "Damn, I'd like to have them as *my* customer." What I said, though, was: "Nope, you're wrong."

I looked around the room, trying to make eye contact with a few people, and then one of them said: "My best customer is a hospital. I don't want to name the hospital, because there are a couple of my competitors in this room."

"I respect that," I said, "but you're wrong."

I looked around the room some more, again trying to make eye contact, until a third attendee spoke up. "Obviously this is some kind of trick question," he said. "Why don't you just tell us what you're driving at?"

"Fair enough," I said. "Here's *exactly* what I'm driving at. None of you will ever get rich taking good customer care of a *company*. (I should probably note that all of the people in this seminar were in *business-to-business* sales, dealing with people at their workplace, not in their homes.)

"I'll grant you that companies have needs," I continued, "but I hope you'll grant me that they don't have any *feelings*. And the whole trust thing — which we've agreed is at the core of the buying decision! — is very much a *feelings* thing. Your customers are not the companies, but the people *within* those companies who trust you to handle some of what they want or need."

Once you understand that, I hope you'll also understand that you can have more than one *customer* within a company — you probably already do! — and you can also have *suspects* and *prospects* within that company. So here's some more Dinosaur Wisdom: *Customer maximization means two things: exploring/educating with your current customers so they know all of what they could be/should be buying from you, and identifying everyone else within the organization who might be buying your products or services.*

Three Levels of Value

Here's another way to look at the customer satisfaction/customer maximization challenge. Each and every one of your current customers provides you with three distinct levels of value. First is the value of what they're buying from you now. Second is the value of what they *could be* buying from you. Third is the value of *influence*; the ways current customers can help you to develop new customers.

What's important about the first level of value is that you *protect* it. What's important about the second level of value is that you *maximize* it. And that's what's important about the third level of value, too — and you do it by *leveraging* that influence.

Protecting The First Level of Value

There are two critical elements to protecting the first level of value: *customer satisfaction* and *customer contact*. The first one is pretty straightforward — meet their quality needs and their service expectations and they'll probably continue to buy from you!

But what if you don't? If you fail on a regular basis, you probably won't keep a customer very long, but what about the occasional quality or service failure? I think we all know that that's possible — and maybe even likely! — and that leads to another one of those "facts" that I know but can't prove: A*nyone who has placed at least ten orders with any company has been disappointed in the quality or service at least once!*

Is that consistent with your experience? I remember a conversation with a buyer who told me that her greatest concern in evaluating a potential new supplier was whether they'd take care of her when something went wrong. And she made it clear that she was talking about *when*, not *if*. "One of my sign suppliers once told me that Murphy's Law runs wild in the sign business," she told me, "and that every order that came into his plant was an accident looking for a place to happen. And this might have been the best sign supplier I ever used! I know they can't always keep their promises of quality, so then it comes down to the promise to take care of me when something goes wrong. Can I trust them to do that?"

There it is again — *trust!* Yes, there have been and will continue to be quality and service failures, but there has never yet been a case where one of those failures ended a relationship. On a much more fundamental level, *the relationships ended because the quality or service failure effected the trust level*, and the salesperson was not successful in restoring that trust.

Restoration Strategy

I hope that tells you something about how you should respond to a quality or service failure. The first step must be to *address the problem* — not to talk about how or why it happened, but to minimize the negative effect on the customer. In recent weeks, I've been involved in three separate situations where the sellers (three of my printing industry clients) had to take immediate action, one that involved a rush reprint, another that involved a physical inspection of 20 cartons of statement forms to make sure that the defective ones were segregated and eventually replaced, and a third situation in which the seller paid for rush shipment of a couple of banners directly to a tradeshow site. In all three situations, the sellers' attitude was *let's get you back in business, and then let's talk about the longer-term implications.*

"I've learned," one of the clients told me, "that you want them to like you when you have to discuss those longer-term implications. You just got done showing them that they can't trust you, and you're going to have to convince them that they can trust you again. The last thing you can afford is one of those 'blame game' situations when tensions are running high."

I think *afford* was an interesting choice of words, and I'll come back to that in a moment. For now, I want you to recognize the importance of *"you just got done showing them that they can't trust you."* Remember what I wrote earlier about *overt* and *implied* promises. You may not actually have said: "I promise that you'll be happy with the quality on this project" or "I promise that it will be delivered on time." But even if you didn't actually speak the words, those promises are *implied* on any order you accept. Here's some more Dinosaur Wisdom: *If a quality or service failure occurred, you broke your promise!*

Temporary Departure

After addressing the problem, your next challenge is to convince the buyer that the quality or service failure was an aberration, a temporary departure from the normal state. Your best strategy, I think, is to *apologize with confidence*. What does that mean? Ideally, you'd like to be able to say something like this: "We don't make many mistakes, and we're all very sorry that we made one that affected you. Here's what we learned from the experience, and how we believe we can prevent this particular aberration from ever happening again."

Now, if this was truly an *occasional* quality or service failure, this strategy has a pretty good chance of working for you. As I wrote earlier, if you fail on a regular basis, you probably won't keep customers for very long. It also helps if they like you at least a little bit, and that takes me back to a promise I made earlier — to note the second of the two instances where the *like factor* is important to a salesperson.

The first is that they like you enough in the very early stages to give you the opportunity to build a relationship based on trust. The second is that they like you enough to give you a second chance when things go wrong. Just remember, they probably won't continue to buy from you just because they like you — remember The Donut Guy's Bad Day! — they will only do that if you're successful at restoring their trust in you.

The "Afford" Issue

There are several layers of cost attached to a quality or service failure. It might cost $1000, for example, to fix a wiring problem with a new electric sign — $10 worth of wire and $990 worth of labor. It could be argued that the labor component of that total is a *soft* cost, since the repair person was going to be paid anyway, whether he/she was working on this problem or on something else, but it's still a cost that has to be considered. It might cost $300 to replace three dozen coffee mugs that were supposed to be white-on-red but got ordered as red-on-white, and that would be mostly *hard* cost, since the mugs themselves would have to be replaced, not just the printing redone.

The point is that there's always going to be a cost attached to resolving a problem. And if you or your company caused the problem, I think you have to bear the cost. What if you didn't cause the problem, though, or if there was shared responsibility? Things get a little grayer then — sometimes quite a bit grayer! — and sometimes it comes down to a decision as to whether a relationship is worth saving.

I can't comment on whether that would be the right decision or the wrong one — it all depends on the specific facts of the specific situation — but I can tell you this: When you dot all the "i's" and cross all the "t's" you have a much better chance of avoiding problems in the first place. An ounce of prevention truly is worth a pound of cure!

I do want to comment on a disappointingly common strategy for dealing with quality failures, though — offering to discount the invoice rather than re-running and/or replacing the sub-standard materials. In my mind, this is the worst sort of cop-out, and it's also really bad business strategy on two different levels. First of all, having shown someone you're capable of *getting it wrong*, I think you need to show them immediately that you're capable of *getting it right*! Second, this discounting strategy establishes your willingness to reduce your price after the fact. Here's some more Dinosaur Wisdom: *Many sellers have learned that many buyers will find post-delivery issues with every order after the sellers established the willingness to try to buy their way out of the problem.*

Contact Failures

There are *two* critical elements to protecting the first level of value: customer satisfaction and customer contact. The issue of *contact failure* relates back to something I wrote back in the chapter on *The Prospecting Stage*, in our discussion of voice mail strategy. As I wrote then, I've seen research which indicates that about 10% of all people who change suppliers say they did so because of quality problems, and another 10% say they changed because of service failures. (Obviously, the salespeople in those situations didn't do a very good job of *addressing the problem* and/or *restoring the trust!*)

Another 15% say they changed because they found "better" prices, and 5% changed for a variety of miscellaneous reasons. The largest group of all, though — fully 60%! — say they changed suppliers mostly because they didn't feel like the one they'd been buying from really valued their business, and over the years, I've heard many variations on that theme: *They were very attentive when they were first trying to win my business, but now I feel like they take me for granted. They used to call on me, now I have to call them. I can't remember the last time anyone over there showed any appreciation at all for the business I give them.*

Here's a quote from a Marketing Manager who now buys all of her printing from one of my clients: "I used to get a monthly call from the (old company's) salesperson, and he used to say 'This is my every-month service call. Do you need me for anything?' Sometimes he also said 'I have an idea I want to share with you' or 'I have some new things to show you.' It was never a hard sell, and I always appreciated the attention. Then that salesperson left, and the only thing his replacement has ever said to me was 'I'm your new sales rep, call me if you need me.' That was probably a year and a half ago, and I haven't called him since. I started ordering from your salesperson, who had been calling on me all along, and I have never looked back."

Interval Strategy

Granted, this was a situation where a new salesperson dropped the ball, but I think the principle is pretty straightforward — if you want to keep your customers, don't leave it up to them to call you! (That's a corollary, by the way, of this Dinosaur Wisdom: *It's not the buyer's responsibility to communicate with the seller, it's the other way around!*)

Here's what I recommend. Go through your customer list and establish an *interval* for each customer — some number of weeks that you will never let go by without either *you hearing from them* or *them hearing from you*. The interval should be related to how much business they give you and how frequently they usually order, and I think two weeks, four weeks and eight weeks might be appropriate options for your top customers, the next level of regular customers, and your "occasional-but-still-appreciated" customers. (It's hard for me to imagine that you wouldn't want to "reach out and touch" any individual customer less than six times each year, which is about what you have on an eight-week cycle.)

Do me a favor, though. Don't ever call me up and say: "Hey Dave, I haven't heard from you for a while!" That happened to me just a few weeks ago — "Hey Dave, I haven't heard from you for a while, and I'm wondering what's going on?" — and I answered: "Let me get this straight. Are you telling me that it's my job to be calling you? No, maybe that's not it, are you *accusing* me of consorting with one of your competitors?"

There was silence at the other end of the line. (I think he might have been wondering what *consorting* means.) Then he said: "I wasn't *accusing* you of anything. I just wanted to check in and see if you needed anything from me."

"Well then why didn't you say that?" I asked him. "Why say something that might be interpreted as confrontational when all you're really trying to do is provide good customer service!"

OK, maybe I'm nitpicking, but I think this is another one of those *little things* that great salespeople do — *little things* that often make *big differences*. Consider the two calls that I've described: "This is my every-month service call. Do you need me for anything?" and "Hey Dave, I haven't heard from you for a while, and I'm wondering what's going on?" Which of those calls would *you* rather be on the receiving end of?

Core Philosophy

Here's some more Dinosaur Wisdom, which has sort of evolved into one of my core philosophies of selling: *You should never expect anything that would not work on you to work for you.* In other words, any time you observe another salesperson's strategy and it turns you off, you probably don't want to be using that strategy in your own selling!

There's a "flipside" to that philosophy that I think is also important: *You have every right to expect that a strategy that does work on you will work on others.* In other words, you should always be paying attention to the way other salespeople sell. Sure, some of what you see and hear will turn you off, but I'm pretty sure you'll also learn things that will impress you and help you to be a better/more effective salesperson.

They say that imitation is the most sincere form of flattery. I say that you should never stop learning!

Education Calls

OK, an interval call strategy will help you to protect the First Level Of Value. It can also help you to maximize the Second Level Of Value. The key is to turn some of your "service calls" into selling calls — specifically into opportunities to *educate* your customer.

Consider this. What percentage of your current customers do you think understands your *product line* and your *strike zone* as well as you do? In other words, what percentage of them fully understands what they *could be* or *should be* buying from you? If you think it's a high percentage, I think you're kidding yourself. As noted, they're *civilians,* and beyond that, most salespeople really don't do a very good job of helping their customers to understand.

What does that mean? Most salespeople's *maximization strategy* consists of a single question: "What else do you buy that I might be able to sell you?" Here's a better strategy. Let's start by *defining* your product line. And then, let's *evaluate* your current customers and determine which parts of your product line they are already buying, and then let's go talk to them about the other parts!

Spreadsheet Format

The best way to do this is a simple spreadsheet. List your top, say, 25 customers in Column A, and then list the main elements of your product line as headers for Columns B, C, D, E and so on. For my nephew, the promotional product salesperson, the categories would include *writing instruments, glassware, trinkets, apparel, medical products, sports-related products*, etc.

If you can picture the spreadsheet, the next step is pretty straightforward. Put an "X" in the box any time *that customer* is buying *that product or service* from you. Put a "Y" in the box if you know *that customer* is buying *that product or service* from somebody else. Put a "?" the box if you're not sure whether *that customer* is buying *that product or service* at all, and put a "0" in the box if you know *that customer* is not buying *that product or service* at all, or that they're buying it from somebody else and you have *no chance* of winning that business.

The "X"s represent the First Level of Value. The "0"s probably reflect dead ends. The "Y"s and the "?"s, though, represent *opportunity* — the Second Level of Value! So, rather than asking your current customers the wrong question — "What else do you buy that I might be able to sell to you?" — let's go to them with something like this: "I've been looking into what you've purchased from me in the past, and I've seen that you've bought a lot of *A* and a little bit of *B*, but you've never bought any *C* or *D*. Is there any *C* or *D* being used in your business? Did you know that they're both part of my product line?"

The answer may be *no, we don't use any of that.* It also may be *yes, we use a lot of that, but we're happy with our current supplier.* If you ask enough people, though, at least occasionally the answer is likely to be *yes, we use a lot of that, and I didn't know I could buy it from you!* Here's some more Dinosaur Wisdom: *Sometimes, all you have to do to get more business from current customers is to* educate *and* ask. Obviously it doesn't always work that way, but if there's an *easy* element to selling, this is probably it!

And remember, by the way, that *we're happy with our current supplier* doesn't necessarily mean that you have no chance at the business. Now that you've determined that they do, in fact, buy that product or service, you can explore their bottom-line level of satisfaction with the status quo. This is another situation where the buyer has *good*, but you may be able to sell *better*!

People Opportunities

Here's another factor to consider. Sometimes it's not that your current customer doesn't fully understand your product line. Sometimes the selling problem is that your current customer is not the right person for that particular product or service! As we discussed earlier, you can have more than one customer within any company, and *customer maximization* is a combination of both *product opportunities* and *people opportunities*.

Again, this is an area where most salespeople ask the wrong question. Most go to their current contact and ask: "Who else in this company buys what I sell?" That's the wrong question for two reasons; first, because the buyer probably doesn't understand the full scope of the seller's product line in the first place, and second, because the bigger the organization, the more likely it is that the left hands won't know what the rights hands are doing!

Here's a better approach. As we discussed earlier it's important to know the titles of the people who order what you sell. For example, it's been established that Human Resources titles buy a wide variety of promotional products. So, if you're a promotional products salesperson like my nephew — and you're not selling anything to Human Resources titles within a company you're getting other business from — the question you really want to ask is: *"Who's in charge of Human Resources?"*

Third Level of Value

That takes us to the Third Level of Value — the value of *influence*, and the ways in which your current customers can help you to develop new relationships. We're really talking about two things here: referrals and testimonials.

Referrals come in two flavors: internal and external. Obviously, "Who's in charge of Human Resources?" is an *internal* referral question, relating to someone in the same company. A more general question might be appropriate for an *external* referral situation; for example, "Do you know anyone else who might have some need for my products and services and might be interested in talking to me?"

That raises the question of when you should be asking for referrals, and as a starting point, I think you should only ask for *external* referrals after you've exhausted all of the *internal* referral possibilities. Why is that? Because it tends to be easier to develop a *horizontal* relationship than a *vertical* one.

Do you see what I mean by that? It's been my experience that the whole process of *suspecting, prospecting* and *convincing* is analogous to *climbing* a ladder — either straight up, or at a very acute angle. *Penetrating* an organization after establishing a relationship with one of the players can be more like *walking* up a ramp. It's not that it's easy, but it's usually not as hard as the initial climb.

I should probably point out that I'm really only talking about the suspecting/prospecting stage of a new relationship here. Remember, *prospecting* is an activity chain that begins with the identification of *suspect* companies, and it ends with your first substantive conversation (hopefully a face-to-face meeting) with the buyer. In the referral scenario, we're not talking about a suspect *company*, but rather a suspect *individual* inside of a company you've already done some business with. You can't fully qualify that individual until you've had that substantive conversation. A referral — specifically an *internal* referral — usually makes it easier to gain a commitment for that conversation.

Introduction

Why is that? The main reason is probably *proximity*, and that leads us to some more Dinosaur Wisdom: *Referrals are great, but there's something even better — an introduction!* Here's an example of the referral conversation I have in mind. You ask: "Who's in charge of Human Resources?" Your current customer (for the sake of discussion, a marketing title) answers: "Annabel Lee." Then you say: "Thank you. I appreciate your help. And in fact, I want to ask you for just a little more help. Would you be willing to walk me over to her office and introduce me?"

Time and distance don't always make that possible, so my backup plan might be: "Would you be willing to make a call or fire off an e-mail to let her know that I'm going to be calling?" The whole idea here is to avoid a *cold call*, and to get a *running start* at setting up a conversation with another suspect/prospect within an organization that's already buying from you. And that's exactly what a referral gives you, a *warm-up touch* and *running start* at both the conversation and the trust-building process that might turn that suspect/prospect into another customer.

On A Pedestal

As I wrote earlier, I use the *pedestal exercise* in seminars to make the point that your customers aren't companies; they're the individuals within those companies who trust you to handle at least some of what they want or need.

I use a continuation of that exercise to reinforce another point. "Please close your eyes again," I say, "and bring back that image of your best customer standing on top of the pedestal. Now open your eyes and tell me what the pedestal is made of."

The most common answers involve granite, steel and money. (I hope you laughed as you read that. The first two are certainly representative of a solid relationship, and the last one, while possibly a selfish perspective, is still a valid one. I'm perfectly OK with you valuing your customers for what they do for you, which is to put money in your pocket!)

After the laughter, I explain that the pedestal I visualize my own customers on is made of brick. "How do you build a brick pedestal?" I ask. The answer I'm looking for is "one brick at a time" — which is exactly the way you build trust, right? It would be nice if all you had to do was walk in and say "Trust Me!" (I don't know about you, but any time I hear those words from a salesperson, I start looking for an exit route!)

Trust takes time to build, which means that seller-buyer relationships take time to build. Once you've built them, though, you can very often leverage them through *referrals* and *introductions*.

External Introductions

It might still be possible to apply an introduction strategy to an external referral. You might remember a story I told earlier, about the salesperson who negotiated a intro luncheon with her customer and three other members of a local business group in return for a small discount on an order. And while "walking me over there" is not as likely on an external referral, a phone call or an e-mail could still do you a lot of good. Anything that warms up your first contact with a buyer is a good thing!

So, obviously, you could ask all of your customers for referrals, both internal and external. I think that raises the question, though, of whether you *should* ask all of your customers for referrals — and I think the answer is *no!* Here's why. When you ask for a referral, you are basically asking your customer to do you a favor. I think you should think about whether your relationship will *support* a favor before you do that.

I am often asked for referrals by salespeople very early in the relationship, perhaps after one or two orders. And in most cases, here's what I'm thinking at that point: *"So far, so good, but I'm not really sure that I'm ready to turn you loose on my family, friends and neighbors!"* Here's another consideration, the best time to ask for a favor is when your customer is happy with you. (The flip side of that, of course, is that you should probably not be asking for referrals right after a quality or service or contact failure!)

Who Else?

Who else, beyond current customers, could be the source of referrals? How about *almost everybody!* I find it interesting that most salespeople seem to understand the concept of asking customers for referrals, but they don't do a very good job of "mining" their family, friends and neighbors. Please understand that I'm not trying to turn you into a sales monster who doesn't think about anything else, I'm just trying to open your eyes to the possibilities. If you pay attention, I think you'll find lots of opportunities to gain referrals from family, friends and neighbors without ever being obnoxious about it.

Please note, though, that I said *almost* everybody. If I were you, I would be very careful about asking current suspects or prospects for referrals. Asking for *names* might be borderline OK, but asking for introductions would not, unless you're *very sure* that the "like factor" you've built will support the favor. The suspect/prospect stage of a relationship really needs to be about *what's in it for them*, not *what's in it for you*! And remember, all a suspect/prospect referral can really say is that they *like you* enough to refer you, while a customer's referral carries the added authority of *first-hand experience* and *trust*.

Testimonials

I'm also a very strong believer in the value and power of testimonials. On one hand, the world is full of salespeople who promise to do a good job for their customers. What's usually lacking is the evidence to support that promise, and that's what a testimonial letter or comment can provide for you.

I made a commitment to myself very early in my career, that anytime somebody told me that they liked doing business with me, or that I had done good work for them, I would ask them to put it in writing. Verbal compliments are always nice, but by themselves they don't do a whole lot for your future. A *written* compliment, on the other hand, has a considerable shelf life — remember what I said earlier about creating your future proposals from "off-the-shelf" components!

I have asked hundreds of customers over the years to write me a testimonial. This may be hard for you to believe, but not one of them ever said no! (Of course, you probably want to keep in mind that I only asked after they told me that they valued my performance!) I've had several customers, though, who promised to write me a testimonial but then didn't follow through on the promise. That raises another question, I think. What should you do in a situation like that? Would it be a good idea to *nag* a customer about doing you a favor?

I think probably not. It's bad enough that we sometimes have to nag them about the details of normal commerce— including little things like paying their bills on time. I *really* don't want to turn a request for a favor into an adversarial situation.

Actually, I remember one specific instance when a customer whom I thought liked me quite a lot promised to write me a testimonial letter and then didn't come through. As I was thinking about calling to remind her, it occurred to me that this might be a wake-up call — that she didn't like me as much as I thought! — and that there might even be some threat to the First Level of Value with this particular customer. So rather than calling to nag her — "Hey, how are you coming with that testimonial letter?" — I called with this question instead: *"Is there anything about our relationship, or about the way we do business together, that you would change if you could?"* (That's the third time you heard me use that particular question, by the way, and I hope you see that it has *defensive* applications in addition to *offensive* ones — offensive is as in *taking customers away from competitors*, not as in *salesjerk!*)

She thought about my question for a moment, and she actually suggested a couple of small things that would improve on the relationship from her perspective. It was obvious pretty quickly that she wasn't mad at me, and in fact at the end of her suggestions she said: "You know, I just remembered, I promised to write you a testimonial letter and I completely forgot. I'll get to that tomorrow!

Looking back on that situation, I think I displayed one of those characteristics of great salespeople that I've been writing about. I didn't *assume*, I found out! And while that certainly represented a happy ending in this particular situation, I'd probably have been just as happy if I'd learned that there was some threat to the First Level of Value — and been able to restore the level of trust and repair the relationship before it turned into a crisis situation!

Reciprocity

Here's another thought on the subject of referrals and introductions. The potential for favors is not limited to current customers or family, friends and neighbors. It also applies to people/companies to whom *you* are the customer. *Reciprocity* has long been one of the guiding principles of commerce. As the old saying goes: "You scratch my back and I'll scratch yours!"

If I were you, I'd start thinking about *reciprocity* and making a list of all of my suppliers, both business and personal. If they buy what you sell, you have some leverage that can be applied to getting them to buy it from you.

Having *leverage* means that you can give them at least a couple of good reasons to buy from you, starting with your *value proposition* and extending to the value of the business you do with them. You can't make them buy from you, though, and that's an important understanding—unless, of course, you do enough business with them to make you the proverbial 800 pound gorilla. (Where does an 800 pound gorilla sit? Anywhere he wants to!)

I would direct my first "reciprocity contact" with a supplier to the person I have the most frequent dealings with, probably a salesperson, but also possibly a CSR, a technician, or even a delivery person. "I'd like to explore the possibility of me being your company's supplier for (what I sell)," I would say, "and I would appreciate it if you'd ask whoever I need to talk to about that to give me a call. Let me also ask you to call me after you've spoken with the right person, to tell me who that is, and when I might expect to hear from him/her."

If a few days went by without a response, I would call my initial contact person to communicate this message: "I'm surprised and disappointed that I haven't heard back from you regarding my request to talk to the person who handles (what I sell) for your company. Let me make two things clear to you; first, I'm not saying that your company has to buy from me, but you do have to *talk* to me. If that doesn't happen, I'm probably going to stop buying from you!"

Don't be unpleasant about this. Your attitude should suggest that you're just stating a fact. But remember, you don't really have any leverage without the threat of taking your business elsewhere. Hopefully you won't have to play that card, but it's there if you need it!

Next Level

When you do speak to the person with decision-making authority, I recommend that you start out by trying to soft-pedal the threat. "I appreciate the opportunity to talk to you about (what I sell)," you might say, "and I want to make it clear that I'm not sitting here right now with the attitude that you have to buy from me or else I won't buy from you. I get value from the money I spend with you, and I'm very confident that you'll get value from any money you spend with me—but the first issue is to talk about your needs to see if there's a match between your needs and our products/services/capabilities."

That should lead you into the same sort of needs-assessment conversation you would have with any other prospect, and remember, in addition to a need, you're also looking for some level of dissatisfaction with the supplier-in-place. It's always easier to convince someone to change when he/she is less than fully satisfied with the current supplier!

Closing Questions

As always, what you learn through your needs-assessment questioning will tell you what to stress in the proposal/presentation stage. Ideally, you'll have identified some problems to which you can suggest solutions. If that's the case, your closing question is "Well, it seems like you do have a problem with your current supplier, and I think we have the solution. What do you think?"

The other side of this coin is when they have no overt problems with their current supplier. In that case, your closing question could be: "Well, it seems like they're doing a pretty good job for you, but let me ask you this. Since we would also do a very good job for you, is there any reason that you wouldn't give us at least some of your business?"

It may be that your supplier does have a reason—valid or otherwise—for not giving you at least some of his/her business. For example, the other supplier might also be a customer, and maybe even a more important customer than you! If that's the case, you may want to exercise your threat and take your business elsewhere.

On the other hand, I'm not suggesting that you cut off your nose to spite your face in a situation like this. Mostly what I want is for you to ask some of the people you buy things from to consider a "reciprocity relationship" which could be a win-win situation for all concerned.

Bad Customers

There's one more important element to consider in this discussion of customers — *what do you do with bad ones?* First of all, I'm pretty sure you'll agree that not all customers are equal in terms of their value to your business. In some cases, that's a reflection of how much they *spend*, but in other cases, it's a reflection of how much they *cost*! My definition of a *bad* customer has two components; first the ones who don't pay their bills are bad customers by any definition, and they shouldn't be tolerated. The second component is simply that bad customers are those who are *more trouble than they're worth.*

OK, what do you do when you have a customer who falls into that category? I'm sure you've heard the phrase *firing a customer*, but that's not what you should do — at least, not until you have tried to change their behavior. This doesn't always work, but I think it's always worth a try! And I think you might be surprised at how often a positive change in customer behavior can be accomplished.

First Step

The first step in this process is to make sure that you *really* understand the problem. I once had a situation where the "bad behavior" was consistently late signoff and return of proofs. (That's a printing industry term for what the printer thinks the printed piece is supposed to look like, submitted to the customer for approval before the actual printing begins. Proofing is an integral part of both the design process and the quality control process.) This was a customer who always had tight deadlines, so we'd put together a tight production schedule, and they'd always foul it up by being late with the proofs — then they'd still expect us to meet their original delivery deadline!

I asked the salesperson handling the account what the problem was. He told me that his contact (a Marketing Coordinator) simply didn't understand the urgency of the schedule. I asked him to set up an appointment with her, and to take me along. It took a few days to set up the meeting, but after just a few minutes of conversation with the Marketing Coordinator, I realized that *she* wasn't the problem. It turned out that she had two Channel Directors and a Vice President in her chain of command, and all three of those individuals insisted on approving every proof before an order could go to press. Apparently there had been a typo once that caused a major problem, and no one wanted to let that happen again.

With this new understanding, I asked the salesperson to invite the Marketing Coordinator, the two Channel Directors and the Vice President to come over for a plant tour. We ended up getting three of the four of them, and the tour emphasized the sheer time it takes for each stage of the production process. We explained how we "backed up" from their delivery deadline to accommodate each stage of production, and we showed them how tight the schedule had to be. At the end of the tour, the general consensus of our visitors was that they had no idea how long everything took, they appreciated us taking the time to educate them, and they committed to making the proofs a high priority. "Carmen (the Marketing Coordinator) has told us that you really need those proofs back faster," the Vice President told us, "but I never really understood why. Now I do. Thank you!"

Another Story

Here's another story about changing customer bad behavior. This one came up with one of my consulting clients, when I made an on-site visit just as a "Job From Hell" was wrapping up. My client had been summoned to a meeting with the buyer, and as we drove over there, he asked me to take the lead at the meeting. "I'm not good at confrontation," he said.

I asked him to tell me the specifics of the situation, and it turned out that about 60% of the problem was the fault of the supplier, with about 40% contributed by the customer. Then I asked him for some guidance on how aggressive he wanted me to be in defending his position. "I figure she's going to fire us anyway," he said, "so you might as well go for it. Take your best shot!"

With those instructions, I opened the meeting by saying: "We appreciate the opportunity to come out here and talk about this, even though you probably hate us right now. Is that too strong a word?"

"Probably not," the buyer said. "You have caused me *huge* problems."

"I understand," I said, "but the thing is, we kind of hate you too." (That was met with utter silence by the buyer, and an anguished sucking of air by my client.)

"Now I'm not trying to be confrontational," I continued, "but we feel that you guys contributed to the problem. So how about this, please tell us your side of this story, and then please listen while we tell you ours. Let's see if we can learn enough to keep something like this from ever happening again."

She spoke for 5-6 minutes, describing her perception of the situation. I nodded my head a lot and took notes. When she wound down, I said: "Most of this happened exactly the way you've described it. We definitely screwed up. But there is more to the story…"

Now I spoke for 5-6 minutes. She nodded her head a lot, although she didn't take notes. And when I wound down, she said: "This is definitely not how I expected this meeting to end, but I realize that I screwed up too, and I'm sorry."

As we drove home, my client said: "We went out there to get killed and we're coming back with a better relationship than I've ever had with her. Amazing!"

Not so amazing. Just good selling strategy. (Remember, by the way, that it's *all selling*, from identifying suspects to setting up meetings to learning about their wants and needs to convincing them to buy from you — and whatever comes after that!)

Identify the problem and then talk about the problem. Sometimes that's all it takes!

Firing Strategy

Sometimes, though, it's not. Sometimes the bad behavior can't be changed. I just hope you'll agree that it's always worth a try!

OK, if you come to the point where a customer has to be fired, how do you do it? The most common approach seems to be a conversation that starts with "We may not be the best supplier to meet your needs..." — a gracious and non-confrontation attempt at ending a bad relationship. I'm all for gracious and non-confrontational, but I don't think this is the best way to fire a customer.

I prefer what I like to call the "Parking Meter" approach, and it's based on the idea that there are two ways to effect the "more trouble than they're worth" equation. One way is to make them less trouble; in other words, the sort of educational conversation described above. The other way is to make them worth more in terms of sales volume and profitability, and you accomplish both of those by raising the prices you quote and charge them. To put *that* in other words, *no more discounts/ low prices for bad customers!*

If you'll embrace this strategy, I'm pretty sure that one of two things is going to happen. One possibility is that they'll go looking for someone with lower prices, and that would certainly accomplish your purpose. The other possibility, though, is that they'll pay the higher prices, and wouldn't that accomplish an even higher purpose? I call it the *Parking Meter Approach*, by the way, because by my definition, anyone who puts enough money in the parking meter is allowed to stay!

Dealing With Customers — Closing Thoughts

I think we've agreed that there are bad customers in the world of commerce. I hope we've also agreed that there's more value in most customers than initially meets the eye. The great salespeople get more of that value than the not-so-great ones, and that's one of the things that differentiates them.

Here's another thing that differentiates them. Great salespeople don't tolerate not-so-great customers. They either change their behavior or they let them cause problems for someone else. In fact, when a great salesperson encounters a not-so-great *suspect* or *prospect*, more often than not, that *potential customer* gets disqualified by the salesperson, not the other way around.

Here's some more Dinosaur Wisdom which I think is elegant in its simplicity: *Let's let the bad customers weaken our competitors.* Remember, the more time and other resources your competitors have to spend dealing with customers who are more trouble than they're worth, the less time and resources they'll be able to spend attacking your good customers. Also remember that you never want to be on the other side of that equation — spending too much of your time and other resources on people/companies who simply aren't worth it.

11
Buying Signals

A lot has been written about selling strategy and technique over the years, much of it contradictory and some of it downright confusing. One of the things that has always confused *me* is an emphasis on the body language of the prospect. I remember another sales training program from my early days in which the trainer demonstrated several examples of body language that he said indicated "I'm ready to buy!" To me, it just looked like he'd had too much caffeine that morning.

I don't reject the idea that there are buying signals, it's just that I've found them to be more audible and behavioral than visual. And in my experience, the importance of body language is more related to "not-buying" signals. For example, when the person you're trying to sell to starts looking at his/her watch or playing with papers on his/her desk, that's probably a pretty good sign that you've lost the initiative.

Early Signals

The great salespeople start looking for buying signals very early in the selling process. "The first thing I hope to see is the willingness just to talk with me," one such salesperson told me. "The 'hard sells' hide behind their secretaries and their voice mail systems, and while that's not to say you don't pursue them — especially if you know that they buy a lot of what you're trying to sell — you still have to recognize that they're not showing you any sort of buying signal and you plan your strategy accordingly. It can be a long haul, just to develop enough of a relationship to get them to talk seriously with you."

The other side of the coin is the prospect who's eager to talk with a salesperson. "That's a great early signal," he continued, "and it usually reflects some combination of three things, two of which are pretty positive. Number 1 is an immediate need, which gets you right into the thick of competition. Number 2 is some level of dissatisfaction with the supplier they've been using, which gives you a competitive edge. Number 3 is the guy who just wants to check your prices, and while that isn't always positive, it at least gets you to the next step in terms of talking to the guy."

It's really important to understand that an invitation to quote is not really a buying signal. At best, it's a *step toward* real interest in buying from you, but often it's not even that. "I'll take a quote from just about anybody," a purchasing agent once told me, "and that's all most of the salespeople who call on me seem to want, an opportunity to quote on my work. I have to admit, though, that I very seldom buy anything from the 'new guys' who give me a few quotes, even if their prices are competitive."

I think most salespeople feel overly positive about an opportunity to quote. Hopefully you're not in that group any more!

A Good Attitude

My own approach to prospecting has always been to look for people with a good attitude. That includes things like taking (or returning!) my phone calls, giving me cooperative and honest answers to my questions, and giving me the opportunity to build the sort of relationship I'm looking for — one that's based on value rather than price. Those attitude and behavioral characteristics are the early buying signals that I'm looking for. When I run into someone who shows me a bad attitude, I make myself sell myself on the idea that this person is worth continued pursuit.

This is important! Most of the salespeople I work with — especially the "selling owners" of small businesses — have significant time constraints. There's a lot more work in their typical day than there is time to do it, and that's usually coupled with a personal preference to do anything rather than selling. The less time you have — or the easier you are to distract from selling activity! — the more important it is that you use your selling time wisely. That means spending it on people who are likely to provide a solid return on your investment.

Remember the definition of a real prospect: (1) they buy, want or need exactly what you sell, (2) they buy, want or need enough of it to make pursuing them worthwhile, and (3) they show some interest in buying from you!

What would make a *suspect* who fails the third test worth pursuing? Only the knowledge that he/she passes the first two tests with flying colors. In other words, someone who buys *a lot* of what exactly what you sell.

Think of it this way: people who buy *just a little bit* are usually about a dime a dozen. That means it's only worth a *little bit of effort to* convince them to buy it from you. If a person with low volume potential shows me a bad attitude, my first impulse is to move on to the next suspect. Once I determine that someone's a marginal prospect in terms of their volume potential, it's a very tough sell to get me to continue the pursuit.

On the other side of that coin, when I determine that someone has large volume potential, I'll hang in for a long time in an effort to develop some interest in buying from me. That can take time, of course, and there's no guarantee of success.

Here's some more Dinosaur Wisdom: *In the suspecting/prospecting stages, you're looking for small customers and large prospects.* If they're small, they need to become customers fast, with a minimum of effort on your part. If they're large, they're worth some time and effort to try to develop real interest in buying from you!

Problems and Opportunities

As we've discussed, any level of dissatisfaction with the current supplier can give you a competitive edge. At the very least, someone who's unhappy with his/her current supplier should be willing to talk to you. Just remember that you still bear the burden of providing a solution to the problem and/or relief for the pain! Most salespeople seem to address this opportunity by *presenting* and then hoping for the best. I can't tell you how many times I've heard some variation of "We had a great conversation" or "He seemed really interested."

These are viewed as buying signals, perhaps, but they're not tangible enough for me. As we've discussed, I'd rather see you flat-out ask your prospect how you did. *Does my proposal make sense to you? Does it seem like a good solution to your problem? Do you think it will provide relief for your pain? Are you sold on the idea of buying from me?*

I think that takes us to the bottom line on *buying signals.* The whole idea is pretty interesting, but great salespeople don't put much stock in a strategy that might fail because a signal was misinterpreted. Great salespeople have the *Courage to Question* that I wrote about all the way back in Chapter 1. They ask provocative questions and they usually profit from the answers — even when the answer is "No, I'm not convinced yet."

So, let's be concerned less with *interpreting* buying signals and more with *making* the sale!

12

FAB and FABEA

Everyone in sales should be familiar with the FAB formula. The basic idea is that every product has *features*, which in turn create *advantages*, which ultimately provide *benefits*. It's been my experience, though, that most salespeople don't use the FAB formula very effectively in their selling, and many don't really understand the way it works in the first place!

The confusion seems to center around the A̲dvantage part of the formula, and specifically about who gets this advantage. It's not the customer! When FAB is applied properly, it's the salesperson!

The key to making the FAB formula work for you is to identify F̲eatures of your offering which provide you with a Competitive A̲dvantage and provide a B̲enefit to your customer as well. If there's no A̲dvantage, you're probably selling a commodity, and the only F̲eature that's likely to help you there is a low price.

An Example

One of the *features* that many of my printing industry clients are promoting these days is online ordering — a capability that applies to a lot of other industries. The *benefit* to the buyer starts with ease-of-ordering, but for many buyers — or more accurately, for many *influencers/originators* — consistency and control are even greater benefits. I think it's fair to say that most printing salespeople don't go much further than talking about ease-of-ordering in their presentations.

The top performers, though, understand all of the potential benefits of online ordering, and they also understand the need to create a competitive *advantage*. So the first part of their selling process is to probe with questions, hoping to find need for or interest in "second-level" benefits. Then, in the presentation stage, they're positioned to say "*Our* online ordering system can do that!" It may very well be that the competitor's online ordering system can do it too, but the points go to the salesperson who takes full advantage of his/her product and service capabilities.

Cui Bono

I read a lot of crime novels, everything from detective stories to courtroom dramas, and one of the key concepts of law and law enforcement I've read about is *cui bono*, Latin for *who benefits*? The basic idea is that, to solve a crime, you look for the person or persons who gain the greatest benefit from it.

Cui bono has applications in selling as well, and that leads directly to another piece of Dinosaur Wisdom: *The person most likely to support a change in the status quo is the person who stands to gain the most from that change.* The complicating factor for many salespeople is that it may not be the person they're currently talking to, or even getting orders from!

When you apply *cui bono* to online ordering of printing, for example, you find two people in most large companies who appreciate the benefits. I call them *the keeper of the company image* and *the watcher of the company money*. *The keeper of the company image* is the person who cares most about the consistency of a company's printed image. That may be the artist who created the logo, or the person in the marketing department who's been pushing a branding program. Consistency of image is one of the key benefits of online ordering, and it's a proven cure for the situation where different people all over a company are ordering different-looking stationery, business cards or other printed materials.

The *watcher of the company money* is a person who's concerned more with *cost* than *price*. This is a person who would appreciate that each individual order might cost more with online ordering — and it often does! — but the overall cost of processing all those orders would be reduced. That may be the Comptroller or possibly the CFO, but it might also be a fairly junior person in the Accounting department who would look good to his/her superiors by championing a cost-saving change to the status quo. It would probably *not* be a purchasing agent. Do you see why? Purchasing agents tend to deal with *price*, not *cost*. I've found that it's a stretch to get many of them to even appreciate the difference.

FEBA

I met a salesperson some years back who introduced me to a new wrinkle on the FAB formula. He was relatively new to his industry, but he had more than 10 years of sales experience as a recruiter for the US Army. In that job, he was taught the FEBA formula, which stands for Facts, Evidence, Benefits and Agreement.

Facts and Features are identical in the application of this selling strategy, and Benefits are too. The difference, of course, is the addition of Evidence and Agreement. The basic idea is that you provide solid evidence to support your benefit claims, and then you ask for commitment.

What sort of evidence are we talking about? Let's say that your questioning process identifies some level of dissatisfaction with the quality a prospect has been getting from another company. Most salespeople would probably address Evidence by showing samples or photos of their own best work, but the great salespeople know that all those samples really prove is that a company is *capable* of producing high quality products. The question in the prospect's mind is: "How do I know that *my* product will look this good?"

I listened to one of my clients explain once that his company's quality control procedures are his most significant competitive advantage, and as evidence, he walked his prospect through a pretty detailed description of that quality control process. "The benefit to you," he said, "is that our attention to detail all through this process is what assures your satisfaction at the end of the process." Then, he handed the prospect three testimonial letters written by current clients. "Now if you'll read these," he said, "I think you'll see that there's more going on here than just a salesman talking. These people took the time to write to let us know that we've consistently met and even exceeded their quality expectations. I think that should give you confidence that you'll have the same sort of experience!"

Agreement

As you might imagine, I listened with pleasure as my client led that conversation. Unfortunately, he didn't take the next step, so I jumped in and asked: "So, does it?"

The buyer said "Excuse me?"

"Does this knowledge of our quality control program and these letters give you confidence that you won't have the same sort of quality problems with us that you had with the other folks? I guess what we really want to know," I said, "is if we've sold you. If you had an order on your desk today, would we be getting it?"

"Well," he said, "your price would have to be competitive."

My client jumped back into the conversation. "Do you remember what you paid for your last order, even just a ballpark figure?"

"Somewhere around $6000," the prospect said.

"OK," said my client, "if my quote on that same project was, say $6300 or $6400, would you consider that competitive?"

There was silence for a moment, and then my client spoke again. "Well, I'm pretty sure we'll be competitive. The important thing is that you believe in our quality. Did we at least convince you of that today?"

The prospect said *yes*, so we accomplished some level of Agreement. I think it's worth mentioning, though, that my client made a tactical mistake by filling the silence that followed his next-to-last question. If he'd waited for an answer — forced the prospect to answer! — we might have accomplished even more on this call. He had *Courage to Question*, but he didn't hang in there long enough to get the answer. We covered that in the "debrief" after the call, though, and I think he'll handle this sort of situation better next time.

FABEA

I think the best "acronymic" selling strategy for a modern salesperson is a combination of FAB and FEBA. Let's call it FABEA — Features, Advantages, Benefits, Evidence and Agreement.

If you want to be a top performer, your first step has to be a complete understanding of your capabilities, and the competitive advantages they provide you with. Then you go looking for situations in which these Features and Advantages provide a Benefit to a prospect or customer. But don't think it will be enough just to tell people how cool you are! Be prepared with Evidence to support your claims, and when you've put all of that on the table, don't forget to ask for Agreement and commitment.

The C Myth

While I'm on this particular acronymic mission, I want to introduce you to "The C Myth." Michael Gerber wrote a book called "The E-Myth: Why Most Small Businesses Don't Work and What to Do About It." *(Harper Business, 1988, ISBN 978-0887303623)* "The C Myth" is the idea that all selling should be targeted at the C Level (CEO, COO, CFO etc.)

In theory, it certainly makes sense to be talking to the *top dog*. In practice, though, most salespeople can't get anywhere near the C Level in most big companies, and beyond that, not every salesperson is really equipped to sell at that level. That's OK, though, because lots of purchasing decisions are either made or influenced at the D Level and the M Level — Directors and Managers — and that's where I think most of your initial sales efforts should probably be focused.

Please note my use of the word *initial*. I want you to build toward C Level relationships eventually. I just don't want you slamming into predictable and probably insurmountable roadblocks by trying to start there. And please note that you may very well be able to start with the president/owner of a small company, especially if you're the president/owner of your company. It's the idea of C Level selling at a big company that I'm talking about here. That would certainly encompass the Fortune 1000, but I think it also applies to most of the companies and/or organizations you'll find on those Top 10/25/50 lists that the business journals and Chambers of Commerce publish.

Now think back on what I just wrote about the *watcher of the company money*, and how that might be a fairly junior person in the Accounting department who would look good to his/her superiors by championing a cost-saving change to the status quo. Many sales trainers advocate selling from the top down. I've always had better success selling to someone who's *on the way up!* Here's some more Dinosaur Wisdom: *When you need to change the status quo, you need to find people who are both* available *and* open to change!

13
Transparency

"I can see right through you," said the buyer to the salesperson. "I know exactly what you're trying to do!"

Question: Is that a good thing or a bad thing? Answer: I think it's a *very* good thing. I believe that the best selling is highly transparent — no tricks, no games, and no subterfuge. The great salespeople don't trick anyone into buying from them; they help their prospects and customers to reach an unmistakable conclusion. When a great salesperson makes a sale, there's no "buyer's remorse", just the confidence that comes from making a good decision.

Selling Is A Game

I should probably clarify this point: the great salespeople don't "play games", but many great salespeople look at selling itself is a game. I think that's a healthy attitude, especially considering that salespeople "lose" more frequently than people in most other job categories. The great salespeople probably lose less frequently, but you still can't win 'em all, no matter what game you're playing.

(Actually, you can win 'em all, over a short period of time. That's called a *streak*. You can also lose 'em all over a short period of time. That's called a *slump*. Great salespeople have both, and just like great athletes, they know both will end. With a *streak*, you try to keep it going by continuing to do what's been working for you. With a slump, you try to make it end by examining what you've been doing and making any changes/adjustments that seem necessary. Just like any other game, selling involves strategies and skills, and you can improve your performance by refining your strategies and/or improving your skills.)

Similarities and Analogies

The "selling is a game" discussion comes up early in most of my seminars. After we agree that it's a healthy way of looking at the job, I ask attendees to consider the similarities/analogies between selling and some other popular sports and games.

Fishing is often suggested as an analogous challenge, and when I ask why, the answer usually has something to do with being in the right place with the right bait. Tennis is another common answer, with its element of each party putting the ball back in the other's court. Chess is another common analogy, and lately I've been hearing a lot about the similarities between selling and poker.

I think those two in particular can help me to make my point, because I think selling at its highest level is a lot more like chess than like poker. Think about the two games. In chess, the whole tactical situation is right out there in front of both players. You won't always know what your opponent is planning to do, but you always know what he/she *can* do. The pieces have proscribed moves, and the player can't change what they can do in the middle of a game.

In poker, on the other hand, there is always hidden information, known only to one player, and because of that, the element of bluffing is of major importance. Now, I'll grant you that there's often an element of bluffing when you get to the negotiation stage in sales, but my point is that bluffing becomes less necessary the more transparent the selling process is up until that point. In other words, the greater the trust, the less important the price!

Transparent Strategy

I've described a selling strategy which includes an introductory letter or e-mail. The gist of that communication is *I'm interested in you (because...), and I think you might be interested in me (because...), so I'm going to call you and ask you to agree to a meeting.* It's pretty straightforward, and I hope you'll agree that it's pretty transparent. To look at it another way, this letter or e-mail says *this is why I'm writing to you and this is what I'm going to do next.* It does not say a great deal about products or services or capabilities or technology or anything else that might be described as a benefit of doing business with you. Why? Because you can't sell that stuff in a letter! The letter or e-mail is only a tool to help you get to that first substantive conversation!

When you make the follow up call, it should also be pretty straightforward: "Hi, this is (your name) from (your company). I wrote to you recently, and I promised that I'd be calling to see if we can set up an appointment. Are you interested in meeting with me?"

Bad Strategy?

I remember being told once that that's a terrible question. "You're just asking for a *no*!" the salesperson said. "You're not going to sell much that way."

"I'm not afraid on a *no*," was my answer. "And I'm not trying to sell my products or services at this point. I'm only trying to sell the meeting. So why not go straight at the issue?"

Here's why I'm not afraid of a *no*. It would give me the opportunity to say something like this: "Before you give me a final *no*, let me tell you exactly what I was hoping to accomplish in a meeting. I have a bunch of questions I want to ask you, some of them about what you buy, but most of them about the way you buy it and receive it and distribute it and the way it works for you. I'm hoping that you buy, want or need exactly what I sell, and if you don't, I'll tell you that right away because I don't want to waste either of our time. Beyond that, though, I want to explore whether there might be a better way to do what you're doing. I'm one of those consultative sales guys, and that, more than anything, is where I think I might be able to bring some value. So let me ask you again, are you interested in meeting with me?"

Meeting Strategy

As we've discussed, I would start out the meeting exactly the same way, with an "opening statement" of my goals and objectives. And let me stress again that this would *not* be a presentation. I don't want to talk about products or services and features or benefits, I want ask questions and talk about *needs* and *wants*! I want to learn what features and benefits would be important to this particular buyer, so I can stress them when I get to the proposal stage of the process. Most salespeople seem to take a "shotgun" approach to selling; in other words, blasting out everything they've got, as quickly as they can, in the hopes that something will hit the target. The great salespeople take a far different approach.

Here's something else the great salespeople know. When you start each stage of the process with a statement of your goals, you can close with a simple question: "How did I do?"

Think about that. You start by telling them what you're hoping to accomplish, and then you close by asking them if you were successful. No tricks, no games, and no subterfuge — just a highly transparent process of open and honest communication.

Here's some more Dinosaur Wisdom: *If that's the way you'd like to buy, it's definitely the way you want to sell!*

14

The Winds of Change

It's been said that nothing is as constant as change, and I think the modern marketplace is living, breathing proof of that old adage. If nothing else, technology has brought incredible change — both to our industries and to our customers' workplace.

Dealing with change is one of the basic challenges of business today, and obviously, some salespeople are handling it better than others. At least, that's true of changes that are "internal" to their industries. I've observed, though, that there are a few "external" change situations that seem to be problems for everyone, even the most progressive salespeople.

One of the most common — and problematic — of those is the situation where change occurs at the customer's workplace; specifically where things change or people change in the customer's organization.

New Buyer, Big Problem

Here's a question I'll bet you've never thought about. How many people will be cleaning out their desks today, and leaving their current position? How many of those people will be moving to something else within their company? How many will be moving to a new job in a completely different company? Based on the size of our population and our economy, I wouldn't be surprised to find that the number of people leaving one job or starting a new job runs in the tens of thousands each and every day.

Now the vast majority of those changes won't affect you at all. I think we're pretty safe in saying that most of the people changing jobs every day have absolutely nothing to do with purchasing whatever it is that you sell. But I also think I'm safe in the speculation that at least two or three decision-makers or decision-influencers do change within your customer base each month!

Think about it! If you're at all typical of the salespeople I work with, your customer/prospect list probably numbers between 200-500. Many of these could be small companies, and the person placing the orders is often a *money-spender* who works at the direction of someone else.

So here's what you have to consider. If you have 200 companies on your customer list, there might be 400 or more people involved in the decision to buy from you. If any of them change jobs, your relationship with that company could be in danger!

Staying On Top Of Change

The first issue we have to consider is staying on top of your customer base, so you know early on when changes are being made. Experience has shown that the earlier you know, the more likely it is that you'll survive personnel changes among your direct contacts and the people who influence their decisions.

This is another application for the *interval strategy* I wrote about earlier. Go through your customer list and establish an interval for each customer — some number of weeks that you will never let go by without either *you hearing from them* or *them hearing from you.* The interval should be related to how much business they give you and how frequently they usually order, and I think two weeks, four weeks and eight weeks might be appropriate options for your top customers, the next level of regular customers, and your "occasional-but-still-appreciated" customers. (It's hard for me to imagine that you wouldn't want to "reach out and touch" any individual customer less than six times each year, which is about what you have on an eight-week cycle.) And ACT, of course (or any other contact manager) is the tool you use to keep track of your interval strategy.

S/he's Not Here Anymore!

So let's say that you haven't heard from Jane Doe at ABC Company for six weeks — the interval you've established for her — so you call to check in. You ask for Jane, and you're told that she no longer works for ABC Company!

I would want to know three things at this point: (1) Who is/will be handling her responsibilities, especially in terms of buying what I sell? (2) Is this person a long-time employee of ABC Company, or a new hire? (3) Who was Jane's immediate superior, and does the new person report to the same boss? (By the way, if you're really on the ball, you already know who your key contacts report to in their own business structure!)

The first of those questions is obvious, I'm sure, but let's explore the reasoning behind the other two. If Jane's replacement is a long-time employee of ABC Company, he/she may already be familiar with the relationship between your two companies. That may provide an incentive toward continuing to do business with you, but then again it may not. The best advice is to *take nothing for granted!* And if Jane's replacement is a new hire, the likelihood increases that he/she will have knowledge of — or relationships with — one or more of your competitors.

Here's what I'd say to Jane's replacement, regardless of whether she was a long-time employee or a new hire: "I enjoyed my relationship with Jane, and I think she always felt good about it too. And I definitely want to keep ABC Company as a customer. But I recognize that Jane is gone, and that I'll have to earn and keep *your* trust and confidence in order to keep ABC Company as a customer, so what do you say I come over there and we start getting to know each other? I can tell you about the things we've done for your company, and hopefully, you can tell me something about your plans."

Please keep this in mind — *you can't just say those words, you have to mean them!* It may not seem fair, but when things change in a customer's organization, your relationship with that company is going to change. If nothing else, you'll have to get used to working with a different person, and things may not go as smoothly as they have in the past. It's your responsibility to make sure that the first order(s) you get from a new key contact go just as smoothly as you'd want the first order(s) to go with a completely new client organization.

Promotions And Transfers

What if your "interval" call reveals that Jane Doe still works for ABC Company, but she's been promoted or transferred and her new responsibilities don't include ordering your products or services? In this situation, you'd obviously still want the name of her replacement, and knowing something about that person's longevity with the company and reporting relationships would still be relevant. But don't stop there! Here's a situation where your "old" customer could be very helpful in building a connection with your new "prospect."

At the very least, I would ask Jane if she had mentioned me to her replacement, and if she could give me any suggestions on how to approach this person. At the other end of the spectrum, the *best case scenario* would be to arrange a visit where Jane would actually introduce me to her replacement.

This is something I've done quite a few times in my own career. One of the most successful examples I remember was a situation in which I invited one of my "Jane Doe's" to lunch to celebrate her promotion and thank her for all of the business she'd given me. When I called to set this up, I said: "Maybe when we get back from lunch, you'll have a minute to introduce me to your replacement." Jane said: "I'll do even better than that. If you want, I'll ask her to come out with us!"

It turned out to be a very interesting lunch. The first thing the new person told me was that she'd worked with several of my competitors at other jobs, and she intended to do business with people that *she* was comfortable with. Then Jane piped in and said: "You ought to at least give Dave first shot at keeping the business, because he's done a lot of good things for our company." She then proceeded to tell stories about several of my "heroic" efforts.

The result? I was given first shot at keeping the business, and that's all I needed! I made sure that the first few things we did for the new buyer went smoothly. I brought her in for a tour of our facilities, made sure to ask often if she had questions about the way we did things, and then answered her questions thoroughly. The bottom line is that I didn't treat her like an "old" customer until I had turned her into one. I'm not sure it would have ever gotten that far without Jane's help.

Upper Level Influence

Not every "change" situation has gone so smoothly for me, though. I remember another case where the new decision-maker was especially independent. He wouldn't even take my phone calls, and at one point, he had his secretary tell me that he had his own ideas and his own suppliers, and even though I'd done a fair amount of work with his predecessor, he was going to stay with the people he knew.

After that conversation, my next call was to his boss (the same person my "old" customer reported to. I had never met the man, but I'd made it my business to know who he was.)

I explained who I was, and said something like this: "I had a pretty good relationship with 'John Doe' and from everything I heard, we never let him or your company down. Now 'John' is gone, and I can't even get the new guy to talk to me. I would never presume that we're automatically going to keep your company's business, but at the very least, I feel like we deserve a chance to sit down face-to-face with the new guy and make our case."

This executive agreed, and promised to talk to John's replacement. Within a few days, the new guy called me and we set up an appointment. It wasn't an easy meeting, but we found enough common ground that he was willing to talk to me again. Over the next couple of months we met several more times, and by the end of six months, I was handling a fair amount of business for this company again. I never got it all back, but I didn't lose it all either!

Now, there's unquestionably some risk involved in going over a buyer's head the way I did, but the way I looked at it, I had already lost the business! The only question was how *hard I would fight to get it back!*

Both Ways!

The two key issues in dealing with change within your customers' organizations are to stay on top of it and then to react intelligently when you discover it. I can't guarantee you that you'll always keep the business when things or people change in your customers' organizations, but I can tell you that you're a lot better off taking a proactive approach — to both key issues!

By establishing a contact interval for each of your important customers, you at least cut down on the length of time that you might be "in the dark" about a personnel change. The shorter that timeframe, the more likely it is that you'll make contact with the new person before he/she gets into the habit of buying from someone else.

And by treating a new buyer like a *prospect* instead of assuming you've still got a *customer*, you'll go a long way toward keeping the business you've been getting from that company! Remember, that may include fighting for the business!

And here's something else to remember. Change doesn't only occur in your customers' organizations. It also occurs pretty regularly in organizations you've tried in the past to turn into customers. The person who's said *no* to you in the past may be replaced by a person who'll say *yes* to you in the future, provided, of course, that you're still out there fighting for new business.

I know that it's easy to get depressed by change that hurts you. Here's some more Dinosaur Wisdom: *The winds of change can blow both ways!*

Value vs. Pain

I have stressed throughout this book that the great salespeople sell *value*, and one of the ways they do that is to identify *pain*. Preventing that pain — or making it go away — reflects considerable value in the minds of most buyers.

It occurred to me that those buyers might have some very interesting things to add to our understanding of *value* and *pain*, so I called a whole bunch of them up and asked them to tell me what hurts and what doesn't. Here are the Top 10 lists that resulted:

Value

At the top of the list of things that create value is **Advice** — defined as the salesperson's willingness to offer suggestions that lead to either improved performance or a lower price. The buyers I spoke with made it clear that it's not always about price, though. "I buy a wide variety of things that make our company go," one said to me, "and I'm not as knowledgeable about all of those things as I would like to be — or as my boss probably thinks I am! A lot of, quote-unquote, 'my' ideas have improved our business, but I have to be honest with you, most of those ideas came from my suppliers. I want to buy from people who make me look good!"

Here's the rest of the list:

2. Familiarity: "The more any supplier knows about our business and the way we do business, the better they'll understand and be able to meet our needs."

3. Absolute Honesty: "Don't hide bad news from me, and don't ever put me in a situation where it's the last minute and I don't have any options. If you can't do something, tell me up front, or else the very minute after you realize we've got a problem."

4. Price: "You don't have to have the lowest price, although you do have to be competitive. The more you give me in terms of value, the more I'm willing to pay."

5. Dependable Quality: "I want all of my orders to look just as good as those samples you've shown me."

6. Sensitivity: "You have to understand that I don't set the deadlines, they're imposed on me by the people I work for. I understand that I cause problems for you, but you need to understand that I'm really passing along a problem that's been dropped on me. If you can help me solve my problem, I'll love you."

7. Additional Services: "When I find someone I like doing business with, I want to do as much business with them as I can. You can't believe how excited I was when I learned that my website guy can also help me to design our catalogs."

8. Desire: "You can see the difference in service when a salesperson really wants you as a customer. I've worked with some who never showed me that, and that's why I don't work with them anymore."

9. Flexibility: "The only constant in my business is how fast things change. I need suppliers who can keep up with the change."

10. Predictability: "I want to know what I'm getting, in terms of quality, service, everything. If I can count on that, I'm a very happy camper."

Pain

At the top of the list of things that cause pain is **Complicating My Life**. "I have a million things going on on a good day," one buyer told me, "and the fact of the matter is that I need help. I need suppliers who will simplify my life, not make it more complicated. I'm even willing to pay more for a helpful supplier, but I won't keep on using one who makes things worse instead of better."

Here's the rest of the list:

2. Unreliable/Inconsistent Service: "I need to know that I can trust you to deliver on time, and to keep me advised about any problems so they don't turn into bigger problems."

3. Unreliable/Inconsistent Quality: "Nothing makes me crazier than when one order looks great and then the next one looks awful. It is really that hard to produce consistent quality?"

4. Miscommunication/Untimely Communication: "It's hard to trust a salesperson who tells you one thing and then a completely different thing happens. And why do they always wait until the very last minute to tell you about a problem?"

5. Order/Acknowledgement Problems: "I still don't understand why they bounce so many orders back to us, saying they need more information. Aren't they supposed to be the experts? If we're doing it wrong, teach us how to do it right!"

6. Untrained Salespeople: "I think I know more about the products than my salesperson does, and I probably know more about selling too. She's nice enough, I guess, but she's really not good for much more than picking up orders and having someone from her office call me back to answer my questions."

7. Additional Charges: "I award the order based on the quoted price, and then I find out that it's a whole different price. If you want to keep my business, you'd better be able to tell me up front how much it's going to cost, and spell out all the possibilities for additional charges so I can avoid them."

8. Procedures Violations: "We have proscribed ways of doing things — requisitions, purchase orders, shipping standards and a requirement for a packing list with every delivery. All our suppliers know this, but they still mess up our procedures most of the time."

9. Lack Of Responsiveness: "There generally are only two times when I'll call a salesperson — when I have something (an order) for them or when I need something from them. Either way, I want to hear back from them quickly."

10. Lack of Empathy: "If my suppliers had to walk in my shoes for a while, I think they'd understand why I'm a 'demanding' customer. I try to understand their problems, but they have to understand mine too."

Two Sides Of The Coin

I think the thing that struck me most about these conversations with buyers is that their perceptions of value and pain reflect two sides of the same coin. In other words, if you give them what they're looking for they look at that as value, and if you don't give them what they're looking for, they experience it as pain. So as Yogi Berra might have said, "All you have to do to have happy customers is to make them happy."

Remember, though, that you can't sell to everyone and you don't really want to sell to everyone. The happiest salespeople I know are the ones whose understanding of value and pain is the same as that of their customers. Here's some more Dinosaur Wisdom: *When there's a good fit, there's usually a good relationship — defined as maximum value and minimum pain on both sides.*

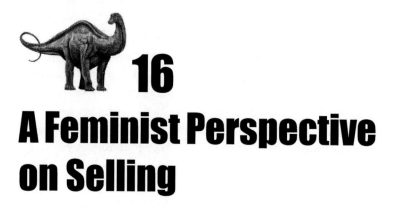

16
A Feminist Perspective on Selling

I can imagine your reaction upon seeing the title of this chapter. "The Old Dinosaur must have interviewed a woman to come up with a feminist perspective on selling." Nope, I didn't need to do that, because I am, in fact, a feminist. I became one on June 12, 1985, the day my daughter was born.

Like many men of my era, I didn't have a whole lot of interest in "women's issues" until I had a tiny one of my own to care about. It was pretty amazing how my perspective changed, and how important things like equal opportunity and equal pay have become. And from my perspective, the sales arena is a pretty good place for women to be in the early 21st Century.

Customers and Salespeople

I don't have any formal research to support this statement, but I think it's pretty widely accepted that the majority of buyers in most product/service categories are women. It may not be true that the majority of *ultimate decision-makers* are women, but the people who place the orders certainly tend to be.

The people who take the orders in many product/service categories also tend to be women — a group which includes both salespeople and customer service employees.

In some categories — construction, for example — there's probably still a bias toward men in the sales role and women in the customer service role. Happily, in most other industries, that bias isn't as strong. In fact, there's a bias *toward* women in the sales role in many segments, for two good reasons and one bad one.

The first good reason is that the majority of buyers seem to be women. The second good reason is that women tend to be less ego-driven and more empathetic than men. The bad reason is that women are often more "affordable" than men — in other words, their compensation requirements are often lower, allowing a company to hire "more woman for the money." From an employer's perspective, of course, that's not a bad thing, but it still offends my feminist sensibilities.

Two Good Reasons

The "two good reasons" are very much interrelated, but I may have to take you off on a little tangent to understand why. That tangent is the idea that most people hate salespeople. In truth, I don't think *hate* is the emotion most people feel toward salespeople, I think it's *fear*! They're afraid that some slick-talking salesperson will push them into making a bad decision!

Men may have less of that fear — or we may hide it better! — but the greater empathy of women tends to make this less of a problem in the first place. If both men and women are less afraid of female salespeople — and if women are more prevalent on the buying side of the equation — that's a pretty strong argument for women in the selling role!

I realize that what I'm about to say next might seem discriminatory, but I want you to read it carefully. *If all other qualifications are equal*, I would choose a woman over a man for a sales job just about every time. Will all other qualifications ever be equal? Probably not. But I do believe that a "typical" female has an advantage over a "typical" male in doing this particular job.

Ego Drive vs. Empathy

In saying that, I draw a distinction between the two most critical elements of selling skill — organizational skills and convincing skills. I draw a further distinction between convincing skills and a convincing attitude. In other words, there's a difference between having the ability to bring someone around to your way of thinking and having a burning desire to do so. That burning desire is often referred to as *ego drive*, and it's one of the characteristics that sales suitability profiles are designed to measure. *Empathy* — defined as the ability to identify with and understand another person's feelings or difficulties — is another of those characteristics.

For most employers, the perfect sales candidate would possess both strong empathy and a strong ego drive. Unfortunately, perfect candidates have proven to be relatively few and far between, especially at the lower ranges of the compensation scale. What employers generally get is a choice, either empathy or ego drive, and my observation is that most of the high empathy/low ego drive candidates seem to be women, while most of the low empathy/high ego drive candidates seem to be men.

So the question is, which is more important? My answer is that I've had lots of success teaching high empathy/low ego drive salespeople to be more *assertive*. In other words, I've been able to develop their convincing skills even without a strong convincing attitude, just by giving them the confidence to ask the right questions and press a little harder for answers.

To put that another way, I've observed that the ego-driven *need* to convince sometimes gets in the way of a relationship sale. The real artists in sales identify pain and problems and offer pain and problem relief. Along with that, they force their prospects and customers to consider that they *do have* pain and problems — that's where the assertiveness comes in! The end result is that, with guidance from the salesperson, the prospects and customers ultimately convince themselves!

One of my coaches back in high school had a favorite saying, that there's no one tougher than a tough gentleman. He was trying to teach us that we could be both good citizens and successful competitors. I think there's a very direct application of that philosophy to this discussion. In selling, there's no one better positioned for success than an *assertive empath*.

R-E-S-P-E-C-T

As I mentioned earlier, I don't think *hate* is the emotion most people feel toward salespeople, but it's certainly true that the sales profession lacks respect in our society. Yes, the serious and talented salespeople gain the respect of both their customers and prospects and their employers, but that respect has to be earned — and then some!

By that, I mean it's not enough to wait and hope for respect. Serious and talented salespeople *demand* respect, in both obvious and sometimes not-so-obvious ways. Here's an "obvious" example. One of my clients told me a story once about a customer who'd gotten more than 60 days behind on his account, and has promised payment several times without coming through. "Fred," this salesperson said, "I think I've worked pretty hard to earn your business, and you know that I've done a lot of things over the years that have made you look good. Right now, you're making me look bad. I don't want to go back to my boss again and make a promise that you're not going to keep, so how about taking care of this *today*." He left with a check — and with very high confidence that he'll continue to be the primary supplier for this customer. "Sometimes, you've just got to explain the rules," the salesperson told me. "It's a respect thing."

Please note the masculine pronoun. Yes, this was one of my male clients, but is there any reason why a female salesperson couldn't have handled this situation the same way? Male or female, it's still a "respect thing" — and respect is not a function of gender unless we let it be.

Here's a not-so-obvious example of demanding respect. I teach all of my clients to use both their first and last names and their company name when introducing themselves or leaving messages. I put special emphasis on this point for my female clients, though, because I don't want them doing *anything* that might diminish the perception of their professionalism. With established customers, I tell them, it might be OK to be "Sally from Superior," but with anyone you're not very well established with, I want you to be "Sally Smith from Superior Manufacturing."

This may seem like a small thing, but as I've written throughout this book, little things in selling strategy and technique often make big differences.

The Sex Thing

Here's some very important advice for women in sales, especially young women: Never flirt! You may think it's harmless, but I've seen and heard of far too many situations where "innocent" flirting led to serious problems, ranging from stress in important customer relationships to sexual harassment complaints. That's not to say that a salesperson can't enter into a romantic relationship with a customer or prospect — although there is some business risk in those situations too. What I'm talking about here is any suggestion that sex might be traded for business.

Within just the last few months, I've had three of my clients tell me that the reason they weren't getting any business from a particular prospect was that the buyer was sleeping with a salesperson from another company. True? Who knows. Talked about? Certainly! A while ago, one of the guys I play basketball with was telling a story about a salesperson who's been calling on him. "I'm pretty sure I can nail her if I give her the order," he said. (That story, by the way, was part of my motivation for including this segment in the book. And I apologize if the explicit language offends anyone, but that's exactly what he said!)

I tell my female clients — and my daughter! — to keep as much distance as possible between themselves and any dangerous or compromising situation. Flirting might be fun, and it may seem harmless, but it doesn't belong in a professional's business behavior!

By the way, I tell all my young male clients exactly the same thing!

Final Thoughts

Here's one more piece of advice I give to my female clients. In many cities, there are "Women In Sales" clubs or networking groups, and if there is one in your area, I would encourage you to check in out. I have mixed emotions about the value of networking groups in general — you'll read about that in the next chapter! — but I've also observed that some of these women-only groups work pretty well. For women who own businesses, you should also consider the National Association of Women Business Owners (NAWBO).

Networking Groups and Media

It's pretty widely believed that most successful salespeople are accomplished networkers. Does that mean, though, that they owe their success to "structured" networking groups or events, ranging from participation in a BNI chapter to attending a local Chamber of Commerce's "Business After Hours" programs? How about the very modern social and businesses networking media, like Facebook and LinkedIn and Twitter? In my experience, some salespeople accomplish a great deal in these structured networking settings and using these modern networking media, but for others, it's a complete waste of time.

Why? Half of the answer is simply that some networking groups, events and media are better than others. The other half is that some salespeople really *work* their networking groups, events or media, while others stand around or play around and hope good things will happen. As with everything else in selling, the harder you work — and the smarter you work! — the more likely it is that you'll be successful.

BNI Background

BNI (Business Network International) is probably the best known of the structured networking groups. It was founded in 1985 by Dr. Ivan Misner, a management consultant with a Ph.D. from the University of Southern California. BNI currently has more than 3200 chapters worldwide, all part of a franchise structure.

That's an important consideration. BNI is a *product*, with a revenue stream that's meant to enrich individual franchisees as well as the franchisor. There's nothing wrong with that, of course, but just as with any other franchised business, there are franchisees who represent the franchise well and others who don't.

BNI's stated mission is "to help people increase their business through a structured, positive, and supportive word of mouth marketing program." Its stated philosophy is that "givers gain." Another part of the BNI equation is that "only one person per professional classification is eligible to join a chapter." In other words, you won't show up to a meeting someday to find a competitor in your group, but you also won't be able to join in the first place if there's already a salesperson who sells what you sell as a member.

It doesn't cost a whole lot to join a BNI chapter. From my research, an annual fee of around $240 seems to be typical. It's not hard to project that a few good referrals will provide a solid return on that investment. Unfortunately, it doesn't always happen, but that's usually more the fault of the salesperson than the networking group concept.

Sometimes, though, it is the group that limits a salesperson's success. I read an article by Dr. Misner in *Entrepreneur* magazine which notes that the referral level often doesn't reach a "critical mass" until a group has more than 20 members. I have also heard stories about much larger groups in which just about everyone fit into the "stand around and hope" category. One of my clients belongs to what he refers to as a "bunch-a duds" group. Having paid his annual membership fee, he's currently on the waiting list to join one of the other groups in his area (all of which have competitors as members right now).

Chambers of Commerce

Another common networking venue is the local Chamber of Commerce. Most CC's state their mission in terms of service to the business community, in areas ranging from support of existing businesses to recruiting new business into the area. There's no question, though, that the networking opportunity is the driving force for many members. In fact, I found a "Top 10 Reasons To Join" list at the website of my own local Chamber of Commerce in Cary, NC, and Number 1 on the list was "Make New Business Contacts." Beyond that, four more of the Top 10 were related to using Chamber membership to develop new customers for your own business.

I know quite a few business owners who have developed significant amounts of business through their membership in a Chamber. On the other hand, though, I know very few employee/salespeople who can make the same claim. Why? Because buyers and sellers tend to hang out at different ends of the Chamber of Commerce spectrum. The senior people in member businesses might forge both friendships and business relationships while serving on a committee together, or perhaps on the Board of Directors. The typical "Business After Hours" event, though, seems to consist of salespeople socializing with other salespeople. Yes, that can be the first step in effective networking toward the decision-makers, but all too often that isn't happening.

Facebook and Twitter

The hot topic in sales training these days seems to be *Social Media Networking*. In fact, I've been turned down for several speaking engagements recently because that's what the organizers think their constituents want/need to hear about.

"Can you put a seminar together on how to use Facebook and Twitter in sales?" I've been asked?

"I could, but I won't," has been my answer. Why? Because most salespeople are wasting enough time already without adding more to the mix.

Networking Good

Let me make this clear, I am not opposed to networking, in fact, I am a very strong proponent of this element of selling strategy. Here's some more Dinosaur Wisdom, though: *The most important part of networking is the* working *part, and that means* two things. First of all, it means that you really have to *work* at it — showing up at a BNI meeting and describing your ideal customer and hoping for some referrals is not net*working*. Nor is showing up at a Chamber Mixer and chatting with a few people and exchanging business cards with a few others. Net*working* involves identification on two levels and follow-up on two more.

The first level of identification is to find people who work at companies or organizations that would seem to be likely suspects. The second level is to identify the person you'll ultimately have to sell to.

The first level of follow-up involves your initial net*working* contact. If he/she is the person you'll ultimately have to sell to, it's to set up a meeting to talk seriously and in depth about his/her wants and needs. (Here's some more Dinosaur Wisdom: *It's unlikely that you can have that conversation in a networking atmosphere.* You really don't want there to be a lot of distractions during this conversation.) If he/she is not the person you have to sell to, the first level of follow up is to gain an introduction to the person you do. That's what I meant by networking *toward* the decision-maker(s).

The second level of follow-up is to identify that person's wants and needs and start the process of convincing him/her that you can meet or exceed them, and provide an improvement over the status quo.

Wasting Time Bad

My problems with Facebook and Twitter have nothing to do with the networking possibilities, which are very real. They have more to do with the *likelihood* that you'll spend 20 minutes "socializing" for every minute of real sales-building activity, so unless all of the Facebook and Twitter time is put in after hours, I think it's pretty likely that some of the real selling hours of each day are going to be wasted.

Wasting time is bad, right? Therefore, anything that makes it easier to waste time is also bad. We'll all be better off with sales and marketing strategies that *maximize* time rather than wasting it.

Real Possibilities

OK, having said all of that, Facebook and Twitter *do* have some real business-building possibilities. The most important thing to understand, though, is that these possibilities are connected to *them*, not to *you* — and by *them*, I mean your suspects, prospects and customers. For the life of me, I can't imagine why anyone would want to follow the life of a typical salesperson in 140 character installments. But by setting yourself up as a *follower* of people you're interested in, you can learn what *they're* interested in, helping you to establish the common ground that often leads to a successful business relationship. Facebook has the same limitations (except for the 140 character part), but provides the same opportunity.

Keep this in mind, though. What you're looking for is still the most *eclectic* interest you share with a suspect, prospect or customer. Remember this element of Dinosaur Wisdom: *You should always be looking for common ground and common interests, but the strongest bonds will be formed around the most eclectic interests.* As noted, here's what that means: You might never be more than just *one of* the salespeople a buyer talks football with, but you might well be the only one he/she talks about ballet with. Part of the artistry in selling is to identify those areas of common ground where you'll really stand out.

Keep this in mind too. With a high-value suspect, prospect or customer, it might be worth *learning something* about one or more of their most eclectic interests. In other words, to *create* some common ground that may not have existed before.

LinkedIn

While Facebook and Twitter are *social* networking media, LinkedIn was intended from the start to be a *business* networking tool. In theory, you can establish a network that contains everyone you do business with, or would like to do business with. LinkedIn also gives you the ability to search on a variety of parameters. For example, I just searched "American Red Cross" for "marketing" titles within 50 miles of my zip code. The first listing that came up was their local Director of Marketing and Communications, and it turns out that she went to the same college my wife attended, at about the same time. We also have two other business connections — people in her network that I also know — and I'm reasonably sure that I could get one of those people to try to provide me with an introduction, based on my relationship with him. The only problem, perhaps, is his relationship with her. Does she know him/like him/trust him enough that she'd meet with me based on his recommendation?

I have used LinkedIn to look up companies that I'm interested in, to help me with that *first level of identification* I mentioned earlier. I have also used LinkedIn to learn more about people I've already identified, to see if I might have some network pathway to them. I'm always looking for something that will increase my likelihood of making a connection, and ultimately selling something.

This is important, though, I don't reach out to my suspects or prospects to say "we have a mutual friend/connection." I reach out to the friend/connection to say "can you introduce me to this person?" Remember this Dinosaur Wisdom: *The only thing better than a* referral *in business is an* introduction!

Manage The Process!

Like every other aspect of selling, your net*working* will be more effective if there's an underlying plan to support the process. The starting point to that plan should be a set of specific goals for the networking component of your overall marketing plan. For example, you might set a goal of gaining 5 new customers over a three-month period from the pool of fellow Chamber members. The specific action plan might be to invite 10 fellow members to come by for an individual tour of your facility each month during that three-month period. You might phrase the invitation as: "I'd love to have you — and anyone else in your organization who might be interested or would be appropriate — come over and see what we do. I think you'll find it interesting and educational, and we might even find that there's a good match between your needs and our capabilities."

I can't guarantee that everyone will accept your invitation, but for planning purposes, a 50% acceptance rate doesn't seem unreasonable. If a third of those people become customers — and again, that doesn't seem unreasonable as a projection — a goal of 5 new customers will have been achieved!

With Facebook and Twitter, I might set my goals this way: Goal 1, to spend 15 minutes each evening, Monday through Thursday, reading tweets and posts from my business targets, and identifying at least 8 elements of common ground each week. Goal 2 would be for all of that social media networking activity to increase my customer count by (X) and my sales volume by ($Y) over a defined period of time.

With LinkedIn, I might set a goal of one new customer gained for each hour spent doing research to identify both buyers and network pathways.

Bottom Line

The bottom line here is that networking groups and media offer a great deal of opportunity, but it doesn't just *happen*. This is not a situation where 90% of success lies in just signing up and/or showing up. Remember this Dinosaur Wisdom: *The key to successful networking is the* working *part*, and remember that the best way to manage the process is a combination of goals and accountability. That's the difference between hoping good things will happen and making good things happen!

Beyond that, please don't kid yourself about how much time you're really spending on this stuff, or when you're spending it. Thirty minutes of dedicated social media networking in the evening will probably put money in your pocket. An hour on Facebook during the working day probably will not.

Tracking Your Progress

Time management, prospecting, questions, proposals, price objections, other obstacles and objections and even a feminist perspective. I think we've covered a lot of ground, and I hope you have some new ideas about how to be an effective salesperson.

The next ground I want to cover is a tool I've developed for measuring progress as you work the process from *suspect* to *prospect* to *customer* to *maximized customer*. It's based on the idea that the distance between *suspect* and *customer* is 100 units, and from *customer* to *maximized customer* is 50 units more.

It's worth noting, I think, that I tend to think of these units as *feet*, although they could be anything else you want them to be — inches, yards, steps, strides, etc. I have a client who's a serious Star Trekkie, and she measures her progress in light years. What's really important here is that we have a unit of measure, and that each major increment has a specific definition.

Increment Definitions

Here's what that means: **0 units** would indicate a very raw suspect; for example, the result of buying a list of all of the companies within a geographic area. If you don't know anything else about these companies — sales volume, business type, number of employees, etc. — they are *very* raw suspects.

10 units would indicate companies/organizations targeted through some sort of *market intelligence*. For example, my printing industry clients know that trade associations represent a good target market, so if a printing salesperson acquired a list of all of the trade associations within his/her territory, they would be ranked at 10.

20 units would indicate a person/company added to your *suspect* list through a referral. As we've discussed, you still have work to do with a referral, but you should have at least a little bit of a head start towards building a relationship with someone you've been referred to — and hopefully *introduced* to!

30 units indicates that your pre-approach research is complete; in other words, you have taken an initial look at the suspect, identified the buyer, and so far, everything you've learned leads you toward further pursuit. Remember what I've written about making a *progressive investment* of your time throughout the suspecting/prospecting stages. If the Internet was involved in your pre-approach research, it should only have been enough time to determine that you want to go further — not the 10-15 minutes of research that would be justified if you actually get to the point of a needs analysis meeting or conversation.

40 units indicates that your introductory letter or e-mail has been sent, and from this point forward, you can start using smaller increments to measure your progress. For example, **41 units** would indicate that you've sent out your introductory letter or e-mail and made a follow-up call, leaving a voice mail message. **42 units** would indicate a second follow-up call and a second voice mail message. (Don't forget that the strategy for the first message is simply to ask them to call you back. If that doesn't work, the strategy for the second voice mail message is to *tell them* why you think they should!) **45 units** could indicate that the person has asked you to get back to him/her at a future date. **48 units** could indicate that he/she has agreed to meet with you, but you haven't yet set a date. **49 units** could mean that you have an appointment set for next week.

Tracking Format

Before I go any further with the definitions, I should probably describe the tracking format where all of these numbers will go. I use a simple Microsoft Excel spreadsheet — not for Excel's computational capabilities, but simply because spreadsheet software makes it easy to organize data in columns. Any other spreadsheet software will do, including Google Spreadsheets or OpenOffice.

Column A in your spreadsheet is for the name of the company or organization. Column B is for the name of your contact. When you have multiple contacts within a company or organization, each one gets their own line, for example "AAA" and "John Smith" in Line 1 and "AAA" and Mary Jones" in Line 2.

Column C should be headed by the date of the next Friday on the calendar when you start the process, and D, E, F, G and so on should be headed by the dates of the following Fridays. As you've probably guessed, that means you'll be updating this tracking tool every week.

Here's a better idea, though, than waiting until the end of the week. Spend a few minutes with your spreadsheet at the end of every day! I don't know about you, but my memory isn't all that it used to be, and if I count on remembering details for any length of time, I usually end up forgetting something important.

No Contact, No Entry

Here's an important element to the use of this tool. If you don't have any contact with a *suspect*, *prospect* or *customer* during the week that you're reporting on, leave the line in that column blank. If you do have contact, enter the number that best represents where you think you are *after* that contact.

Here's what that means on a daily basis. Let's say that you ended last week with "AAA/John Smith" at 40 units, indicating that your intro letter or e-mail went out prior to the end of the week. On Monday, you made your first follow-up call and left a voice mail message, so you would enter "41" in this week's column. You had no contact on Tuesday, so you just left "41" in that column as you updated the spreadsheet at the end of the day. Then on Wednesday, you called again and left your second voice mail message, so you changed the number in the column to "42". No contact on Thursday, so the number in the column stayed the same, but on Friday you called again, connected with your suspect, talked for a little while and set an appointment for the following week, so you changed the number to "49" and that's how you ended the week.

To compare that to another scenario, let's say that you ended the previous week with "BBB/John Jones" at 30 units, indicating that your pre-approach research was complete. You did not send out your intro letter or e-mail this week, though, and in fact, there was no contact at all with Mr. Jones. That means there'd be a blank box in the column at the end of this week.

In this way, in addition to having a snapshot of your progress with each *suspect/ prospect/customer*, you'll also have a snapshot of how long it's been since you had any contact with them. With this tool backing up ACT, or whatever other contact manager you may be using, it gets pretty hard for anyone to slip through the cracks!

Failing Memories & Minimum Equipment Lists

As I mentioned, my memory is not all that it used to be. I do remember some things pretty well, though. I'm a pilot, though not an active one these days, but I still have my license, and I still remember much of what I learned in pilot training. One of the things I learned is that you don't always have to scrub a flight because a piece of equipment isn't working. Most airplanes carry equipment that is not absolutely required for safe flight, and most also have redundant systems for the critically important stuff. There are certain pieces of equipment, though, that must be onboard and operable or else you can't fly — legally or safely — and those are documented on that airplane's Minimum Equipment List, or MEL.

I remember a salesperson telling me that is was important for him to feel well-equipped when he went out on his calls. "I'm not confident," he said, "unless I have all my brochures and samples and give-aways and all the rest, so I know I'll be prepared for anything I might run into."

I'm all for preparation and confidence, believe me, but I don't think you should postpone any sales activity just because you don't have all of your tools available. In fact, I think a salesperson's MEL consists of just three items: something to write with, something to write on, and solid questioning skills. Beyond that, all the rest is gravy!

By the way, when I was much younger, I used to laugh at my father for pulling out the pen and notebook that he always carried and writing things down, sometimes many times in a day. I can picture him smiling at me now and asking: *"Now do you understand?"*

Definitions, Continued...

OK, back to the increment definitions. **50 units** indicates that the first substantive conversation — hopefully a face-to-face meeting! — has been held, and **60 units** indicates that a second meeting has been held. Hopefully, to this point, you will have completed your *needs and wants* analysis and presented your proposal.

Please remember that you can use smaller increments to indicate contact — and hopefully progress — between 10-unit levels but still short of the next level. For example, you might talk on the phone the week after your first meeting and raise the tracking number to "52" or "53". On the other hand, you might talk on the phone but not feel that you made any progress, so you'd enter "50" again. The fact that there's a number in the column indicates *contact*. The number itself can indicate *progress*.

(*Can*, by the way, reflects the possibility that a relationship can move backward, or that you realized that it was not really as far along as you previously reported. Be honest and objective, and if anything, *conservative* in your evaluation of progress!)

70 units indicates a level of high confidence in the likelihood of turning a *prospect* into a *customer*. In fact, "70" is the point where a *suspect* turns into a *fully qualified prospect* — where you *know* (not just think!) that they buy exactly what you sell, and you *know* (not just think!) that they buy enough of it to make pursuing them worthwhile, and you *know* (not just think!) that there's real interest in buying from you. "70" means: "*I'm continuing with my follow up plan, and this prospect is definitely receptive. In fact, I'm starting to believe that I have at least a 50-50 chance of winning some business here!*"

80 units indicates that the prospect has decided to buy from you, but there's no immediate need for your products and/or services. "80" means: "*I expect to have an order from this buyer within 90 days.*" **90 units** means: "*I expect to have an order from this buyer within 30 days.*" And "100" is not open to interpretation — when you get that first order, they have arrived at **100 units!**

Customer Definitions

100 units indicates the passage from *prospect* to *customer*, but as noted, you're probably still a long way from *maximized customer* — and the first issue is the customer's satisfaction with that first order! **105 units** indicates First Order Satisfaction Assured. **110 units** indicates that you have completed both the *product opportunity* and *people opportunity* evaluations, and **115 units** indicates that you have formulated a *maximization plan*, with a specific timeline and benchmarks. **120 units** indicates the beginning of the implementation of that plan, and you can note your progress from there with smaller increments, adding a point every time you talk about a new product or service, and maybe a couple of points every time that activity gains you a new order. When you're confident that you're getting it all — or at least all you can reasonably expect — you indicate that with a score of **150 units**. And from that point, having maximized the *Second Level of Value*, don't forget that you still have to protect *First Level of Value,* and don't ignore any ongoing testimonial/referral possibilities reflecting the *Third Level of Value!*

Modifiers

In addition to the progress increments, this tracking tool also uses several *modifiers* to indicate specific circumstances. "D" indicates a disqualification; for example, you've decided that you're unlikely to get anywhere with "CCC/Tom Payne" after numerous attempts at following up on your introductory letter. After your "full court press" they're still at 44 and you've made all the investment that you're willing to make, so you enter "44D" and that's that.

A variation on that theme would be a suspect you've decided to *recycle* rather than disqualify — in other words, to try again later. In that case, you would enter "44R" and schedule the next attempt in your contact management tool. What's the difference between a "D" and an "R" situation? As I wrote earlier, I'll usually try again later with someone I think has significant volume potential, but I won't invest any further time on a *minnow* with a bad attitude!

Here are the other modifiers: "Q" to indicate any situation where you have a live quote out; "X" to indicate a new *product opportunity* order; and "P" to indicate a *people opportunity* referral. Please feel free to develop additional modifiers to further flesh out your own situations.

Tracking Your Territory

My father was a big fan of Broadway musicals, and half of the soundtrack in our house growing up was the Original Cast Recordings of *My Fair Lady*, *Oklahoma*, *The Music Man, Camelot, Gypsy* and many other great shows. (The other half, of course, was the Beatles and Bob Dylan and Buffalo Springfield and Joni Mitchell and the rest of that 60's rock and folk music that my dad never quite understood.) What does any of that have to do with selling? Well, I quoted a line from *The Music Man* just the other day. It comes from the first song in the show, titled "Rock Island," which introduces the main character, a con man/musical instrument salesman named Harold Hill. "He's just a bang beat, bell ringing, big hole, great go, neck-or-nothing, rip roarin', every time a bull's eye Salesman," the lyrics tell us.

"But," they also tell us, and I told one of my clients yesterday, *"you gotta know the territory!"*

This client doesn't believe in assigning salespeople to territories, and I think it's very poor management strategy not to.

Organizational Tool

"I don't want to limit anyone's effectiveness," he told me, "and I don't want to lose out on any opportunities. What if one guy has a relationship with a buyer in another guy's territory, or else one guy hasn't ever made any progress with a buyer, and I want to give another guy a shot at him?"

"Neither of those things rules out a territory strategy," I answered. "There's a lot more to this than geography."

Let's start with this understanding, a territory strategy is all about *organization*. It can be geographic organization, or vertical market segment organization, or target list organization, or a combination of all of the above, but the most important consideration is that most salespeople need help with organization and time management. A sales territory is simply a tool that can provide that help, and I hope you realize that what we're really talking about here is a *sales management* tool.

If you are the Sales Manager in addition to your individual sales responsibilities, I hope you'll see the value in assigning territories — either geographic or by vertical market segment or by target list or by any combination of the above — and using the reporting process I've just described with the people you manage. In my Sales Coaching activities, this tracking spreadsheet is the foundation of most of my conversations with my coaching clients. It gives me *visibility* into both their activity level and their progress with individual *suspects, prospects* and *customers*. We have lots of conversations about what to do next, especially in situations where the salesperson is *stalled* with a particular individual.

If you're not the Sales Manager, I hope you'll see that this can be a very powerful *self-management* tool, giving you an objective look at both your progress and activity levels. Remember this Dinosaur Wisdom: *If your company doesn't assign you to a specific sales territory, you should* define *one for yourself!*

For what it's worth, I have tried several times to integrate this process into ACT, without success. As I wrote back in our discussion of time management, ACT does have a tool to measure progress — the Opportunities Tab — but it doesn't give you the same sort of snapshot visibility, nor does it show the timeline as clearly. I recognize that keeping both ACT and this tracking process up-to-date represents "double work" to some degree, but in my judgment, the benefit derived from that work more than justifies the time and effort.

19
Looking For A Sales Job

Since this is a book on the fundamentals of selling, I think there's a good chance that you're in the early stages of your selling career. You might even be in the "pre-career" stage, since I also wrote this to serve as the textbook for a course I'm teaching at a local college. In either case, there's a pretty good chance that your current or first sales job won't be your last one, so I thought it would be appropriate to cover some of the fundamentals of looking for a sales job.

First and foremost, this is an exercise in selling yourself, and I hope you'll remember that most salespeople face two core selling challenges. The first is to sell themselves. The second is to "close the sale" on a product or service. When you're looking for a sales job, you get both of those challenges rolled into one!

Critical Questions

When I interview sales candidates, my first two questions are usually "Why sales?" and "Why (the specific product or service that you'll be selling if you get this job)?" Let's set "Why sales?" aside for just a moment, and talk about the other *why*. In my experience, the great salespeople usually have a pretty good reason for selling what they're selling.

In some cases, that reason might better be described as a *passion*. For others, it's more coldly logical. In my own case, for example, when I decided that I'd had enough of restaurants and that I wanted to try sales, I went looking for a job selling restaurant equipment and supplies. I knew that I didn't know anything about selling, so I went looking for a job selling something I knew something about!

One of my neighbors sells sports equipment and supplies — his big sale last month included a blocking sled and a tackling dummy for a local high school. His customers — and suspects and prospects! — are mostly coaches and athletic directors, and he has a real passion for both his products and his market. He's worked for a number of different companies since he got out of college 20+ years ago, but he knew from the start that he wanted to work in that marketplace.

You may not have a particular product/service *passion*, but I still expect you to have a good answer to my question. Here are a few good ones I've heard recently, and one bad one:

- "I want to sell something that gets used and then has to be replaced, but not something that's a pure commodity." (Industrial Cleaning Equipment)
- "I want to sell something where quality and personal service really matter." (Fine Men's Clothing)
- "I want to sell something that will give me a residual income, a sale that will be renewed from year to year." (Insurance)
- "I want to sell a good brand into a distribution network — selling to the stores where people will go to buy the products, not to the end users themselves." (Power Tools and Accessories)
- "I can sell anything!" (I hope you realize that's the bad one, and why.)
- "I started on the production side of the business, and I think my product knowledge is going to be an asset, both to me and my customers." (Printing)

That last one was actually part of the answer to the other question — "Why sales?" — recently. The other half of this particular candidate's answer was: "I've been earning a pretty good living in production, but I've been watching some of our salespeople earn a *very* good living. I don't think they're any smarter than I am, and I don't think there's any magic to what they do. If it takes brains, I think I've got enough, and if it takes guts, I think I've got more than enough. Is there any reason someone like me wouldn't be successful at selling?"

I hope you can see why I liked that answer. On a fundamental level, he gave me a good, logical reason for wanting to be in sales. On another level, he used good selling strategy by putting the ball in my court — *Is there any reason someone like me wouldn't be successful at selling?"* On still another level, he demonstrated the guts he says he has and the courage I'm looking for by asking a fairly provocative question. That's not all there is to selling success, especially when the product you're trying to sell is *you*, but it's a pretty good start!

By the way, if you didn't get why "I can sell anything" is a bad answer, I'll be happy to elaborate. It's not a thoughtful answer to what I intended as a serious question. I'm looking for commitment to the product, not just commitment to a career in selling. Someone who can sell anything might be looking for something else to sell before to very long.

Here's something else to keep in mind, especially for young, aspiring salespeople. When I interview a candidate, I'm not looking for or expecting a lifetime commitment. But I am looking for someone who'll probably be around for at least 3 years. If your resume indicates that you're a shorter-term job-hopper, you probably won't even get to the interview stage with me.

Why Sales?

Here are some other good and not-so-good answers to "Why sales?":

- "It's where my strengths lie. I'm good at getting to the heart of the matter, and I'm good at coming up with solutions. People seem to like me, but more importantly, they seem to trust me."
- "I'm a people person. I really like getting to meet different people and learning all about them."
- "I want to earn a good living and I want to have control over my own destiny."
- "All my friends say I should be in sales because I'm a really good talker."
- "I love the challenge. I love the hunt and I love the kill."

Those aren't all exact quotes, but I think they reflect the flavor of many of the answers I get to that question. As you've probably guessed, I like #1 and #3, and I don't like #2 and #4. (#4 is an exact quote, by the way. Scary, but true!)

I'm not sure about #5. Here's some more Dinosaur Wisdom: *There are two distinct culture in sales. One is all about the customer, the other one is all about making the sale.* I tend to like people who embrace the former, although I recognize that there's a place for hunters and killers too. Car salespeople, for example, really have to have that make-the-sale mentality. Their success rate goes way down if a customer leaves the lot to shop some more, or even to "think about it." The same holds true for any product or service that's really a "one time sale."

On the other hand, I like salespeople who enjoy the challenge. Ultimately, what I'm looking for is someone who's going to be motivated to succeed. Whether it's money that provides that motivation, or the satisfaction of winning, or even the thrill of the kill, it all boils down to getting results. The point I'm trying to make is that you need to be prepared to tell an interviewer what motivates/will motivate you.

Money: Part 1

Many sales job seekers — especially younger people — seem reluctant to talk about the money part of motivation. There's a sense, I think, that a person should have a higher calling in life than making money. I would phrase that differently. I think a salesperson should have a higher calling *in addition to* the desire to make money. I think that's a pretty good definition for the kind of consultative, problem-solving salesperson that I hope you are, or will be!

Having said that, I think most employers think they're looking for "money-motivated" salespeople, and I think they're wrong. Here are my three most important criteria: *intelligence, a competitive nature,* and *an appreciation for the finer things in life.*

Intelligence is at the top of my list, simply because bright people learn faster than not-so-bright people, and because intelligent people generally do better at the conceptual elements of selling. Please note that you don't have to be brilliant, but it helps to be bright.

A competitive nature provides two things. First is the motivational power of wanting to win. Second is the understanding of what to do when you lose. I have a bias toward people who've played competitive sports, because I know that I learned something very important to selling in my many years of competitive athletics. (I often refer to myself as an aging jock. When my wife's in the room, she says "ag*ed,* dear, you're way past ag*ing.*") What I've learned through sports is how to lose— and I want to make it clear that I've never learned to like losing! What I learned was how to *react* to a loss, which is to get yourself up and dust yourself off and give some thought to why you didn't win, and then refine your strategy and/or practice your skills and then look for another opportunity to compete. You don't always win in sports — even if you're Tiger Woods! — and you definitely don't always win in selling. But if you compete every day, you'll find that you can make a pretty good living with a relatively small percentage of *yeses.*

An appreciation for the finer things in life is important because it's really not money which motivates most money-motivated people — *it's what you can do with the money!* I'm looking for people who want to drive nice cars and live in nice houses, who want to own nice things and go to world-class destinations on their vacations. I'm *not* looking for people who are going to be satisfied with the lesser things in life.

Money: Part 2

There are two reasons why a sales job-seeker shouldn't be afraid or ashamed to talk about money. The first is your opportunity to convince me that you are someone I can motivate with the power of the paycheck. The second is your opportunity to make sure that the job I'm offering will meet your earnings *wants* and *needs*. I have an ongoing problem with business owners and sales managers who overstate the earnings potential of their positions. I also have an ongoing problem with salespeople who think they'll earn more than what the opposite of those owners and sales managers tell them a job will likely be worth.

I should probably rephrase that. There are people who will tell you that the sky is the limit, and that what you'll earn is only limited by how hard you're willing to work. Those people are lying to you. Every sales job has a range of earnings possibility. For example, I worked with one of my printing industry clients just last week to define a range. We started with three sales volume projections for the first year, one that would represent a solid performance, another that would represent an outstanding performance, and a third that would represent the worst performance that would allow the salesperson to keep his/her job into Year 2.

Next, we extended those *solid, outstanding* an *barely tolerable* projections into the second and third year. Then, I asked my client how much she was willing to pay for each level of performance. The end result of that conversation was the determination that this was probably a $35,000/year job in the first year, with the possibility of as much as $39,000 for an outstanding performance. By the third year, the range would be $60,000 for *solid* to $68,000 for *outstanding*. This is how well-run companies develop their compensation plans, with reasonable performance expectations considered right alongside profitability. (Remember, no one wants to give you all of the profit from what you sell. When you're in sales, *you* are a means to an end for the company that employs you!)

I explained to my client that the numbers we'd just come up with placed some real limits of who she could hire for the position. "What do you mean?" she asked. "It's really pretty simple," I answered. "We've just determined that this is a $35,000 to $39,000 job. That means you can't hire someone who *wants* or *needs* any more than that to do the job.

Why? It's pretty straightforward really. If you *need* to make $5000 per month right from the start, and you take a job that pays $3000 per month right from the start, you'll be $2000 behind your earnings curve at the end of the first month — and you'll get farther and farther behind! How long are you going to stay with a job that doesn't pay you what you *need*?

Now *want* is a different issue. If you *need* to earn $3000 per month and *want* to earn $5000 per month, you'll be OK with a job that starts at $3000 per month but gives you a reasonable shot at getting to the *want* level.

My third and fourth questions in an interview are usually "How much do you need to make?" and "How much do you want to make?" Sadly, most of the people I'm interviewing don't seem to get the difference, and they don't seem to understand why it's an important difference. My advice is to prepare yourself for your next interview with an answer to both of these questions.

As I tell my clients, you don't have to guarantee the *want* figure, although you do have to provide a very reasonable opportunity to make it. You do have to guarantee the *need* figure, and if the *need* is greater than what the job's likely to be worth — or what you can pay and still remain profitable — you simply can't hire that candidate. *It's all just arithmetic*, I tell them, *the economics of your situation tell you exactly how much salesperson you can afford.*

Here's some more advice for you. Don't be afraid to discuss money in an interview, and don't be afraid to challenge — or at least ask for amplification — when you're told how much you can earn on the job. I'm not going to hate you if you ask me what my expectations are based on, and if other salespeople have had the kind of earnings success that I'm predicting. And if the answer to that question is *no*, I'm not going to hate you if you ask me why I feel they were less successful than they should have/could have been. In fact, I think I'm going to be impressed with your willingness to ask assertive and provocative questions — *because that's what it takes to be successful on this selling job we're talking about!*

Common Errors

Here are a few more common errors I'm seeing from sales job-seekers:

- **Not sending a cover letter with a resume.** Some sales positions draw literally hundreds of applicants. You will immediately face the challenge of standing out in that crowd. A cover letter — or a couple of cover paragraphs in the text box of an e-mail — gives you that opportunity. It can be as simple as this: *Dear Sir/ Madam, You'll find my resume attached. As you'll see* (here you highlight the experience you think is relevant to this position). *Please let me know what the next step should be.* Don't let that relevant experience hide in the body of your resume. If you don't highlight it in the cover letter/e-mail, it might never be seen. And don't write things like *I would welcome/appreciate the opportunity for an interview.* Of course you would! I hope you'll see how *please tell me what the next step should be* is a stronger and more assertive closing statement.

- **Poorly named resume files.** If I was attaching my resume to an e-mail, the file name would be *David Fellman Resume.doc* or possibly *David Fellman Resume.pdf.* It would not be *daverez* or *davesresume* or *resume* or *resume12.* This is another one of those little things that can make a big difference. Remember, you are seeking a professional position. Portray yourself as a professional!

- **Questionable e-mail addresses.** If I was looking for a sales position — or any kind of job for that matter — I would set up a special e-mail account to use in all of my job-seeking communications: DavidFellman@ (aol.com, gmail.com, yahoo.com, etc.). Last week I received a resume from freakflirt@, and other recent addresses have included BoneCrusherPhil@, swordsman@, and grandmasherry@. If this is the sort of thing you want to use as your personal e-mail address, that's all right with me, but in a job-seeking situation, it makes me question two things — the first of those being your judgment! The second is whether you might push the weird-meter, dork-meter or jerk-meter past my tolerances.

Interview Strategy

I've been told that the "Dinosaur Interview" is much different from what most people expect. I've already told you about the first four questions I like to ask. After that, I generally switch gears and start talking about what I'm looking for in a candidate, in terms of background, experience, skills and attitudes. Then I say: "OK, here's your opportunity to convince me that you have all that I'm looking for. The floor is yours!"

On one hand, I'm hoping for a thoughtful and organized discourse which will address each of my issues. "Wow," you may be asking yourself, "how would someone remember all of those issues and keep them straight?" The answer is, by taking notes while I'm talking! Remember what I wrote earlier about a salesperson's MEL — Minimum Equipment List — consisting of three items: something to write with, something to write on, and solid questioning skills. You should always be prepared to take notes on a sales call, and a job interview may be the ultimate sales call.

Now, think about that for a moment, and think back on what you've read here about selling being an interrogatory process. Is there any reason why you can't take control of this "sales call" by *asking me* what I'm looking for in a candidate, in terms of background, experience, skills and attitudes? I would be truly impressed if you did that, and then even more impressed if you followed with that thoughtful and organized discourse which would address all of my *needs* and *wants*.

Here's the most important element of this sort of interview strategy. It will not be enough for you to tell me "yes, I have those skills and attitudes." You have to back up your statements with evidence! I would love to hear you say: "Here's a story which I think demonstrates that I have this particular skill or attitude."

In many ways, what you're doing is as much of an *audition* as an interview. And even if you're "just" a kid getting out of college, you have the opportunity to impress people — maybe not with *sales experience*, but with *sales instincts*.

Following Up

The end of the interview is another good place to ask "what should the next step be?" You'll probably hear a lot of "well, we're going to be interviewing some other candidates, we'll get back to you if we want to take a next step."

OK, again, let's remember that this is a sales call, and just about everything you have read to this point applies. So I hope you're thinking about asking: "Based on what you've seen and heard today, is there any reason that you would *not* consider giving me the job?" (If you weren't thinking that, you may need to go back and re-read the chapter on *Preparing and Presenting Your Proposal!*)

If there are negative issues, you will (hopefully) have the opportunity to discuss them further. If not, you'll have the opportunity to ask: "If you were me, what would you do in terms of following up on this opportunity?"

In the absence of any contrary answer to that question, here's what I would want to do. First of all, I would make sure that I had the interviewer's e-mail address before I left, either getting it directly from him/her (perhaps on a business card?) or by stopping at the receptionist's desk on my way out. Second, I would write a brief message, along these lines:

I enjoyed meeting with you (yesterday/earlier today) *and I wanted you to know that there are* (three) *things that really jumped out at me during our conversation*: (here you list those things, for example, that your company is a leader in its industry, that the market for your products/services is going to grow, that it's exactly the sort of opportunity that I'm looking for). *In addition, there are* (three) *things that I hope jumped out at you about my background/experience/skills/attitudes:* (and here you list those things that you think portray you as the right salesperson for the job). *Beyond all of that, I want you to know that I want the job! Please let me know if there's anything else you need from me at this point. I'll look forward to our next conversation.*

If you want the order, ask for the order. If you want the job, ask for the job!

20
Now What?

The little box at the bottom of my Microsoft Word window tells me that I've written more than 100,000 words to you so far. As you can see, there are not too many more to go. We've come to the point where probably both of us are thinking *now what?*

I truly hope the answer will be that you'll use some of what I've written to help you to make more money, or to achieve whatever would represent your own individual definition of success. As I wrote earlier, I recognize that you may not be motivated totally by money, but I hope you'll recognize that making money is the end result of doing everything right in a sales job. That means everything from prospecting effectively to presenting great proposals to managing your time effectively to closing the sale. And money is a good thing in almost every way; you can spend it on yourself, you can spend it on your loved ones, you can give it to people who may need it more than you do, you can use it to support good causes — if you have some and you don't know what to do with it right now, you can save it or invest it to do whatever you want with it later on!

The ball's in your court, though. You've read all of my Dinosaur Wisdom, so here's my closing thought: I've been paid for writing this book. The question now is whether you'll reap a payoff for reading it.

I truly hope so!